T0244584

LADY
KATHERINE
GREY

LADY KATHERINE GREY

A DYNASTIC TRAGEDY

CONOR BYRNE

For my mum

Jacket Illustrations: Portrait miniature of Lady Katherine Seymour, *née* Grey holding her infant son. (Belvoir Castle, Leicestershire, UK/Bridgeman Images); Floral motifs in an antique fresco. (Orietta Gaspari/iStock)

First published 2023

The History Press
97 St George's Place, Cheltenham,
Gloucestershire, GL50 3QB
www.thehistorypress.co.uk

British Library Cataloguing in Publication Data.
A catalogue record for this book is available from the British Library.

ISBN 978 0 7509 9970 0

Typesetting and origination by The History Press
Printed and bound in Great Britain by TJ Books Limited, Padstow, Cornwall.

Trees for Life

Contents

Acknowledgements

I would like to thank the staff at the British Library, the Bodleian Library, the National Archives, Lambeth Palace Library, Surrey History Centre, Staffordshire Record Office, Gosfield Hall, Ingatestone Hall, Belvoir Castle, the Victoria and Albert Museum and Salisbury Cathedral for assisting with my research enquiries, as well as the various image libraries for their helpfulness. I would additionally like to thank Mark Beynon and the team at The History Press for making this book possible and for being flexible with deadlines. Thanks are also due to Melanie Taylor for her support, advice and encouragement over the years, as well as Rebecca Larson for hosting my article on Katherine Grey on her Tudors Dynasty website. Anthony Wilson accompanied me to Salisbury Cathedral for research and kindly looked over the manuscript. Finally, I would like to thank my family and friends for their support over the years.

List of Illustrations

Introduction

According to the last will and testament of Henry VIII, when Elizabeth I died on 24 March 1603, she should have been succeeded by the 41-year-old Edward Seymour, Lord Beauchamp, eldest son of Lady Katherine Grey. Instead, upon Elizabeth's death James VI of Scotland became the first Stuart king of England. James' accession to the English throne was not predestined – yet its seeming inevitability has arguably served to marginalise the dynastic significance of Katherine Grey and her heirs. While Katherine herself remains a somewhat obscure figure, her tragic story can be regarded as one of the most significant 'what ifs' in British history, and Elizabeth's determination to exclude Katherine and her heirs from the succession ultimately resulted in the realms of England and Scotland being united under one monarchy in consequence of James' inheritance of the English throne.

Henry VIII's decision in the 1540s to reinstate his daughters Mary and Elizabeth in the line of succession created a situation in which the issue of female royal inheritance could, and did, become a matter of dynastic and political significance in the decades ahead. While the king likely did not envisage that his reinstatement of the two women would have practical results, given the hope that his only surviving male heir Edward would produce legitimate sons of his own, female royal inheritance in fact arguably became one of the most pressing issues, if not the most, in the English political sphere upon the death of the childless

9

Edward VI in 1553. It occupied both a crucial and a controversial place in the dynastic politics of Tudor England because, from the death of Edward to the execution of Mary, Queen of Scots in 1587, the leading claimants to the throne were female. Moreover, by barring the descendants of his elder sister – the Scottish line – from the English succession in favour of those of his younger sister – the Suffolk line – Henry set a precedent that was to prove significant, namely that the monarch could ignore existing laws of succession and instead nominate an heir according to their own preferences.

Katherine is popularly remembered as a tragic figure in Tudor history. Her secret marriage to Edward Seymour, earl of Hertford incurred the wrath of Elizabeth I and led to the imprisonment of both Katherine and her husband. Separated from the earl and her elder son, Katherine died in January 1568 at the age of only 27. However, her life was more than a tragic love story. Henry VIII's last will and testament recognised her as the lawful heir to the throne until such time that Elizabeth married and produced a legitimate heir. Politicians, courtiers and diplomats – both in England and on the Continent – offered support for Katherine's claim to the throne, whether to safeguard a Protestant monarchy, to protect England's national interests from the ills of foreign rule or to prevent the succession of a candidate who threatened the interests of another foreign power. In some cases, these goals were intertwined. While James of Scotland ultimately succeeded Elizabeth peacefully in 1603, the English succession was the most controversial and politically charged issue of Elizabeth's long reign, and its resolution was never guaranteed.

It is possible to regard Katherine's demise in 1568 as both a personal and a political tragedy. Perhaps best known as the younger sister of the ill-fated Lady Jane Grey, Katherine has not attracted the same degree of scholarly or popular interest as either her sister or her rival for the succession, Mary, Queen of Scots, although she features in all studies of the Elizabethan succession.[1] In addition, a number of modern novels have explored her turbulent life.[2] This book treats seriously her claim to the throne and identifies her as, arguably, the leading candidate to succeed

Elizabeth during the first decade of the queen's reign, from Elizabeth's accession in 1558 to Katherine's untimely and unexpected death ten years later. In doing so, it will draw on a wide range of contemporary sources, including state papers, ambassadors' dispatches, chronicles and histories, letters and succession tracts, alongside documents pertaining to the investigation into her clandestine marriage.

While the sadness of Katherine's life and her death at a young age has understandably led historians to identify her as a tragic figure, the issues of her political ambition and importance as the leading claimant to succeed Elizabeth have arguably been marginalised as a result. Katherine's relationship with Hertford was a love story that ultimately ended in tragedy, but the question of her ambition during the first years of Elizabeth's reign to be publicly recognised as the queen's successor deserves to be considered. She was the leading rival to Mary, Queen of Scots and, according to Henry VIII's preferences, possessed a superior claim to the Scottish queen. Resident ambassadors at court and politicians alike were keenly aware of Katherine's status as a figure of considerable dynastic and political significance. As one of her earlier biographers noted, Katherine was 'a princess of the blood and a person of international importance'.[3] This importance derived from her royal blood and was strengthened by the recognition of her inheritance rights in Henry VIII's will and testament, while being intensified by the reality that Elizabeth's successor was never firmly established, mostly due to the queen's understandable – if risky – reluctance to name an heir. Prior to her ultimately fatal decision to marry Hertford without securing Elizabeth's permission, it can be argued that Katherine might have had a strong chance of succeeding the queen. Her secret marriage, instead, led to both her ruin and that of her husband. Having never received the queen's forgiveness, Katherine's story tragically concluded with her untimely death on a cold January morning in the Suffolk countryside, far from the royal court in which she had once lived and loved.

1

A Godly Family

Katherine Grey was the second daughter of Henry Grey, marquess of Dorset and later duke of Suffolk, and Frances Brandon. She was born on 25 August 1540, according to tradition at her family home of Bradgate Park in Leicestershire. It is possible, however, that Katherine's birth actually took place at Dorset House in Westminster.[1] The seventeenth-century ecclesiastic and historian Peter Heylyn reported that Katherine was named for Queen Katherine Howard, fifth wife of Henry VIII.[2] The royal couple's wedding had taken place at Oatlands Palace on 28 July, a month before Katherine Grey's birth. Like her namesake, Katherine Grey would suffer a tragic fate as a result of incurring royal displeasure, although she fortunately escaped the axe.

Katherine's two sisters, Jane and Mary, were born in 1536 and 1545 respectively.[3] The Grey sisters possessed royal blood as great-grand-daughters of Henry VII, the first Tudor king. His youngest surviving daughter, Mary – briefly queen consort of France – clandestinely married her brother Henry VIII's closest friend Charles Brandon, duke of Suffolk, in 1515; their eldest daughter was Frances, who married Henry Grey in the second half of 1533 or early in 1534.[4] Frances' marriage took place only months after the death of her mother on 25 June 1533, who continued, even after her marriage to Brandon, to be referred to as the French queen. The herald and chronicler Charles Wriothesley, for example, recorded her death thus: 'This yeare, on Midsommer eaven, died the French Queene, sister to the Kinge, and wife to the Duke of Suffolke, and was buried at Sainct Edmondesburie in Suffolke.'[5] The royal blood of Frances' three daughters was to prove a curse for them all. While Jane, famously, was executed as the so-called 'Nine Days' Queen', Katherine and Mary both suffered the consequences of secretly marrying without obtaining the permission of Elizabeth I. At Katherine's birth in 1540, however, the consequences of her possession of royal blood could not have been anticipated. In fact, Henry VIII had married for the fifth time that summer with the hope of siring sons – a dynastic imperative that the Tudor king could not afford to ignore, given his own history: his accession to the throne in 1509 had occurred only because his elder brother, Arthur, had unexpectedly died seven years earlier, in the spring of 1502. With only one male heir, the 2-year-old Edward, this family history made the need for a 'spare' heir all the more pressing.

Katherine spent her childhood in the idyllic setting of Bradgate Park. The seventeenth-century author Thomas Fuller believed that Katherine was born there, 'in the same place' where her elder sister Jane was born, although modern historians have determined that Jane was probably born in London.[6] Henry Grey had inherited the property in 1530 on the death of his father Thomas, second marquess of Dorset.[7] In addition to her Tudor blood, Katherine was descended from Elizabeth Wydeville, consort of the first Yorkist king, Edward IV, by her first marriage to the Lancastrian knight Sir John Grey of Groby. Following Thomas Grey's death, Henry VIII ordered 1,000 masses to be said for his soul. Dorset's 'well-beloved' wife Margaret was appointed her husband's chief executor, and the marquess stipulated that his son and heir Henry was to remain under the care of his schoolmaster Richard Broke.[8] Henry held a position in the household of the king's illegitimate son Henry Fitzroy, duke of Richmond and Somerset. Prior to his father's death, it was suggested that Henry would marry Katherine Fitzalan, daughter of the earl of Arundel, but when he refused to honour the betrothal following his fourteenth birthday, his mother was still required to pay the earl 4,000 marks in annual instalments of 300 marks.[9] Henry succeeded his father as marquess of Dorset following the latter's death in 1530.

In March 1533, Margaret Grey reached an arrangement with Charles Brandon, duke of Suffolk, concerning the wardship and marriage of her son. The duke paid 2,000 marks for the wardship and £1,000 for the king's consent for a marriage between his daughter Frances and Henry.[10] When the couple married either later that year or early the following year, Frances was 16 years old and Henry either 16 or 17. Frances' 'high descent, and the great care of King Henry the Eighth to see her happily and well bestowed in marriage, commended her unto the bed of Henry, Lord Marquess Dorset … a man of known nobility and of large revenues'.[11] In 1538, when he was 21 years old, the marquess was described as 'young, lusty, and poor, of great possessions, but which are not in his hands, many friends of great power, with little or no experience, well learned and a great wit'.[12] Another contemporary believed Dorset to be 'an illustrious and widely loved nobleman of ancient lineage, but lacking in circumspection'.[13] His relations with his mother were fractious: in 1538, Dorset reached his majority and was in a position to take control of his estates and move to Bradgate Park (thus forcing his mother to leave the residence), leading Margaret to write to the king's chief minister Thomas Cromwell seeking his intercession, for she was 'a poor widow unkindly treated by her son the Marquis, and not suffered to have her own stuff out of her own house'.[14]

Frances Brandon's reputation has traditionally been negative. She has long been condemned for both her alleged dynastic ambition and physical cruelty to her daughters. Alison Weir, for example, asserted that Frances was possessed of 'aggressive ambition'. She 'was forceful, determined to have her own way, and greedy for power and riches. She ruled her husband and daughters tyrannically, and in the case of the latter, often cruelly, and was utterly insensitive to the feelings of others.'[15] It is suggested that both she and her husband beat their daughters.[16] In her biography of Lady Jane Grey, Alison Plowden commented that Frances was 'a buxom, hard-riding woman who, as she grew older, began to bear an unnerving resemblance to her late uncle Henry [VIII]'.[17] She also alleged that Frances and Henry did not show affection to their daughters.[18]

Plowden's suggestion that Frances physically resembled her uncle the king is based on the traditional belief that a portrait created by Hans Eworth and held in the National Portrait Gallery, dating to 1559, is a likeness of Frances and her second husband Adrian Stokes. This early identification was problematic, however, given that the ages inscribed above the sitters' heads (36 and 21) do not correspond with Frances' and Adrian's known ages in 1559. The portrait was re-identified in the late twentieth century as a likeness of Mary Fiennes, Baroness Dacre and her eldest son from her first marriage, Gregory. The female sitter bears a marked similarity to the sitter in an earlier portrait of the baroness painted by Eworth, both of which feature a woman with the same distinctive ring on the fourth finger of her left hand. Elizabeth Honig commented that, in such images, the man was usually positioned on the left and the woman on the right. The double portrait emphasises 'her son's superficiality and almost feminine youthfulness', in contrast to the 'masculine consolidation of self which power, cemented by experience, has given Mary'.[19] The baroness is presented in 'her first husband's place as the keeper of the Dacre dynasty',[20] following his execution in 1541. The misidentification of the sitter in this portrait as Katherine Grey's mother served only to worsen her already poor reputation, in giving rise to the suggestion that her alleged physical resemblance to her uncle Henry VIII reflected the tyrannical and cruel nature that Frances shared with the king. She has also been condemned for her allegedly hasty second marriage to Stokes following the execution of her first husband in 1554.

As Leanda de Lisle noted, Frances' reputation as a child abuser is based on *The Schoolmaster*, written by the future Elizabeth I's tutor Roger Ascham, which stated that Jane had characterised her parents as 'sharp' and 'severe' when he visited her at Bradgate in 1550.[21] According to Ascham, Jane proclaimed that:

One of the greatest benefits that ever God gave me, is, that he sent me so sharp and severe parents, and so gentle a schoolmaster. For when I am in presence either of father or mother; whether I speak, keep silence, sit, stand, or go, eat, drink, be merry, or sad, be sewing, playing, dancing, or doing any thing else; I must do it, as it were, in such weight, measure, and number, even so perfectly, as God made the world; or else I am so sharply taunted, so cruelly threatened, yea presently sometimes with pinches, nips, and bobs, and other ways (which I will not name for the honour I bear them) so without measure misordered, that I think myself in hell, till time come that I must go to Mr Elmer; who teacheth me so gently, so pleasantly, with such fair allurements to learning, that I think all the time nothing whiles I am with him. And when I am called from him, I fall on weeping, because whatsoever I do else but learning, is full of grief, trouble, fear, and whole misliking unto me. And thus my book hath been so much my pleasure, and bringeth daily to me more pleasure and more, that in respect of it, all other pleasures, in very deed, be but trifles and troubles unto me.[22]

On one level, Jane's treatment at the hands of her parents, as apparently described to Ascham, could be interpreted as a conventional aspect of the society in which she lived. The twentieth-century historian Lawrence Stone, for example, famously suggested that the early modern family was a 'low-keyed, unemotional, authoritarian institution', while relations between parents and children were remote in an age in which 'individuals ... found it very difficult to establish close emotional ties to any other person'.[23] Stone's interpretation of early modern family relations, however, has been increasingly questioned based on his problematic use of evidence, while a wide range of material illuminates the 'close emotional ties' that did exist in early modern England.

One difficulty with Ascham's account is that it was only published after the deaths of both Jane and her parents. Other evidence for the cruelty of Frances and her husband is the suggestion that when Jane initially refused to marry Guildford Dudley in the spring of 1553, she was punished by being beaten until she capitulated. However, the Suffolk gentleman Robert Wingfield, who wrote an account of Mary Tudor's successful coup in 1553 entitled the *Vita Mariae Angliae Reginae*, offered an alternative narrative. Wingfield reported that Henry and Frances were reluctant to agree to a marriage between Jane and Guildford because of their dynastic ambitions for their eldest daughter, having long hoped that she would wed Edward VI prior to his untimely death. Their agreement to the Dudley marriage was based, according to Wingfield, on Henry Grey's fear of Guildford's father, the duke of Northumberland, who 'seemed to be like Phoenix in his companionship with the king and second in authority to none' in the spring of 1553.[24] Finally, the most convincing interpretation of Ascham's account is that, in recording Jane's alleged words, the scholar sought to prove an educational moral, namely that children learn better with a kind teacher.[25]

Evidence dating from Jane's lifetime presents a more balanced view of her relations with her parents. John Aylmer wrote to Henry Bullinger on 29 May 1551, noting that Dorset 'loves her [Jane] as a daughter'.[26] There is no evidence that any of the Grey sisters were physically abused by their parents, and Jane's younger sisters seem to have had a good relationship with Frances.[27] The suggestion that Henry and Frances 'were incapable of affection, or of differentiating, emotionally, between their girls'[28] is not supported by contemporary evidence. While the suggestion that the marquess and marchioness of Dorset treated their daughters cruelly in pursuit of their dynastic goals can, therefore, be dismissed, it is nonetheless apparent that Katherine and her sisters would have grown up with a strong sense of their royal lineage. At Katherine's birth in 1540, both of Henry VIII's daughters were illegitimate and there was, as yet, no indication that the king would name them in the line of succession should his only male heir die without having produced heirs of his body. Rumours circulated at court during Katherine Howard's brief queenship about the possibility that the queen was with child, all of which proved to be false. During the early 1540s, therefore, the Grey sisters' place in the Tudor succession may not have attracted a great deal of attention, but the illegitimacy of Henry's two daughters, even when they were reinstated in the succession by Act of Parliament in 1544, created an ambiguous dynastic situation, as would become apparent during the reign of Edward VI.

By virtue of her status as the king's niece, Frances and her husband were visible figures at court during the final years of Henry VIII's reign. The marquess of Dorset undertook a number of important political and military activities during the last years of the reign, but there is little evidence to suggest that the king had a particularly high opinion of his abilities. Indeed, a later account claimed that Dorset 'had few commendable qualities which might produce any high opinion of his parts and merit'.[29] He undertook ceremonial duties at court and commissions of the peace, for example in Somerset, Wiltshire and Devon, but did not participate in the wars with Scotland during the 1540s or in the subsequent negotiations for peace.[30] He was also not appointed to the Order of the Garter during Henry's reign, only gaining that honour in Edward VI's reign, a period in which he acquired greater political significance through, for example, serving on the Privy Council. Dorset was known for his fervent reformist beliefs and, instead of viewing the Grey sisters' childhoods as unhappy and characterised by physical and emotional abuse, it would be more fruitful to consider the religious climate of the 1540s in which Katherine and her sisters spent their childhoods for insights into the household in which they grew up.

As a result of Henry VIII's determination to annul his marriage to Katherine of Aragon and marry Anne Boleyn, the king's chief minister Thomas Cromwell had overseen the break with Rome and the resulting religious reforms that led to the establishment of the Church of England, including the aggressively efficient dissolution of the monasteries during the 1530s. Both the crown and the nobility, irrespective of individual religious beliefs, benefited financially from the dissolution of the monasteries. The suppression of papal authority went hand in hand with attempts to extirpate traditional Catholic practices and symbols, including the use of images, statues and rood screens, all of which were denounced by reformers as idolatrous. These measures met with active resistance, most notably with the outbreak of the rebellion known as the Pilgrimage of Grace in 1536. Some historians have argued that it was Henry, rather than Cromwell or other prominent figures like Archbishop Thomas Cranmer, who was the driving force behind the unprecedented religious changes in England.[31]

The king's attitude to the Reformation remains contentious. It is generally agreed, nonetheless, that he became increasingly opposed to the radical direction in which the religious reforms of the late 1530s were heading. The Act of Six Articles (1539) upheld traditional Catholic practices and beliefs, including transubstantiation and clerical celibacy. The execution of Cromwell the following year was perceived as another victory for conservatives at court. However, both reformers and conservatives alike were harshly treated if their religious activities were perceived as threatening to royal supremacy. In 1540, the French ambassador offered his opinion on the king's recent decision to execute both papists and reformers for their religious practices:

> [I] t is difficult to have a people entirely opposed to new errors which does not hold with the ancient authority of the Church and of the Holy See, or, on the other hand, hating the Pope, which does not share some opinions with the Germans. Yet the Government will not have either the one or the other, but insists on their keeping what is commanded, which is so often altered that it is difficult to understand what it is.[32]

The execution of Katherine Howard in 1542 has traditionally been interpreted as a setback for the conservatives at court, most notably the queen's uncle Thomas, duke of Norfolk, but other developments, including the publication of the *King's Book* in 1543, defended traditional religious beliefs and practices. Henry VIII's sixth and final marriage to Katherine Parr was welcomed by the reformers in view of the queen's active support for the reformist cause, most notably in publishing her own work, although rumours of heresy in her household placed her queenship, if not her life, in danger, if the later account of the martyrologist John Foxe is to be believed. Certainly, the brutal torture and execution of Anne Askew for heresy in 1546 was a clear demonstration of the king's determination to exterminate heresy from the kingdom. However, Henry's decision to provide for a regency council ultimately ended the reign on a triumphant note for reformers at court, given that the conservatives who would have been placed on it to assist in governing during his son's minority – including Norfolk and Bishop Stephen Gardiner – fell foul of the king. As a result, reformers such as the king's brother-in-law Edward Seymour, earl of Hertford, found themselves in positions of strength at the death of Henry VIII in 1547.

In this climate of religious toing and froing during the final decade of the reign, Katherine Grey's father was firmly committed to the reformist cause. His eldest daughter Jane was celebrated both during her lifetime and posthumously for her devout Protestant beliefs, and the shaping of her faith was in large part a result of the climate in which she grew to maturity. In 1550, the reformer John of Ulm noted that Dorset 'has exerted himself up to the present day with the greatest zeal and labour courageously to propagate the gospel of Christ. He is the thunderbolt and terror of the papists, that is, a fierce and terrible adversary.'[33] It is plausible that the marquess' religious beliefs became increasingly radical during Edward VI's reign, given the unprecedented scale of reform within the kingdom in those years. The Edwardian Reformation was marked by widespread iconoclasm as a result of the commitment to the destruction of traditional religion and establishment of a godly commonwealth. These measures were encouraged by the celebration of the young king as the biblical King Josiah, whom reformers praised for having brought his people back to God's word. The king's reformist beliefs had been actively shaped by the tutors selected for him by Henry VIII, including Richard Cox and John Cheke. Foxe celebrated Edward as a 'godly imp'.

Dorset's piety influenced his selection of tutors for his three daughters. These included the Cambridge scholar John Aylmer and Michelangelo Florio; the latter instructed Jane in Italian. All three of

Dorset's daughters studied Latin and Greek, while Jane also learned Hebrew. The family's chaplains John Haddon, Thomas Harding and John Willock – all of whom held reformist beliefs – were also involved in the girls' education.[34] The books owned by the youngest daughter Mary later in life, moreover, demonstrate her knowledge of French and Italian.[35] Modern historians have long acknowledged Jane's formidable intellect, and some have unfairly contrasted her scholarly abilities with those of her younger sister Katherine. Hester Chapman, for example, claimed that both Katherine and Mary were brought up in the shadow of their sister, due to Jane's 'superior intellect and stronger personality', and suggested that Katherine may have felt the need to compete with, even outstrip, her sister later in life.[36] No evidence supports Chapman's assertion, and while the marquess and marchioness of Dorset may understandably have focused their ambitions on Jane, as their eldest daughter, it is clear that Katherine and Mary were not neglected in the education that was provided to them. The assumption that Katherine was foolish or intellectually limited is usually the result of comparisons with her gifted elder sister, while knowledge of Katherine's politically unwise decision to marry the earl of Hertford secretly has also informed assumptions about her intelligence. An unverifiable historical tradition claims that she was the most attractive of the three Grey sisters.[37] Certainly, her portraits – which will be discussed later – testify to her physical charms. By contrast, the youngest Grey daughter, Mary, suffered from a physical deformity that was described as leaving her 'crooked backed'.

The correspondence of the Swiss reformer Henry Bullinger has been viewed as evidence that the household at Bradgate 'clearly took over as the principal aristocratic nursery of reform in England' during the 1550s.[38] Aylmer, who tutored the Grey daughters, informed Bullinger that their family 'is both well disposed to good learning, and sincerely favourable to religion'.[39] Jane's correspondence with leading European reformers is well known. The marquess and marchioness were clearly desirous of raising their daughters to be godly maidens, to behave virtuously with a desire to honour both their royal lineage and the noble house of Grey. They would have been expected to possess the virtues of 'chastitie, shamefastnes, and temperaunce' associated with women, as noted by the Cambridge scholar John Cheke.[40] While Dorset's committed reformist beliefs influenced the nature of education that his three daughters received, it is highly likely that his wife Frances also played an important role in this sphere. In the spring of 1551, in a letter to Sir Nicholas Throckmorton, Sir Richard Morysine referred to Frances' 'heats' in commenting that 'so goodly a wit waiteth upon so forward a will'.[41] Indeed, she 'was of greater spirit' than her husband.[42] Such characterisations of the marchioness serve as evidence of her forceful, spirited personality. In addition to their formal education, Frances would have ensured that her three daughters were instructed in the conventional pursuits deemed essential for young women of the nobility and gentry in sixteenth-century England, including sewing, embroidery, dancing, music and singing. Katherine and her sisters would also have acquired the necessary skills to manage a household. Evidence from later in her life suggests that Katherine was fond of animals, a passion that may well have begun in childhood.

With royal blood in their veins, Katherine and her sisters could anticipate prestigious marriages once they had reached maturity. The marquess and marchioness of Dorset nurtured ambitions that Jane would marry Edward VI, the only surviving child of Henry VIII by his third wife Jane Seymour. It has been suggested that Jane was carefully educated in view of her parents' ambition for her 'to be the pious Queen of a Godly King, the rulers of a new Jerusalem that Dorset intended to help build'.[43] Following the death of Henry VIII, however, Edward Seymour, Lord Protector and duke of Somerset – uncle of the young Edward VI – regarded Jane as a possible bride for his son and heir, Lord Hertford. In view of Katherine's young age, it is understandable why the issue of her marriage was not raised prior to 1553. Her step-grandmother Katherine Brandon, duchess of Suffolk, conveyed her disapproval of children being married at too young an age to William Cecil, then secretary of the duke of Somerset: 'I cannot tell what unkindness one of us might show the other than to bring our children into so miserable a state as not to choose by their own liking.'[44] In the last years of the fifteenth century, Henry VII's consort Elizabeth of York and his mother Margaret Beaufort had voiced similar opposition to the intended marriage of the royal couple's eldest daughter Margaret with James IV of Scotland, in view of her youth, and had insisted that the wedding take place at a later date. There was, as yet, no urgent need to arrange a marriage for Katherine.

Little evidence survives of Katherine's childhood. Growing up in the Leicestershire countryside, she could have had no awareness of the developments at court, as Henry VIII's reign drew to an end, that were to have a profound bearing on her future and that of her sisters. Despite infamously marrying six times, as Henry increasingly contemplated mortality he was left with the realisation that he had only one male heir – still a child – to guarantee the survival of the Tudor dynasty. The 1544 Succession Act had reinstated the king's illegitimate daughters Mary and Elizabeth in the line of succession, but Henry's decision not to restore their legitimacy ultimately left them in ambiguous positions that would become especially problematic during the following reign. The 1536 Succession Act empowered the king with the right to appoint his successor by his will, and this right was confirmed in the 1544 Act.[45] On 30 December 1546, the king implemented a final revision to his last will and testament, which was signed with a dry stamp. John Edwards has noted that one provision in the 1544 Succession Act later proved crucial: the right of the sovereign to amend the order of succession further in a subsequent will and testament, for 'this was a move of great constitutional significance since it meant that the succession was now in effect to be determined not by legitimacy of birth or by hereditary right, but by the will of the sovereign acting under parliamentary statute'.[46] A number of questions would arise during the 1560s' succession controversy of Elizabeth I's reign about the validity, or otherwise, of Henry VIII's will, but for now it is important to note that the king's will affected Katherine and her sisters in that it named them in the line of succession.

Upon Henry's death, he would be succeeded by his only son, Edward, then aged 9 years old. The will appointed sixteen executors to sit on a regency council to govern during Edward's minority, headed by the prince's maternal uncle Edward Seymour, earl of Hertford. Although neither Mary (daughter of Katherine of Aragon) nor Elizabeth (daughter of Anne Boleyn) were recognised by their father in his last will and testament as being legitimate, he nonetheless decreed that they could in turn succeed their brother Edward if the latter died without siring heirs.[47] The king also stipulated that both Mary and Elizabeth would lose their places in the succession if they married without the consent of the councillors in office during Edward's minority; thus their place in the succession was conditional.[48] If, however, Mary and Elizabeth both also died childless, then the crown 'shall holly remayn and cum to the Heires of the Body of the Lady Fraunces [Brandon] our Niepce, eldest Doughter to our late Suster the French Quene [Mary Tudor] laufully begotten', and then to 'the Heyres of the Body of the Lady Elyanore [Brandon] our Niepce, second Doughter to our sayd late Sister the French Quene laufully begotten'.[49]

It remains unknown why the king overlooked his niece Frances in favour of her offspring. It is possible that she was excluded because of Henry's low opinion of Frances' husband, which also seems to have been the case regarding the list of councillors nominated by the king to govern during his son's minority – Dorset was absent.[50] According to contemporary hereditary and dynastic succession customs, Mary, Queen of Scots – granddaughter of the king's elder sister Margaret – should have had precedence over Lady Jane Grey and her sisters, but Henry VIII ignored existing beliefs about primogeniture in royal succession.[51] Historians have puzzled over Henry's reasons for excluding the descendants of his elder sister – the Scottish line – from the line of succession in favour of those of his younger sister, but undoubtedly the king had no reason to believe that his three children would in turn die childless, thus creating a succession controversy at the heart of English political culture during the second half of the sixteenth century. Given that Edward inherited the throne at the age of 9 years old and was not, contrary to popular belief, constantly plagued by ill health, there was every reason to believe that the young king would marry and sire heirs of his own with which to ensure the continuation of the Tudor dynasty. That was not, in fact, the case, and his final, fatal illness in 1553 would change the lives of Katherine Grey and her sisters, Jane and Mary, forever.

2

'Tempests of Sedition'

Upon Henry VIII's death on 28 January 1547 at Whitehall Palace, his 9-year-old son Edward became king of England. Katherine's father acted as chief mourner at the late king's funeral, a role granted him as a male kinsman of the new king.[1] He and the other twelve mourners 'prepared themselves in their mourning habits, as hoods, mantles, gowns, and al other apparels, according to their degrees; and were in good order and readiness at the Court, to give their attendance when they should be called'.[2] On 3 February, the marquess assembled with the other mourners 'in the pallet chamber, in their mourning apparel' and proceeded to the hearse, Dorset's 'train born after him'.[3] The marquess made an offering 'with the rest following after him in order two and two', after a requiem mass had taken place and 'the chappel singing and saying the ceremonies therto appertaining, in most solempn and goodly wise, to the offertory'.[4]

On 13 February, three solemn masses were sung, after which Dorset, as 'chief mourner, accompanied with al the rest of the mourners, offered for them al'.[5] The mourners and prelates subsequently withdrew to the Presence Chamber to dinner.[6] The following day, the marquess rode 'next to the chariot ... alone, his horse trapped al in black velvet', followed by the twelve mourners, as the funeral procession made its way through Charing Cross, Braintree and Syon to

St George's Chapel, Windsor, where the king had directed that he would be buried beside the mother of his son and heir, Jane Seymour.[7] The burial itself took place on 16 February. Dorset also officiated as Constable of England at the coronation of Edward VI four days later and rode in front of the king during the coronation procession, carrying an upturned drawn sword.[8]

At the coronation service, Archbishop Cranmer hailed the new king as a second Josiah, exhorting further reformation of the English Church and calling for the 'tyranny' of the Pope to be expunged from the realm. Edward's reign has been described as a period of 'evangelical revolution', and both the duke of Somerset and the earl of Warwick – the respective leaders during the king's minority – actively worked to create 'King Josiah's purified Church'.[9] Church property continued to be confiscated and the chantries were dissolved. The 1549 Book of Common Prayer, which was criticised by reformers for not being radical enough, was replaced by that of 1552, which removed many of the traditional sacraments and religious observances. Edward's reign was characterised by widespread iconoclasm as part of the concerted effort to suppress idolatry and superstition. Reformed doctrines, such as justification by faith alone, were made official.[10] For Catholics, the new king's accession meant that 'the observance of Catholic piety was put to flight and abolished, as far as the public government could prevail, and heresy and schism brought in place'.[11]

As the religious revolution of Edward's reign progressed, Katherine Grey and her sisters grew to maturity within the godly atmosphere at Bradgate. However, from Katherine's perspective, perhaps the most significant development in the spring of 1547 was not Henry VIII's death but the placing of her elder sister in the household of the Lord Admiral, Thomas Seymour, maternal uncle of Edward VI and brother of the Lord Protector, the duke of Somerset. Sir John Harington, friend and servant of the Lord Admiral, was sent to Dorset House shortly after Edward's accession to suggest that Jane reside in Seymour's household, with the promise that he would arrange Jane's marriage to the king. Harington described Jane as:

as handsom a Lady as eny in England, and that she might be Wife to eny Prince in Chrestendom, and that, if the King's Majestie, when he came to Age, wold mary within the Realme, it was as lykely he wold be there, as in eny other Place, and that he wold with it.[12]

Given that the Lord Admiral's brother, the duke of Somerset, hoped to marry Jane to his son Edward, earl of Hertford, it is possible that in securing Jane's wardship, Seymour sought to thwart his elder brother's ambitions.[13] William Parr, marquess of Northampton, later testified that Seymour had confided to him 'that ther wolde be moch ado for my Lady Jane, the Lord Marques Dorsett's Doughter; and that mi Lord Protector and my Lady Somerset wolde do what they colde to obtayne hyr of my sayd Lord Marques for my Lord of Hertforde; butt he sayd, they should not prevayle therin, for my sayd Lord Marques had gyven hyr hollye to hym, upon certeine Covenants that wer betwene them two'.[14] The Lord Admiral offered Dorset a loan of £2,000 in return for permitting Jane to join Seymour's household as his ward.[15]

It has been suggested that Dorset initially agreed to be the Lord Admiral's friend and ally as a result of the marquess' ill treatment at the hands of the Lord Protector, namely by ennobling Parr as marquess of Northampton (formerly, Dorset had been the only marquess in the realm) and excluding Dorset from the Privy Council.[16] The marquess later claimed that, at Seymour Place, the Lord Admiral 'used unto me at more length the like persuasions as had been made by Harrington for the having of my daughter, wherein he showed himself so desirous and earnest, and made me such fair promises'.[17] Dorset subsequently agreed to send his daughter to the Lord Admiral's household once Seymour had promised £2,000 in return for her wardship and a future marriage with the king.[18]

Jane's departure from Bradgate marked a formative change in her life. There is no way of knowing whether Katherine enjoyed a close relationship with Jane, although historians have usually contrasted Jane's pious and scholarly nature with Katherine's alleged frivolity. Some, including Chapman, have asserted that Katherine was jealous of Jane.[19]

There is no evidence for this and unfortunately the nature of their relationship remains uncertain, although Katherine would certainly have been aware of her parents' ambitions for Jane, namely their desire for her to marry Edward VI. Katherine's relations with her younger sister Mary are similarly obscure.

In view of his duty to produce an heir to ensure the continuation of the Tudor dynasty, the subject of the young king's marriage attracted considerable interest in diplomatic circles during his brief reign. While the marquess and marchioness of Dorset hoped that he would marry their eldest daughter, and accordingly ensured that Jane received an education suitable for a godly queen consort, foreign ambassadors speculated about the possibility of Edward marrying into one of the European royal houses, primarily those of France and Scotland. In February 1547, only a month into Edward's reign, it was claimed that King François I of France, who had formerly favoured a marriage between Edward and Mary, Queen of Scots as a means of securing the restitution to him of Boulogne, might 'now attempt to renew these negotiations'.[20] The imperial diplomat Jean de St Mauris also reported the French king's willingness to encourage a marriage between Edward and Mary as a means 'for the recovery of Boulogne' and 'on the condition that, if he brought about the said marriage, he should be set free of his obligation to pay the two millions in gold, by which he thinks he would be doing for England far more than the value of the said two millions'.[21] Towards the end of that year, St Mauris noted that the Lord Protector had sent a delegation to Berwick to speak with the Scottish envoys about a marriage between Edward and Mary as a way of obtaining 'an understanding between the English and Scots' and to come to terms with France, Scotland's long-standing ally.[22]

Following her departure, Jane spent her time alternately at Seymour Place and at Chelsea, the residence of the dowager queen, Katherine Parr. She seems to have become part of Katherine's entourage. The dowager queen secretly married Seymour sometime that spring, only months after Henry VIII's death, although the exact date is unknown.

It was only in July, for example, that the imperial ambassador François van der Delft informed the Holy Roman Emperor that Katherine:

> was married a few days since to the Lord Admiral, the brother of the Protector, and still causes herself to be served ceremoniously as Queen, which it appears is the custom here. Nevertheless when she went lately to dine at the house of her new husband she was not served with the royal state, from which it is presumed that she will eventually live according to her new condition.[23]

The previous month, he had reported that 'a marriage is being arranged between the Queen Dowager and the Lord Admiral brother of the Protector'.[24] A fictionalised account of Seymour's relationship with Katherine claimed that the Lord Protector actually encouraged their courtship as a means of putting his younger brother 'in a great position', and accordingly the duke and Katherine discussed and arranged her marriage to the Lord Admiral, 'which was performed by the Archbishop of Canterbury, and was known all over London the next day'.[25]

Irrespective of the circumstances of her marriage, Katherine's devout Protestantism surely exerted a strong influence on Jane, helping to shape the young girl's renowned piety. The martyrologist John Foxe noted that Katherine possessed 'virtues of the mind' as well as 'very rare gifts of nature, as singular beauty, favour, and comely personage'.[26] As queen, she had been 'very much given to the reading and study of the holy Scriptures'.[27] Jane would undoubtedly have flourished under the care of the scholarly and pious dowager queen, who had published a number of religious works since 1544 including *Prayers or Meditations* (1545), later translated by her stepdaughter Elizabeth into Latin, French and Italian as a New Year's gift for Henry VIII. The more radical *The Lamentation of a Sinner* was published after Henry's death. The eldest Grey daughter would have spent time during this period with Elizabeth, also in residence in Katherine's household, although it does not appear that the two were close, despite their shared love of learning.

It is almost certain that Jane learned of the scandal involving Seymour and Elizabeth, which culminated in the dowager queen expelling her stepdaughter from her household in an attempt to protect both her reputation and that of the Lord Admiral.[28] Seymour had visited the teenaged Elizabeth in her bedchamber at Seymour Place when she stayed at that residence with the dowager queen, coming up 'every Mornyng in his Nyght-Gown, barelegged in his Slippers, where he found commonly the Lady Elizabeth up at hir Boke'.[29] Such behaviour led Elizabeth's governess Kat Astley to warn Seymour that 'it was an unsemly Sight to come so bare leggid to a Maydens Chambre; with which he was angry, but he left it'.[30] At Chelsea, the Lord Admiral:

> wold come many Mornyngs into the said Lady Elizabeth's Chamber, before she were redy, and sometyme before she did rise. And if she were up, he wold bid hir good Morrow, and ax how she did, and strike hir upon the Bak or on the Buttocks famylearly, and so go forth through his Lodgings; and sometyme go through to the Maydens, and play with them, and so go forth: And if she were in hir Bed, he wold put open the Curteyns, and bid hir good Morrow, and make as though he would come at hir: And she wold go further in the Bed, so that he could not come at hir.[31]

Elizabeth's cofferer Thomas Parry believed that the Lord Admiral:

> loved her but to well, and hadd so done a good while; and that the Quene was jelowse on hir and him, in so moche that, one Tyme the Quene, suspecting the often Accesse of the Admirall to the Lady Elizabeth's Grace, cam sodenly upon them, wher they were all alone, (he having her in his Armes:) wherfore the Quene fell out, bothe with the Lord Admirall, and with her Grace also.[32]

Nowadays, Seymour's relations with Elizabeth are interpreted as predatory, tantamount to child abuse, and the potentially treasonous nature of the affair caused sufficient scandal to prompt the Privy Council to order an investigation into the goings on.

Jane accompanied the dowager queen, then pregnant, to Sudeley Castle in the summer of 1548 following the departure of Elizabeth from Katherine's household. In August, Dorset visited Jane there and informed her that, among other news, her sister Katherine was studying Greek with the family chaplain Thomas Harding.[33] Unfortunately, there is no record of whether Katherine enjoyed these lessons, but it is usually assumed that she lacked her elder sister's scholarly nature. Katherine Parr died on 5 September at the age of 36 from childbed fever, only six days after giving birth to a daughter, Mary. Jane officiated as chief mourner at the dowager queen's funeral, which has been described as the first Protestant funeral held in English. The dowager queen's death resulted in Jane returning to Bradgate, but it is ridiculous to assert that her parents regarded her 'as a failure' and were disappointed as a result of her unexpected return to their care.[34]

In fact, the marquess and marchioness were eager for Jane to return to them. Dorset was 'fully determined, that his Doughter the Lady Jane shuld no more com to remaine with the Lord Admirall', but the Lord Admiral did not take no for an answer, being 'so earnest ... in Persuasione', namely regarding his promise to arrange Jane's marriage to Edward VI.[35] The courtier Sir William Sharington, a friend of Seymour, likewise persuaded Frances 'to let the sayd Lady Jane come to my Lord Admirall'.[36] Seymour also confessed to Dorset his antipathy to the Lord Protector and declared that 'he wold have the King to have Thonor of his own Things; for, sayd he, of his Yeres he is wise and lerned'.[37] On 17 September, less than two weeks after his wife's death, Seymour wrote to Dorset:

After my most hartye commend unto your good Lordship. Whereby my last Lettres unto the same, wrytten in a Tyme when partelye with the Quene's Highnes Deathe, I was so amased, that I had smale regard eyther to my self or to my doings; and partelye then thinking that my great Losse must presently have constrayned me to have broken upp and dissolved my hole House, I offred unto your Lordeship to sende my Lady Jane unto you, whensoever you wolde sende for her, as to him whome I thought wolde be most tendre on hir: Forasmuche as sithens being bothe better advised of my self, and having more depelye disgested wherunto my Power wolde extend; I fynde indede that with God's helpe, I shall right well be hable to contynewe my House together, without dyminisheng any greate parte therof. And therfore putting my hole Affyance and Trust in God have begonne of newe to establish my Houshold, where shall remayne not oone-lye the Gentlewomen of the Quene's Hieghnes Privey Chamber, but allso the Maids which wayted at larg, and other Women being about her Grace in her lief Tyme, with a hundred and twenty Gentlemen and Yeomen, contynualle abeyding in House together; saving that now presentlye certaine of the Mayds and Gentlemen have desyred to have Licence for a Moneth, or such a thing, to see theyr Frends; and then immedyately returne hither again. And therfore doubting, least your Lordship might think any unkyndness, that I shoulde by my saide Lettres take occasion to rydd me of your Doughter so soon after the Quenes Deathe: For the Prof both of my hartye Affection towards youe, and good Will towards hir, I mynd now to keape her, untill I shall next speak with your Lordshipp; whiche should have been within these thre or four Dayes, if it had not been that I must repayr unto the Corte, aswell to help certane of the Quenes pore Servants, with soome of the Things now fallen by her Death, as allso for my owne Affayrs; oneles I shalbe advertysed from your Lordship of your expresse Mynd to the contrarye. My Ladye, my Mother, shall and wooll, I doubte not, be as deare unto hir, as though she weare hir owne Doughter. And for my owne Parte, I shall contynewe her haulf Father and more; and all that are in my House shall be as dili-gent about her, as your self wolde wyshe accordinglye.[38]

The dowager queen's death meant that it would have been inappro-priate for Jane to reside in the widowed Lord Admiral's household. Recognising this difficulty, Seymour sought to put her parents' minds at ease by explaining that his mother, Margery, Lady Seymour, would assume responsibility for Jane's care. In October, then about 12 years old, Jane wrote to Seymour thanking him for the 'goodnes' he had shown her:

My dutye to youre lordeshippe in most humble wyse rememberd withe no lisse thankes for the gentylle letters which I receavyed from you Thynkynge my selfe so muche bounde to your lordshippe for youre greate goodnes towardes me from tyme to tyme that I can-nenot by anye meanes be able to recompence the least parte thereof: I purposed to wryght a few rude lines unto youre lordshippe rather as a token to shewe howe muche worthyer I thynke youre lordshippes goodnes then to gyve worthye thankes for the same thes my letters shall be to testyfe unto you that lyke as you have becom towardes me a louynge and kynd father so I shall be alwayes most redye to obey your momysons and good instructions as becomethe one uppon whom you have heaped so manye benyfytes. and thus fearynge leste I shoulde trouble youre lordshippe to muche I moste humblye take my leave of your good lordshyppe
    your humble servant durynge
    my life jane graye[39]

Neither of Jane's parents were convinced of the merits of returning Jane to the Lord Admiral's household, instead believing that she should stay at home under her mother's supervision. Dorset wrote to Seymour from Bradgate thanking him for his 'most frendly Affection towards me' and Jane in offering 'thabode of my Doughter at your Lordeshypes House', but explained that:

Nevertheless considering the State of my Doughter and hyr tendre Yeres, wherin she shall hardlie rule hyr sylfe as yet without a Guide, lest she shuld for lacke of a Bridle, tak to moche the Head, and conceave such Opinion of hyr sylfe, that all such good behauior as she heretofore hath learned, by the Quenes and your most holsom

Instructions, shuld either altogither be quenched in hyr, or at the leste moche diminishid, I shall in most hartie wise require your Lordeshippe to committ hyr to the Governance of hyr Mother; by whom for the Feare and Duetie she owithe hyr, she shall most easilye be rulid and framid towards Vertue, which I wishe above all Thinges to be most plentifull in hyr.[40]

Dorset sought 'in thes hyr yonge Yeres, wherin she now standeth, either to make or marre (as the common saing ys) thadressing of hyr Mynd to Humilytye, Sobrenes, and Obedience'.[41] In alluding to his desire for Jane to be guided by her mother in learning virtuous behaviour, Dorset voiced the contemporary belief that 'the archetypal good woman was a godly matron' in a culture in which medical understanding of the female body supported religious beliefs about women's inferiority.[42] Reformers identified a godly woman as one who obeyed her husband, cared for her children and servants, and dutifully attended to private devotion.[43] Given that the marquess and marchioness were ambitious for Jane's marriage to Edward VI to take place, understandably they were desirous of ensuring that she acquired the virtues of 'Humilytye, Sobrenes, and Obedience' as she grew to maturity, so that she appeared an attractive candidate for the king's hand in marriage.

Dorset's expectation of his eldest daughter's virtuous conduct undoubtedly extended to her sisters Katherine and Mary within the godly household at Bradgate. Jane's complaint to Roger Ascham in 1550 about her parents' high expectations (referred to in Chapter 1) should be considered alongside Dorset's belief, expressed to Seymour, that Frances' role was to 'correcte' Jane 'as a Mystres, and monishe hyr as a Mother'[44] following the death of Katherine Parr, who would have been responsible for taking on this role prior to her death. Jane's speech to Ascham indicates that she struggled with the high expectations of her parents, but there is no way of knowing whether Katherine – or her sister Mary, for that matter – felt similarly about the Dorsets' ambitions. Chapman has suggested that Jane's parents may have treated her more harshly than her sisters because of her 'abrupt frankness that sometimes bordered on insolence'.[45] It is possible, although unproven, that Katherine's relations with her parents were less tense both because their ambitions were focused on Jane and because of the two girls' differing personalities. Frances wrote to Seymour at the same time as her husband, requesting 'that I may have the Oversight of hir [Jane] with your good Will', promising 'to use your Counsaile and Advise in the bestowing of hir, whensoever it shall happen'.[46]

Seymour, however, did not take no for an answer. He travelled to Bradgate to speak with the marquess and marchioness in person. As Dorset later reported, the Lord Admiral 'was so earnestly in hand with me and my wife, that in the end, because he would have no nay, we were contented she should again return to his house', Seymour having promised to promote Jane's marriage to the king.[47] Sharington likewise 'travailed as earnestly' with Frances 'for her good-will to the return of' Jane.[48] By the end of October, Jane was in residence at Seymour Place under the care of the Lord Admiral's mother. Seymour had successfully persuaded Henry and Frances to permit Jane to return to his household, with the promise that he would arrange a marriage for her with the king.[49]

In addition, Dorset assured Seymour that he would 'defend him against all men, save the King'.[50] The Lord Admiral's disaffection with his brother's government was, however, to prove his downfall. Although she did not encourage his attentions, Seymour apparently desired to marry Elizabeth in pursuit of his political ambitions. Her cofferer Thomas Parry believed, incorrectly, that Elizabeth was receptive to the idea of marrying Seymour, and he discussed the matter with the Lord Admiral.[51] Recognising the dangers of plotting to secretly marry the king's half-sister — whose marriage required permission from both the king and the Privy Council — Seymour's intimates tried to dissuade him. One advised him: 'Beware, it were better for you if you had never been born, nay, that you were burnt to the quick alive, than that you should attempt it.'[52] On the night of 16 January 1549, Seymour:

attempted to outrage the person of the young King by night, and has been taken to the Tower. The alarm was given by the gentleman who sleeps in the King's chamber, who, awakened by the barking of the dog that lies before the King's door, cried out 'Help! Murder!' Everybody rushed in; but the only thing they found was the lifeless corpse of the dog. Suspicion points to the Admiral, because he had scattered the watch that night on several errands, and because it has been noticed that he has some secret plot on hand, hoping to marry the second daughter of the late King, the Lady Elizabeth, who is also under grave suspicion.[53]

It was rumoured that Seymour, by nature a reckless individual, 'had planned to marry the late King's second daughter, and kill the King, the Lady Mary, and the Protector, to ensure a more peaceful, or rather more despotic reign'.[54] The Lord Admiral was said to have begun 'to make a party and confederation, whereof himself would be head; and got rules and offices into his hands, and retained many gentlemen and yeomen in his service', and intended 'to take the King into his own hands and government, and so to rule the affairs of the realm; and endeavoured to engender a hatred in the King's heart against his uncle the Protector'.[55] Seymour's interest in Elizabeth was 'judged to be a traitorous aspiring to the crown of the realm, and to be King of the same'.[56]

Jane returned to Dorset House, the Grey family's residence in London, while her father was questioned about the Lord Admiral by the king's councillors.[57] Seymour was arrested and imprisoned in the Tower. He was convicted of treason in March 1549 and his execution took place at Tower Hill on the 20th. Van der Delft reported that Seymour:

was sentenced to death by Parliament, without being allowed to present his defence. Some claimed in Parliament that he ought to be heard personally, but their opinions availed him little. He was condemned almost unanimously (with two or three dissident votes only) on the evidence produced in proof of 31 charges brought against him, the most important being that he had planned to marry the Lady Elizabeth without consent of the Council; that he had planned to ally the King with the daughter of an English nobleman; that he had plotted to kill the Protector; and had amassed a large sum of money; that he had induced 400 young lords to join his side, some with money, some with promises, so that the greater number of the gentlemen of the King's chamber were with him. From this, and from the fact that he tried to get the King to sign a letter to Parliament in which he enjoined them to give entire faith to whatever the Lord Admiral his uncle told them from him, and recommended his (the Admiral's) person to them, it was deducted that, following the example of Richard III, he wished to make himself King.

He was charged, besides, with having favoured pirates; connived at the passage of the Queen of Scots to France, and received a pension from a foreign prince, who is said to be the King of France. He refused persistently to answer any of these charges in the Tower, saying he had a right to a public hearing. This contumacious behaviour is punishable with capital punishment by the English law; which decrees that the accused must declare the defence he intends to make, when charged to do so. This was one of the reasons why Parliament sentenced him unheard.[58]

Wriothesley recorded that, on 20 March, 'Sir Thomas Seymor, Lord of Sidley and High Admirall of England, and brother to my Lord Protector, was beheaded at the Towrehill, which said Lord Admirall was condemned of high treason by the hole Perliament, as by an Act made by the same more plainlie appeareth'.[59] While the Lord Admiral undoubtedly plotted against his brother, historians have questioned whether he was actually guilty of treason. Elizabeth Norton has argued that 'he was, rather, the casualty of his dispute with his brother'.[60]

The year 1549 proved, in several respects, to be a turbulent one. Rebellion broke out that spring and summer across the realm, motivated by social and economic grievances, alongside opposition to the Edwardian religious settlement; these uprisings are known as Kett's

Rebellion and the Prayer Book Rebellion respectively. Sir John Hayward later claimed that 'such tempests of sedition tumbled in England'.[61] On 11 June, the Lord Protector wrote to Dorset and the earl of Huntingdon warning them of the presence of rebels in the region.[62] Katherine's father acted alongside Huntingdon in suppressing discontent in Rutland and Leicestershire.[63] On 17 August, the marquess wrote to the Privy Council asking for his brother, Lord Thomas Grey, to be sent to him to help in maintaining order in the county, but Lord Thomas was already needed to assist Lord John Grey in defending Ambleteuse after King Henri II of France declared war.[64] Ultimately, both rebellions were defeated by the royal forces and thousands of rebels were slain, including the leaders.

During these years, Katherine spent her childhood at Bradgate, far away from court. That the evidence for Katherine's life and upbringing during this period is fragmentary is understandable given that the marquess and marchioness of Dorset were then focusing their attention on their eldest daughter, in view of their ambitions for her future. The downfall of Seymour and the outbreak of rebellion the same year would have been a tense and unpredictable time for the Grey family, but the scattered evidence for this period of Katherine's life seems to suggest, in more normal circumstances, a close and supportive family environment. As an example of this, Frances and her daughters visited the home of George Medley at Tilty in Essex in November and December 1549, and they also spent time with the king's elder half-sister Mary that year, perhaps at her residence of Hunsdon in Hertfordshire.[65] Frances and her daughters travelled to Mary's residence at Beaulieu on 26 November. While there, Jane Grey walked with one of Mary's attendants, Lady Wharton, to the chapel; when the latter curtseyed towards the altar as a sign of her obeisance, Jane asked her whether Mary was in the chapel, and when Lady Wharton informed her that she curtseyed 'to Him that made us all', Jane retorted, 'how can He be there that made us all, and the baker made Him?'[66] This conversation provides an early example of the Protestant piety for which Jane became so well known. A few days later, on 2 December, Katherine and her younger sister Mary 'came to sup' at Tilty in the company of 'a great many gentlemen'; they were joined there by their parents, elder sister and uncle Lord John on the 16th.[67] In January 1550, Katherine and her family departed from Tilty to the residence of the marquess' sister Elizabeth, Lady Audley at Saffron Walden, before returning to Tilty afterwards.[68]

A number of important developments, both political and personal, affected Katherine's family during the early years of Edward's reign. In November 1549, Dorset was appointed a privy councillor probably as a reward for his loyalty to John Dudley, earl of Warwick, whose coup that autumn resulted in the overthrow of the Lord Protector. Van der Delft declared that:

> no mention has as yet been made of restoring religion, and those who desired to see this step taken have been displeased to see that the Marquis of Dorset and the Bishop of Ely, both of them entirely won over to the new sect, have recently been admitted to the Council, which may well have been done by the Earl of Warwick in order to strengthen his party.[69]

As she approached her tenth birthday, Katherine experienced a change of scene following her father's appointment, since her family began to spend more time in London and at the court from February 1550 onwards.[70] The young and impressionable Katherine surely would have found London an exciting and vibrant city, especially when contrasted with the idyllic rural setting of Bradgate in which she had spent her early years. Some years later, it was described as being:

> the metropolis of the kingdom, and truly royal, being with reason regarded as one of the principal cities of Europe, whether it be from the abundance and convenience of whatever is required for the use of man, or from the amount of its population, estimated ordinarily, including the suburbs and the town of Westminster, which serves as a suburb, at 185,000 souls. It has handsome streets and buildings,

especially the bridge, which has 19 arches, all of solid stone, over the river, and the cathedral church of St. Paul. But yet more beautiful is the site of the City, placed, as it is, advantageously on the banks of the Thames, from which, besides beauty, it derives great wealth, from the vast concourse of ships, of three and four hundred Venetian tons burthen, which enter the river from every quarter, being aided by the strong ebb and flow of the sea, although more than 60 miles from the city.[71]

During the 1550s, Katherine's father was awarded a number of honours and offices, including the appointments of steward of the King's Honours and constable of Leicester Castle.[72] In early 1551, he was appointed Warden of the Marches but surrendered the office shortly afterwards.[73] In April 1551, the imperial ambassador Jehan Scheyfve reported that:

> the Marquis of Dorset, who has been appointed the King's lieutenant in the North Country, set out in that direction a short time ago with 80 horse, and my Lords of Westmorland and Grey, who was captain of Boulogne, have done the same, and have taken up their quarters there.[74]

The hoped-for marriage between Jane and the king may, by now, have become uncertain as a result of the execution of Seymour, who had done so much to persuade the marquess and marchioness of Dorset of his desire to achieve it. Before his downfall in the autumn of 1549, the Lord Protector had nurtured hopes that the eldest Grey daughter would marry his son and heir Edward, earl of Hertford. In the spring of 1550, following his release from the Tower, Somerset once again sought Jane's hand in marriage for his son, while his eldest daughter Anne would marry Jane's teenaged uncle Henry Brandon, duke of Suffolk.[75] However, Katherine Brandon, dowager duchess of Suffolk and stepgrandmother of Jane, voiced her hostility to the suggested marriages on account of the parties' young ages, and Somerset's eldest daughter eventually married Lord Lisle, Warwick's eldest son.[76] Thus, there is no evidence to support the suggestion that a marriage contract was drawn up between Hertford and Jane around this time,[77] especially given that Jane's parents continued to hope that their eldest daughter would one day wed the king.

Following their move to the capital, the Grey family initially resided at Dorset House. However, Katherine's father was granted the dukedom of Suffolk in October 1551 as a result of the deaths of Frances' half-brothers Henry and Charles in the summer of that year from the sweating sickness, and the family moved from Dorset House to Suffolk Place as a result.[78] The deaths of Henry and Charles Brandon occurred during a particularly virulent outbreak of the sweating sickness, for that summer 'died verie many of yong men and women', including 'booth ... rich yong mene and other' in London.[79] The creation of Henry Grey as duke of Suffolk took place on 11 October at 'a great solemnitie kept at the Kinges Maiesties Court at Hampton Court'.[80] Remarking on Suffolk's elevation, Hayward asserted that the duke was 'a man for his harmelesse simplicitie, neither misliked nor much regarded'.[81]

The duke's 'harmelesse simplicitie' can arguably be discerned in the nature of his association with the earl of Warwick, who had acquired the dukedom of Northumberland on the very day that Dorset was elevated to duke of Suffolk. Suffolk's association with Northumberland, both during the early 1550s and in the events leading to the coup of 1553, indicates that the latter was the stronger personality and that Suffolk was easily guided, perhaps even manipulated, by Northumberland. Regarding the events of 1553, it would be claimed that Suffolk, who was 'timid and trustful', feared Northumberland on account of his 'fierce nature'.[82] Contemporary evidence reveals Suffolk's involvement in the downfall of the duke of Somerset. Reporting Somerset's arrest in October 1551 for having 'committed a very great offence', Scheyfve noted that 'the Duke was taken secretly from his house to the Tower by water, by means of the persuasions of the Treasurer, now Marquis of Winchester; Herbert, Master of the Horse, and the new Duke of

Suffolk'.[83] Somerset had allegedly plotted to have his colleagues murdered at a banquet, while also intending 'to seize the Tower of London and the royal treasury, bombard the town to revenge himself for his former imprisonment, and occupy several other castles and strong places in the country'.[84]

Somerset's trial took place on 1 December at Westminster Hall. The duke was acquitted of treason and 'lese-majestie' but was convicted of felony 'for having held illicit assemblies'.[85] Later that month, it was rumoured that Somerset would be granted a pardon and released from confinement.[86] This report, however, proved false and Somerset was executed on 22 January 1552 at Tower Hill. In view of the duke's popularity with the public, the government ordered that the execution should take place earlier than usual: 'three or four hours before the accustomed time, they took him from the Tower to the scaffold and beheaded him, although many of the people who had come to behold … made a great outcry, as though they would have delivered him'.[87] Somerset:

> tooke his death very patiently, but there was such a feare and disturbance amonge the people sodainely before he suffred, that some tombled down the ditch, and some ranne toward the houses thereby and fell, that it was marveile to see and hear; but howe the cause was, God knoweth.[88]

The imperial ambassador related that Somerset was 'deeply mourned by the people, who are far from satisfied with his execution, when he had only been convicted of felony', and after the execution 'a great crowd assembled all day long at the place, talking about the Duke and bewailing his death. Those who could come near washed their hands in his blood, and others dipped their handkerchiefs in it.'[89] Following Somerset's death, the duke and duchess of Suffolk acquired the late duke's property of the Charterhouse at Sheen.[90]

Irrespective of the ambitions of the duke and duchess of Suffolk for Jane's marriage to the king, a number of candidates were put forward for King Edward's hand in marriage during the early 1550s. A commission in May 1551 comprising William Parr, marquess of Northampton, Thomas, bishop of Ely, Sir John Mason, Sir Philip Hoby, Sir William Pickering, Sir Thomas Smith and Dr John Oliver was appointed to sign a marriage treaty between Edward and the Queen of Scots with the agreement of Henri II of France; failing that, the commissioners were instructed to press for a marriage with Elisabeth, daughter of the French king.[91] The king's diary noted in May that the terms for the marriage would stipulate, 'first, to have the dote 12,000 marcs a yere, and the dowrie at lest 800,000 crounes. The forfaieture 100,000 crounes at the most, if I performed not; and paiing that to be delivered. And that this shuld not empeach the former covenauntes with Scottlande; with many other braunches.'[92] In June, it was rumoured that, if Edward married Elisabeth, 'it is thought the Pope will excommunicate both'.[93] By August, discussion of a marriage between the king and the French king's daughter had given rise to 'much talking', as reported by Peter Vannes, dean of Salisbury, who was then writing to the Council from Venice.[94]

In addition to the king's marriage, there were other concerns at court – one of which was a lack of religious uniformity at the heart of the royal family. As the Edwardian Reformation progressed, the young king's government became concerned with his half-sister Mary's opposition to the religious reforms, especially when she began attending mass up to four times a day. This defiance was further demonstrated on Whit Sunday 1549, when she celebrated the mass of Pentecost according to the old Latin rite at Kenninghall.[95] The government permitted Mary to have private celebrations of mass in Latin, although she later feared that this concession would be withdrawn.[96] In 1550, van der Delft reported Mary's 'forebodings' and the ambassador expressed his concerns for Mary's welfare on account of the actions of Northumberland and his followers, including 'the Marquis of Northampton, who has two wives, and the Marquis of Dorset, a senseless creature ... they are all of them Sacramentarians, as they publicly declared in Parliament quite lately'.[97] As a result, 'they will never permit the Lady Mary to live in peace'.[98] Mary became so concerned about the government's hostility to her religion that she contemplated secretly escaping from England in 1550, although her Habsburg relatives ultimately persuaded her that doing so would destroy any hopes she harboured of becoming queen of England one day. In 1557, when Mary was queen, the Venetian ambassador would write of:

> the degradations, the injuries, the threats, and the affronts endured by her after the change of the religion and the spoliation of the churches and their final ruin, from her never having chosen to apostatize, nor to adhere to the heretical opinions of those who ruled in the time of her brother King Edward.[99]

Historians have traditionally questioned whether Katherine shared her elder sister's commitment to reform but, as she grew to maturity in a godly household, she would undoubtedly have learned of the tensions between the king and his half-sister on the matter of religion, alongside the government's apprehension that the Catholic Mary would succeed Edward should he die childless, and her family's reformed beliefs surely shaped Katherine's perceptions of the religious struggle between the king and Mary, as was presumably also the case for Jane. Jane's biographers have explored her reformed education and its role in shaping her uncompromising religious beliefs, to the extent that she would only years later be described as having 'surpassed men in maintaining the cause of Christ'.[100] Mary's faith was similarly uncompromising, and like her half-brother she refused to give way when it came to her religious beliefs and practices. It was reported that:

> although the King her brother and his Council prohibited her from having the mass celebrated according to the Roman Catholic ritual, she nevertheless had it performed in secret, nor did she ever choose by any act to assent to any other form of religion, her belief in that in which she was born being so strong that had the opportunity offered she would have displayed it at the stake, her hopes being

placed in God alone, so that she constantly exclaims: '*In te Domine confido, non confundar in æternum: si Deus est pro nobis, quis contra nos?*'[101]

Irrespective of tensions within the royal family on the matter of religion, a number of glittering occasions were of interest to the Grey family during Edward's short reign. Katherine's parents were at court to welcome Marie de Guise, widow of James V of Scots, in November 1551. The dowager queen had arrived in Portsmouth and stopped at Southwick, Warblington, Stanstead (the residence of the earl of Arundel), Cowdray (home of Sir Anthony Browne) and Guildford prior to her arrival at Edward's court, 'to all which places she was conducted by the noblemen and gentlemen of the respective counties in great state':[102]

> At Guildford she was met by Lord William Howard, with the nobility and gentry of Surrey, who conducted her to Hampton Court, at a mile from which the Marquis of Northampton, with other nobles, came on part of his Majesty to congratulate her, and at the house she was received by the Marchioness of Northampton and other ladies. There she abode Allhallow-day, and on the following went by water, accompanied by numerous barges, to London, where she was lodged at the Bishop of London's palace. Next day the Duke of Suffolk, the Earl of Huntingdon, and others visited her from his Majesty, and on the following, which was yesterday, the 4th inst., her Grace, accompanied by Lady Margaret Douglas, the Duchesses of Northumberland and Suffolk, and others, came to the Court, where, being met by the Lord Chamberlain and other officers of the household, she was most honourably and princely received and welcomed by the King's Majesty in the hall, and led up to her chamber on the Queen's side, where his Majesty dined with her, and in the afternoon departed; she taking her leave of him with most hearty and earnest thanks for the kingly usage of her and hers.[103]

It was reported that the dowager queen had 'gret chere' at the English court.[104] The king gave Marie a diamond ring at their meeting.[105] This splendid occasion visibly demonstrated the honoured status that Katherine's parents enjoyed at court, both as members of the royal family and as respected nobility of the kingdom. One person who was not present, however, to welcome the dowager queen was the king's half-sister Mary, whose ill health prevented her from attending court. It is possible that this was an excuse invented by Mary to avoid being pressured by the king to renounce her religious practices.[106] In January that year, the king himself upbraided Mary for her defiant behaviour, and she had earlier refused to attend court out of fear that she would be compelled to conform to the new liturgy.[107] If Mary had been ill, she had sufficiently recovered by the time that Katherine, her sisters and mother arrived at Mary's townhouse of the former Priory of St John of Jerusalem at Clerkenwell in the same month as the dowager queen's visit.[108] The family, including the duke's younger brothers Lord Thomas and Lord John Grey, spent Christmas 1551 at Tilty.[109]

Both these occasions at court and family visits during the holidays indicate that, despite the duke of Suffolk's reputation for godliness, it would be erroneous to view the Grey household as one that was devoid of merriment. The Cambridge divine James Haddon served as chaplain to the duke and wrote a number of letters to Bullinger about his patron's household. In a letter discussing games of cards and dice, Haddon noted that 'the duke has forbidden all his domestics to risk any money upon amusements of this sort; but yet he himself and his most honourable lady with their friends, not only claim permission to play in their private apartment, but also to play for money'. Haddon disapproved of such activities: 'As to myself, however, I am of opinion that I can nowise admit it to be allowable for a Christian so to risk his money at any game whatsoever, as to leave off as a winner, with some pecuniary advantage, or else as a loser, to his pecuniary loss.'[110]

By the spring of 1552, the hope of the duke and duchess of Suffolk that their eldest daughter would marry the king may have been renewed when the mooted marriage between Edward and Elisabeth of Valois fell through.[111] The evidence for Katherine's whereabouts that summer is fragmentary. Given that Frances fell ill in August while in residence at the Charterhouse,[112] it is possible that her daughters were then with her at this property that had been granted to the duke of Suffolk after Somerset's execution. It seems that the duchess' illness was serious enough to give cause for concern because her husband immediately left court upon receiving word of her condition, as he explained in a letter written to William Cecil on 26 August, reporting that Frances was suffering from 'three diseases', including 'a hot burning ague', 'the stopping of the spleen' and 'hypochondriac passion'. The duchess recovered from her illness but it had evidently been a worrying time for the Grey family.

The court celebrated Christmas that year at Greenwich. The king's Lord of Misrule 'ordered the sports and pastimes for the King's diversion; which were in as great variety and royal pomp, as scarcely ever had been seen before'.[113] On 10 February, the king's half-sister Mary rode through Fleet Street to Westminster to visit Edward; she was attended by a number of ladies including Frances, duchess of Suffolk.[114] Upon her arrival 'at the outward court, there met her the Dukes of Suffolk and Northumberland, the Marquis of Winchester, the Earls of Bedford, Shrewsbury, Arundel, the Lord Chamberlain, the Lord Admiral, and a great number of knights and gentlemen'.[115] It was reported that Mary was now looked upon 'as the rising sun, the King being in a consumption'.[116] It is unlikely that Henry and Frances were among those who looked upon Mary as such, in view of their antipathy to Mary's Catholic faith, while, more to the point, should Edward's illness result in his death, their hopes for a marriage between Jane and the king would be dashed. As the winter of 1553 gave way to spring, however, preparations for marriage were set in motion not only for Jane, but also for her younger sister Katherine Grey.

3

Sister to the Queen

In the spring of 1553, Edward VI fell ill. The king's health appears to have been robust until he caught a feverish cold in February and deteriorated during the spring. His doctors believed him to be suffering from a suppurating tumour on the lung, alongside experiencing a persistent and racking cough and the outbreak of ulcers on his body.[1] The imperial ambassador Scheyfve reported that, when Edward's half-sister Mary visited court in February, 'the King was attacked by a fever caused by a chill he had caught, and was so ill that the Lady Mary could not see him for three days'.[2] Later, in his bedchamber, 'the King received her very kindly and graciously, and entertained her with small talk, making no mention of matters of religion.'[3]

By late April, however, Scheyfve recorded that:

the King withdrew to Greenwich a few days ago. There seems to be no improvement in his condition, and he has only shown himself once, in the gardens, the day after his arrival. I hear from a trustworthy source that the King is undoubtedly becoming weaker as time passes, and wasting away. The matter he ejects from his mouth is sometimes coloured a greenish yellow and black, sometimes pink, like the colour of blood. His doctors and physicians are perplexed and do not know what to make of it. They feel sure that the King has no chance of recovery unless his health improves during the next month.[4]

In the same dispatch, the ambassador also related news of Jane Grey's betrothal to Guildford Dudley, a younger son of the duke of Northumberland. This union was hardly the glittering marriage to Edward VI that her parents had long nurtured ambitions for. Scheyfve reported that 'during the last few days he [Northumberland] has found means to ally and bind his son, my Lord Guilford, to the Duke of Suffolk's eldest daughter, whose mother is the third heiress to the crown by the testamentary dispositions of the late King, and has no heirs male'.[5] The betrothal was made 'with the consent and approval of the King and his Council. Their marriage is to be solemnized at Whitsuntide.'[6]

An enduring historical tradition claims that Jane was beaten into submission by her parents when she initially refused to marry Guildford. In his *Historia delle cose occurse nel regno d'Inghilterra*, Giulio Raviglio Rosso asserted that Jane was 'urged by the mother, and beat by the father'.[7] A later Italian account alleged that, while Jane's father was persuaded by Northumberland to agree to the marriage, 'the Duchess of Suffolk with all her household would not have wished [it], and the daughter was forced there by the father, with beating as well'.[8] Conversely, the Suffolk gentleman Robert Wingfield claimed that the duke and duchess of Suffolk had to be persuaded to permit Jane to marry Guildford, having entertained hopes that she would marry the king.[9] Wingfield explained that:

Suffolk, as I freely allow, feared the fierce nature of the man [Northumberland] more than he ought to have done on the two particular grounds that Northumberland was believed to be dangerous and that he seemed to be like Phoenix in his companionship with the king and second in authority to none. The timid and trustful duke therefore hoped to gain a scarcely imaginable haul of immense wealth and greater honour of his house from this match and readily followed

Northumberland's wishes, although his wife Frances was vigorously opposed to it, but her womanly scruples were of little avail against the opponents of such wealth and power.[10]

Any disappointment that the duke and duchess felt regarding Jane's marriage is understandable in view of their dynastic ambitions. Their hope for a union between their eldest daughter and the king was well known. As the reformer John of Ulm had informed Conrad Pellican in 1551, Jane 'is to be married, as I hear, to the king'.[11] Notwithstanding the frustration of their ambitions, on 25 May three weddings took place at Durham House, Northumberland's London residence, including that of Jane and Guildford. Her sister Katherine, then 12 years old, wed Henry Herbert, heir of the earl of Pembroke, while Northumberland's daughter Katherine married Henry Hastings, heir of the earl of Huntingdon. This marked the most significant moment in Katherine Grey's life thus far. Marrying Herbert offered an attractive future as countess of Pembroke, but it was not a matter in which she had a choice: like her elder sister, she would have been keenly aware of her dynastic duty. In addition, two other marriages were planned: Northumberland's youngest son Henry would marry Margaret Audley, and Katherine Grey's cousin Margaret Clifford would marry Northumberland's brother Andrew. Mary Grey was betrothed to Lord Grey of Wilton.[12]

A letter from Northumberland to Sir Thomas Cawarden, Master of the Revels, was sent in advance of the weddings. In it, the duke issued an order for two masques – one of men and the other of women – that are 'rich' and 'seldom used' for entertaining the nobles and dignitaries who would be in attendance. Northumberland promised that Cawarden's servants would be rewarded.[13] In April, a warrant was issued to deliver 'wedding apparel' to Jane, Katherine and Northumberland's daughter Katherine and their respective bridegrooms, as well as their mothers and Lady Northampton. The apparel consisted of 'certain parcels of tissues, and cloth of gold and silver, which had been the late Duke's and Duchess's of Somerset, forfeited to the King'.[14]

Wingfield noted that 'a most magnificent marriage was celebrated in the great palace of the bishop of Durham by the Thames; the French ambassador was present, and most of the English nobility dignified the ceremony with their attendance'.[15] The imperial ambassador similarly informed the emperor that:

On the 25th of this month were celebrated the weddings of my Lord Guilford, son of the Duke of Northumberland, to the eldest daughter of the Duke of Suffolk; of the Earl of Pembroke's son to the second daughter; and of the Earl of Huntingdon's son to the daughter of the Duke of Northumberland. The weddings were celebrated with great magnificence and feasting at the Duke of Northumberland's house in town.[16]

Despite the splendour of the occasion, the day was marred somewhat by Jane's husband Guildford, 'one of his brothers, the Admiral and other lords and ladies' falling 'very ill after eating some salad at the Duke of Northumberland's, and are still suffering from the results. It seems the mistake was made by a cook, who plucked one leaf for another.'[17] Following her marriage, Katherine went to live with her husband and his father at Baynard's Castle, a residence of the earl.[18] Little evidence survives for Katherine's activities following her marriage. She would play only a minor role in the dynastic crisis that characterised the last weeks of Edward VI's reign, while her elder sister would take centre stage.

With an awareness of the events of the spring and summer of 1553, both contemporary and modern authors have regarded the weddings in a sinister light, namely as part of Northumberland's scheme to exclude Edward VI's half-sisters from the succession and have his son Guildford made king instead by right of his wife Jane Grey. A later account declared that 'the men of intellect, and who knew how the King was faring, waiting to see strange things, judged this wedding to be the first act of a tragedy'.[19] Richard Grafton, who served as King's Printer to both Henry VIII and Edward VI, asserted that the:

mariages were compassed and concluded chiefly vpon purpose to chaunge and alter the order of succession to the crowne, made in the time of king Henry the eight, from the said kings daughters, Mary, & Elizabeth, and to conuey the same immediatly after the death of king Edwarde to the house of Suffolk in ye right of the said Lady Fraunces.[20]

Of the king's involvement in this scheme, Grafton believed him to have been 'an earnest trauailer in the time of his sicknesse', because of his determination to ensure that neither of his half-sisters succeeded him.[21] In his *Universal History*, the Elizabethan clergyman William Harrison reported that 'certain wise men thought more than they spake of these combinations, but ye common sort spake more than either ... first crying God save ye king and defend him from his enemies'.[22]

In the seventeenth century, it was suggested that 'the noise of these marriages bred such amazement in the hearts of the common people, apt enough in themselves to speak the worst of Northumberland's actions, that there was nothing left unsaid which might serve to shew their hatred towards him, or express their pity toward the King'. Yet Northumberland 'was so little troubled at that' and 'resolved to dissemble no longer'.[23] However, David Loades noted that the duke initially attempted to marry Guildford to Margaret Clifford, daughter of the earl of Cumberland. That he preferred the Cliffords to the Greys indicates that his matrimonial schemes were unconnected with the succession issue.[24] Eric Ives similarly affirmed that it is unlikely that the weddings of May 1553 had an ulterior motive; they seem to have been straightforward aristocratic alliances.[25] The ambassadors resident at court did not connect the weddings that spring with a plot allegedly concocted by Northumberland to usurp the throne for his son.

In the seventeenth century, Heylyn believed that Katherine's marriage to Herbert was arranged because 'Dudley had made' the earl of Pembroke 'privy to all his counsels'.[26] The imperial ambassadors, writing shortly after Mary I's accession, reported that Northumberland had claimed that Pembroke, 'whose son married Lady Jane's younger sister,

Catherine of Suffolk', had favoured the marriage between Jane and Guildford.[27] 'The said Pembroke had schemed with Northumberland to bring about the troubles, amply described heretofore to your Majesty, and was of the Duke's party.'[28] If this account of Pembroke's involvement in the arrangements for the marriage between Jane and Guildford is true, then it is plausible that he may have instigated the union between his heir and Katherine; as a great-granddaughter of Henry VII, she was undoubtedly an attractive bride for his son.

Given that the duke and duchess of Suffolk had opposed Jane's marriage to Guildford, their attitude to Katherine's marriage deserves consideration. Unlike Jane, there had been no suggestion of a royal match for Katherine, and thus her parents may well have been satisfied with a marriage for their second daughter that would one day see her become a countess. The question of whether Katherine's marriage was consummated is somewhat contentious. Heylyn later asserted that Pembroke 'found some means to procure a sentence of divorce, almost upon the very instant of the consummation'.[29] The couple would claim that their union had been consummated when Herbert's father sought an annulment, but it is likely that this was a lie arising from their feelings for one another and desire not to be separated.[30] The duke and duchess of Suffolk almost certainly expressly insisted that Katherine's marriage remain unconsummated until she had reached a suitable age. Scheyfve reported on 30 May that 'the marriage between the Duke of Northumberland's son and the daughter of the Duke of Suffolk has taken place, but is not yet to be consummated, because of their tender age'.[31] It has been convincingly suggested, however, that Scheyfve confused Jane with Katherine, because Jane's marriage to Guildford was certainly consummated.[32] In early modern England, childbirth was approached by many women with fear, for it involved 'great danger' and 'great pain and peril'.[33] Frances would surely have been aware that her great-grandmother Margaret Beaufort had given birth to the future Henry VII at the age of only 13; it was perhaps significant that she did not go on to bear any more children. Katherine's youthful age would have been a sensible reason to delay consummation.

Aware that he was dying, that spring the young king composed a draft document entitled 'My Deuise for the Succession'. It has been described as 'a miniature imitation of Henry VIII's will'.[34] Edward stipulated that neither of his half-sisters, Mary and Elizabeth, were to succeed him because both were illegitimate. He was also opposed to Mary becoming queen because 'she would subuert all his lawes and statutes made concerning religion, wherof he was most careful'.[35] The king's provisions to alter the succession were a direct contravention of the 1544 Succession Act, as well as the line of succession ordained by Henry VIII in his last will and testament. The 'Deuise' laid out Edward's wishes:

> For lakke of issu masle of my body, To the L Fraunceses heires masles, if she haue any of such issu befor my death to the L Jane and her heires masles, To the L Katerins heires masles, To the L Maries heires masles, To the heires masles of the daughters wich she shal have hereafter. Then to the L Margets heires masles. For lakke of such issu, To theires masles of the L Katerins daughters and so forth til you come to the L Margets daughters heires masles.[36]

Originally, Edward decreed that the crown would pass to the male heirs of Lady Jane Grey, but as the king's illness worsened, he inserted 'and her' before 'heires masles' in the recognition that Jane would not produce a son before his death. Thus, with the insertion of these two words, Jane was named heir to the throne.

The question of responsibility for the decision in the spring of 1553 to ignore Henry VIII's provisions for the succession has long been a matter of historical controversy. Writing shortly afterwards, the Spanish merchant Antonio de Guaras claimed in his account of Mary I's accession that Northumberland, who was obeyed by the nobility 'as if he had been the true King', had 'caused the King to bequeath his kingdom to the daughters of the Duke of Suffolk'.[37] The duke 'wrought so much with the King and the nobles', gaining 'over some by fear, and others by promises, and others by gifts'.[38] Dale Hoak's assertion that 'the scheme to alter the succession originated in Northumberland's camp and not in King Edward's brain'[39] is characteristic of the traditional view that Northumberland manipulated the young king into excluding his half-sisters from the succession to instead nominate the duke's daughter-in-law Jane Grey as Edward's successor to ensure a Dudley triumph. Mortimer Levine alleged that 'Northumberland decided on a bold gamble that might, if successful, ensure the continuance of both his life and his power' by securing the throne for the Dudley family through a marriage between his son and Jane, before 'inducing the compliant young king to name their male heir as his successor'.[40]

Modern historians, however, have increasingly emphasised the king's agency in overturning the provisions of his father's last will and testament. Far from merely being a cipher, the evidence shows that, as Edward neared the age of 16, he was acting with independence and authority.[41] Rather than Northumberland masterminding the 'Deuise' to achieve his political ambitions, 'Edward's detailed revisions demonstrate that he had thought very deeply over the nature of the English succession.'[42] Stephen Alford alluded to Edward's reasons for making these revisions: he 'set out to preserve his godly legacy and, implicitly, his political establishment'.[43] The king took wide counsel from the men around him, including Thomas Wroth, Henry Sidney, John Cheke and William Petre.[44] Perhaps the issue is best summarised by John Guy, who suggested that 'if, however, Northumberland had little choice but to usurp power, Edward himself wished to exclude his sister Princess Mary from the throne'.[45] The imperial ambassador Scheyfve's report, dated 4 July 1553, is instructive:

I hear for a fact that the King of England has made a will, appointing as true heir to the Crown, after his death, Suffolk's eldest daughter, who has married my Lord Guilford, son of the Duke of Northumberland. The Princess [Mary] has been expressly excluded on religious grounds and because she is asserted to have disobeyed the King and his Council, and infringed the decrees of Parliament. Some folk say the Duke of Suffolk is to succeed to the Crown and that the Princess is to be declared a bastard, others that this is not to be done, partly for fear of your Majesty and partly in order to be able to declare the Lady Elizabeth a bastard, as the King is said to have done in his will. This instrument, with its clauses of exclusion, was written by the King's own hand, and he requested the Council to sign his last will and testament, which they signed and swore to observe rather out of fear than for any other reason.[46]

On 12 June, the judges of the King's Bench were summoned by the Council to discuss the succession. They were shown the king's 'Deuise' and were instructed to turn it into a legal will; when they expressed fears of committing treason, Edward ordered them to obey his wishes.[47] Scheyfve recounted that:

Lord Shrewsbury, the Lord Treasurer, the Lord Warden, the Privy Seal and other members of the government demurred and made many difficulties before consenting, especially the Earl of Arundel, who was made a councillor on the same day. Several gentlemen of the King's Bed-chamber, certain lords who had been summoned to Court, and some of the judges and legal authorities who were consulted on the preparation of the will, affixed their signatures to the instrument.[48]

The privy councillors and crown officers were reluctant to accept the 'Deuise', as there was doubt as to whether, as a minor, Edward could legally overturn his father's provisions. Sir Edward Montague, the Lord Chief Justice, believed that no letters patent could overthrow an existing statute (namely the 1544 Succession Act) without it being repealed in Parliament.[49] Edward's insistence on his 'Deuise' becoming legally binding is understandable in view of the speed at which the king's health was deteriorating. Those at court were aware that Edward's death was imminent. The imperial ambassador informed the emperor in early July that:

As for the King, his condition is still as I reported to your Majesty on the 27th of last month, though since then he has shown himself at a

window at Greenwich, where many saw him, but so thin and wasted
that all men said he was doomed, and that he was only shown because
the people were murmuring and saying he was already dead, and in
order that his death, when it should occur, might the more easily be
concealed. The people believed that the King was to show himself
again last Sunday, the 2nd of the month, and a great crowd went to
see, but they were told it should be done the following day. A large
gathering then assembled, but a gentleman of the Bed-chamber came
out and told them that the air was too chill. As far as I am able to
ascertain, Sire, the King is very ill to-day and cannot last long. He
will die suddenly, and no one can foretell whether he will live an
hour longer, notwithstanding his having been shown to the people,
for that was done against the physicians' advice. It seems there is at
present about the King a certain woman who professes to understand
medicine, and is administering certain restoratives, though not inde-
pendently of the physicians.[50]

On the evening of 6 July, Edward VI died at Greenwich Palace at the
age of 15. His cause of death is uncertain. Some of his contemporaries
believed that 'he was poyssoned'.[51] Later that month, the imperial envoys
claimed that Northumberland 'decided to kill the late King Edward, as
every one supposes and the course of the malady demonstrates. It is generally said that he poisoned the King',[52] probably on the basis of gossip
circulating at court. Indeed, some feared that Northumberland had poisoned the king over a sustained period of time: 'he resolved, as has been
bruited, to kill the King by poison; and the poor innocent languished
for seven months'.[53] Despite contemporary reports, however, there is no
evidence that Northumberland poisoned the king, as he had the most
to lose by Edward's death.[54] Others suggested that he had died of 'consumption in his lunges, so as there was no hope of his recouery'.[55] The
Venetian ambassador Giacomo Soranzo stated that Edward 'was seized
with a malady, which the physicians soon knew to be consumption,
and in a few days his life was despaired of'.[56] Modern historians have
indicated that the king may have suffered from a pulmonary infection,

while the reported swelling of his lower body could suggest kidney fail-ure.[57] Alternatively, secondary effects of tuberculosis (aggravated by an earlier instance of measles) and a later onset of septicaemia and cyanosis may have caused Edward's death.[58]

Jane had been in residence at Chelsea in the final days of Edward's life, where she lay sick. On the day of the king's death, she was sum-moned to Syon House in the company of Lady Mary Sidney, her sister-in-law, where Northumberland announced the death of the king and explained that Jane had been named by Edward as his succes-sor.[59] As is well known, she reacted with shock and protested that she had no right to be queen, for that title rightly belonged to the king's half-sister Mary. Jane 'refused to desire to accept such great weight, not meet to her own weak wits; nonetheless with many tears she was in the end persuaded by the Council, by the Duke, and by the father (he was content to do their bidding)'.[60] Heylyn noted that Jane 'sub-mitted unto that necessity which she could not vanquish; yielding her head with more unwillingness to the ravishing glories of a crown than afterwards she did to the stroke of an axe'.[61] The reaction of Katherine to the news of Jane's elevation is unrecorded, but she would surely have been astonished to learn that she was now sister to the queen of England – and, until such time as Jane produced a child, Katherine's as yet unborn offspring were in line to inherit the throne, as set out in the late king's 'Deuise'.

Following the king's death, the new queen's regime was immediately established. On 9 July, 'alle the hed offesers and the gard' were sworn unto Jane as their queen.[62] A contemporary chronicler recorded that on 10 July:

the duke of Northumberlande, with his adherentes, did proclaime lady Iane (daughter to the duke of Suffolke, and wife to Gilforde Dudley) quene, the whiche duke incontinently made an armie against the lady Mary, right inheritour to the crowne of this realme. But his attempt (for as muche as it was not of God, coulde not come to any good successe.)[63]

That day, Jane arrived at the Tower at around 3 o'clock in the afternoon. She was received there by the lords and nobility, 'the duches of Suffoke her mother, bering her trayn, with mony lades, and ther was a shot of gunnes and chamburs has nott be sene oft be-tweyn iiij and v of [the clock]'.[64] At 5 o'clock, Edward VI's death was proclaimed and it was also announced that the king 'had ordained by his letters pattents bearing date the 21. of June last past that the Lady Jane should be heire to the Crowne of England, and the heire males of her body, &c'.[65]

The imperial envoys provided further details about Jane's arrival at the Tower, a visible and public demonstration of her inheritance of the kingdom:

[A]t about four o'clock this afternoon the ceremony of the state entry was performed at the Tower of London with the accustomed pomp. The new Queen's train was carried by her mother, the Duchess of Suffolk; and there were not many people present to witness the act. When it was over, criers at the street-corners published an order given under the Great Seal of England, by which, by the new Queen's authority, the Lady Mary was declared unfitted for the Crown, as also the Lady Elizabeth. Both ladies were declared to be bastards; and it was stated that the Lady Mary might marry a foreigner and thus stir up trouble in the kingdom and introduce a foreign government, and also that as she was of the old religion she might seek to introduce popery. However, no one present showed any sign of rejoicing, and no one cried: 'Long live the Queen!' except the herald who made the proclamation and a few archers who followed him.[66]

In 1909, the writer Richard Davey claimed that the Genoese merchant Sir Baptist Spinola observed Jane's arrival at the Tower and left the following account of it:

To-day I saw Donna Jana Graia walking in a grand procession to the Tower. She is now called Queen, but is not popular, for the hearts of the people are with Mary, the Spanish Queen's daughter. This Jane is very short and thin, but prettily shaped and graceful. She has small features and a well-made nose, the mouth flexible and the lips red. The eyebrows are arched and darker than her hair, which is nearly red. Her eyes are sparkling and red. I stood so long near Her Grace, that I noticed her colour was good, but freckled. When she smiled she showed her teeth, which are white and sharp. In all, a *graziosa persona* and *animata* [animated]. She wore a dress of green velvet stamped with gold, with large sleeves. Her headdress was a white coif with many jewels. She walked under a canopy, her mother carrying her long train, and her husband Guilfo [Guildford] walking by her, dressed all in white and gold, a very tall strong boy with light hair, who paid her much attention. The new Queen was mounted on very high chopines to make her look much taller, which were concealed by her robes, as she is very small and short. Many ladies followed, with noblemen, but this lady is very *heretica* and has never heard Mass, and some great people did not come into the procession for that reason.[67]

Although many historians subsequently repeated this description in their account of Jane's arrival at the Tower, Leanda de Lisle established that Davey invented Spinola's report of Jane.[68] However, there is no doubt that it was a glittering and unforgettable occasion as well as being an unimaginable triumph for the Grey family, irrespective of public opinion. De Guaras asserted that, when Jane was proclaimed queen, 'the people, amazed at this great innovation, gazed at one another as astonied', while 'great shows of heralds' were made 'to intimidate the people'.[69] Katherine and her husband were present at Jane's arrival at the Tower and remained there, with Pembroke, until the 19th.[70] It is likely that, during the days that followed, the earl kept Katherine informed of developments.

The proclamation of Jane's queenship reads as follows:

IAne by the grace of God Quene of England, Fraunce and Ireland, defendor of the faith, & of the Church of Englande, & also of Irelande vnder Christ in earth the supreme head. To al our most louing,

faithfull, and obedient subiects, and to euery of them greting. Where
our moste dere cousin Edwarde the vi. late King of Englande, Fraunce
and Irelande, defendour of the faith, and in earth the supreme head
vnder Christ of the Church of Englande and Irelande, by his letters
patentes signed with his owne hand, and sealed with his great seale
of Englande, bearing date the xxi. day of Iune, in the vii. yere of his
reigne, in the presence of the most parte of his nobles, his counsail-
ours, Iudges, and diuerse others graue, and sage personages for the
profite and suretie of the whole realme therto assenting, and sub-
scribing their names to the same, hath by the same his Lettres Patentes
recited, that forasmuch as the Imperiall croune of this realme, by an
Acte made in the xxxv. yere of the reigne of the late King of woor-
thy memory King Henrie the viii. our progenitour, and great vncle,
was for lacke of issue of his bodie lawfullie begotten, and for lacke of
issue of the bodie of our saide late cosin King Edwarde the vi. by the
same act limited, and appointed to remaine to the Ladie Marie, by the
name of the ladie Marie his eldest Daughter, and to the Heires of her
bodie lawfully begotten, and for default of such issue, the remainder
therof to the Ladie Elizabeth, by the name of the Ladie Elizabeth his
seconde Daughter, and to the heires of her bodie lawefully begotten,
with such condicions, as shoulde be limited, and appointed by the
saied late King of woorthie memorie, King Henrie theight our progenitour, and great vncle by his letters patentes vnder his great Seale,
or by his last wil in writing signed with his hande. And forasmuch
as the saied limitation of Thimperial croune of this realme, being
limited (as is aforesaied) to the said Ladie Marie, and Ladie Elizabeth
being illegitimate, and not lawfully begotten, for that that the mariage had betweene the saied late King, King Henrie theight our
progenitour, and great vncle, and the Ladie Katherine mother to the
saied Ladie Marie, & also the mariage had betwene the saied late king,
King Henrie theight our progenitor and great vncle, and the ladie
Anne mother to the saied ladie Elizabeth, were cleerely, and lawfully
vndone by sentences of deuorces, according to the woorde of God,
and the Ecclesiasticall lawes: And which saied seueral deuorcements

haue beene seuerally ratified, & confirmed by auctoritie of parlament, and especiallie in the xxviii. yere of the reigne of King Henrie theight our said progenitor, and great vncle, remaining in force, strength, and effect, wherby aswel the said Ladie Marie, as also the said Ladie Elizabeth, to all ententes, and purposes, are, and been cleerely disabled, to aske, claime, or chalenge the saied Imperiall croune, or any other of the honours, castelles, manours, Lordshippes, lands, tenements, or other hereditaments, as heire, or heires to our said late cosin king Edward the vi. or as heire, or heires to any other person, or persons whosoeuer, aswel for the cause before rehearsed, as also for that that the saied Lady Marie, and Lady Elizabeth were vnto our saied late cosin but of the halfe bloud, and therefore by the ancient lawes, statutes, and customes of this realme be not inheritable vnto our saied late Cosin, although they had beene borne in lawefull Matrimonie, as in dede they were not, as by the saied sentences of deuorce, and the saied statute of the xxviii. yere of the reigne of King Henrie the eight our saied progenitor and great Vncle, plainly appeareth.

And forasmuch also as it is to be thought, or at the least, much to be doubted, that if the saied ladie Marie, or ladie Elizabeth should hereafter haue, & enioy the said Imperial croune of this realm and should then happen to marry with any Stranger borne out of this realme, that then the same Stranger hauing the gouernmente and the Imperiall crowne in his handes, would adhere and practise, not onely to bring this noble free realme, into the tirannie and seruitude of the Bishoppe of Rome, but also to haue the lawes and customes of his or their own natiue countrey or countreys to be practised, and put in vre within this realme, rather then the laws, statutes, and customes here of long time vsed, wherupon the title of inheritance of all and singular the subiects of this realme dooe depend, to the peril of conscience, and the vtter subuersion of the common weale of this realme wherupon our saied late dere cosin weighing and considering with himselfe, what waies and meanes were most conuenient to be had for the stay of the said succession in the saied Imperiall croune, if it should please God to call our said late cosin out of this transitory

life, hauing no issue of his body, and calling to his remembrance that
wee and the Lady Katherine, and the Lady Mary our sisters, being the
daughters of the lady Fraunces our naturall mother, and then and yet
wife to our naturall & most louing father Henrie Duke of Suffolke,
and the lady Margaret, daughter of the lady Elianour then dece-
assed sister to the said lady Fraunces, and the late wife of our cosin
Henrie Erle of Comberland, were very nigh of his graces bloud, of
the part of his fathers side our said progenitour and great vncle, and
being naturally borne here within the realme, and for the very good
opinion our said late cosin had of our, and our said sisters and cosin
Margarets good education, did therefore vpon good deliberation
and aduise heerein had and taken, by his said Letters Patents declare,
ordre, assigne, limit, and appoinct, that if it should fortune himselfe
our said late cosin king Edward the sixt to decease, hauing no issue
of his body lawfully begotten, that then the saied Imperiall croune
of England and Ireland, and the confines of the same, and his title
to the croune of the realme of France, and all and singular honors,
castles, prerogatiues, priuiledges, preheminences, aucthorities, iuris-
dictions, dominions, possessions, and hereditaments to our said late
cosin King Edward the sixt, or to the said Imperiall croune belonging, or in any wise appertaining, should for lacke of such issue of his
body remain, come, and be vnto the eldest sonne of the body of the
said lady Fraunces lawfully begotten, being borne into the world in
his life time, and to the heires males of the body of the same eldest
sonne lawfully begotten, and so from sonne to sonne, as he should
be of auncienty in birth, of the body of the said lady Fraunces lawfully begotten, being borne into the world in our said late cosins life
time, and to the heires males of the body of euery such sonne lawfully begotten: and for default of such sonne borne into the world in
his life time, of the body of the said lady Fraunces lawfully begotten,
and for lack of heires males of euery such sonne lawfully begotten,
that then the sayd Imperial croune, and all & singular other the premisses should remain, come, and be to vs, by the name of the lady Iane,
eldest daughter of the said lady Fraunces, & to the heires males of our

body lawfully begotten, and for lacke of such heire male of our body lawfully begotten, that then the sayd Imperial croune, and all other the premisses should remain, come, & be to the sayd lady Katherine our sayd second sister, and to the heires males of the body of the sayd lady Katherine lawfully begotten, with diuerse other remainders, as by the same letters patents more plainly & at large it may and doeth appere. Sithens the making of which letters patents, that is to say, on Thursday, which was the vi. day of this instant moneth of Iuly, it hath pleased God to cal to his infinite mercy our sayd most dere & entirely beloued cosin Edward the vi. whose soule God pardon, & forasmuch as he is now deceased, hauing no heires of his body begotten, & that also there remaineth at this present time no heires lawfully begotten of the body of our sayd progenitor, and great vncle king Henrie theight, and forasmuch also as the sayd lady Fraunces our sayd mother, had no issue male begotten of her body, and borne into the worlde, in the life time of our cosin King Edward the sixth, so as the saied Imperiall croune, and other the premisses to the belonging, or in any wise appertayning, now be, and remaine to vs in our actuall, and royall possession, by auctority of the sayd letters patents: wee doe therefore by these presents signifie vnto all our most louing, faithfull, and obedient subiects, that like as we for our part shall, by Goddes grace, shew our selfe a most gracious, and benigne Souuereine Queene, and Lady to all our good Subiects in all their iust, and lawfull sutes, and causes, and to the vttermost of our power shal preserve and maintaine Gods most holy word, christian policy, and the good laws, customes, and liberties of these our realmes & dominions: So we mistrust not, but they, and euery of them wil again for all their partes, at all times, and in all cases shew themselues vnto vs their naturall liege Queene, and Lady, most fayvthfull, louing, and obedient subiects, according to their bounden duties, and allegiances whereby they shall please God, and doe the thing that shall tend to their own preseruation, and sureties: Willing, and commanding all men of all estates, degrees, and condicions, to see our peace, and accord kept, and to bee obedient to our Lawes, as they tender our fauor, and will answere for the contrary, at their extreme perils. In witnes whereof, wee haue caused these our letters to bee made patents. Witnesse our selfe at our Towre of London, the tenth day of Iulie, in the first yeere of our reigne.

God saue the Queene.[71]

The proclamation established the validity of Jane's queenship and asserted that neither of the late king's half-sisters could inherit, given that both were illegitimate and thus disqualified from the succession. It also warned of the dangers that could arise if either Mary or Elizabeth married a foreign prince, namely that English laws and customs would be subverted in favour of those of a foreign land. In the context of mentioning Jane's sisters and cousin, the proclamation explicitly noted that Katherine was her sister's heir and would, by law, become queen of England if Jane should die childless.

In the days that followed, as the privy councillors received word of Mary's steps to claim the throne, further attempts were made to emphasise the legitimacy of Jane's title. Those who failed to rally behind Jane were warned that they would be guilty of treason and would be punished accordingly. Six days after the proclamation of Jane's queenship, the following letter was issued in her name admonishing her subjects to remain loyal to her as their duty:

Trusty and wellbeloved we greet you well albeit that our estate in this imperial crown whereof we be actually and really possessed as partly may appear by our proclamation wherein our title is published is not he can be any wise doubtful to all such our good faithful subjects as setting blind affection apart, do with reason and wisdom consider the very foundation and ground of our title with the great commodition thereby coming through Gods providence to the preservation of our commonwealth and policy, yet for that we understand the Lady Mary doth not cease by letters in her name, provoked thereto by her adherents, enemies of this realm, to publish and notify slanderously to divers of our subjects, matter derogatory to our title and dignity royal with the slander of certain of our nobility and council. We have thought meet to admonish and exhort you as our true and faithful subjects to remain fast in your obeysance and duty to the imperial crown of this realm, whereof we have justly the possession and not to be removed any wise from your duties by slanderous reports or letters dispersed abroad either by the said Lady Mary or by her adherents. For truly like as the nobility of our realm, our council, our prolates, our judges and learned men and others, good, wise, godly and natural subjects, do remain fast and surely in their allegiance towards us, ready to adventure their lives, lands and goods for our defence, so can a great number of the same nobility, councillors, and judges truly testify to all the world with safety of their conscience how carefully and earnestly the late king of famous memory, our dear cousin King Edward the sixth, from time to time motioned and provoked them partly by persuasions, partly by commandments, to have such respect to his succession if god should call him to his mercy without issue as might be the preservation of the crown in the whole, undefiled English blood. And, therefore, of his own mere motion both by grants of his letters patents and by declaration of his will, established the succession as it is declared by our proclamation that for the testimony hereof to the satisfaction of such as shall conceive any doubt herein. We understand that certain of our nobility have written to you at this present in some part to admonish you of your duties and to testify their knowledge of the truth of our title and right. Wherefore we leave to proceed further therein being assured in the goodness of god that your hearts shall be confirmed to owe your duty to us your sovereign Lady, who mean to preserve this crown of England in the royal blood and out of the dominion of strangers and papists with the defence of all you our good subjects, your lives, lands, and goods in our peace against the invasions and violences of all foreign or inward enemies and rebels. Given under our signet at our Tower of London. the 16th day of July in the first year of our reign.[72]

The letter was signed 'Jane the Quene'. It was a powerful assertion of royal authority, seeking to rally the country behind Jane in the defence of her 'title and right'. Another letter was issued two days later on 18 July. Addressed to Sir John St Lowe and Sir Anthony Kingston, Jane commanded the recipients to 'repair with all possible speed towards Buckinghamshire for the repressing and subduing of certain tumults and rebellions moved there against us and our crown by certain seditious men'.[73] In a further effort to bolster support for Jane's queenship, on the very day that the first letter was issued the bishop of London preached at Paul's Cross in support of her right to the throne, on the basis that Mary and Elizabeth were 'illegitimate and not lawfully begotten in the estate of true matrimony accordinge to Gods lawe'.[74] This did not meet with the intended response: 'the people murmured sore at' the bishop's words.[75]

Despite the public proclamation of Jane's queenship, the late king's half-sister Mary had no intention of relinquishing her right to the throne. She began rallying her supporters in a bid to seize the crown from what she perceived as the unlawful regime in London. On 9 July, only three days after the king's death, Mary had written to Sir Edward Hastings as 'Marye the Quene', explaining that she had inherited the throne 'by act of parliament and by the testament and last will of our late dearest father King Henry the Eighth', and instructed Hastings to secure 'the surety of our person, the universal quietness of the whole realm, specially that of our counties of Middlesex and Bucks'.[76] On 11 July, the imperial ambassadors noted that Mary had 'caused herself to be proclaimed Queen in Norfolk, and is continuing to do so in the neighbouring districts, both verbally and by means of letters', including to the Council in London.[77] Privately, however, the envoys doubted whether Mary's bid for the throne would prove successful unless she received support from the emperor, for they believed that she would fall into the hands of Northumberland within days since 'the Duke is raising men wherever he can and is strong on land and by sea'.[78]

The lengthiest account of Mary's coup was written by Robert Wingfield, who was responsible for hosting Mary in Ipswich on her triumphal progress to London in 1553 and was later granted a life annuity of £20 for his service.[79] Due to his proximity to Mary, it has been noted that 'no other commentator can rival Wingfield's detailed account of events in East Anglia during the coup', and Wingfield expressly declared that his intention was to record the events of the coup to illuminate 'the famous deeds of such a godly Queen'.[80] In Wingfield's view, Mary's accession was providentially ordained and the success of her coup demonstrated divine approval of her claim to the throne.

The actions of Northumberland in the summer of 1553 meant that Mary was compelled to assume the traditional male role of military leader in order to establish her sovereignty.[81] She also needed to do so in order to assert her authority, as an unmarried female claimant to the throne. In the course of her coup, Mary 'manipulated her gender – and her sexuality – to fashion an image as a powerful ruler with masculine attributes while conforming to the model of sexually chaste womanhood'.[82] Wingfield's account of her seizure of the throne testified to her success in presenting herself as powerful, 'with masculine attributes', while upholding her reputation as chaste and virtuous. In doing so, Wingfield provided evidence of what Sarah Duncan referred to as Mary's ability to manipulate contemporary gender expectations. When her commanders informed her of their readiness to engage in battle, Mary 'set a day when she would come from the castle to view and muster her army, and gratify her soldiers, who deserved so well of her, with her presence'.[83] After riding out from Framlingham Castle to inspect her troops, Mary ordered:

> that no harquebusier should fire his gun, nor any archer release his arrow until her majesty had inspected the army. When this order was given, such was the respect that everyone felt for their sovereign that no harquebusier nor archer fired after the command; but the soldiers bowed low to the ground and awaited their beloved mistress's arrival with as great an obeisance as they could manage.[84]

Wingfield's account attested to the respect that Mary's troops held for her royal authority, in obeying her and following her commands in the same way as they would have those of a king, as was perhaps demonstrated most symbolically in their public shows of obeisance, bowing 'low' to her and by doing so publicly recognising her claim to the throne. However, it is noteworthy that the narrative is underpinned by references to Mary's gender, on one level perhaps to further stress her effectiveness as a leader in the coup and to call attention to her unique status as England's first queen regnant; but on another level, it was associated with the providential nature of her cause, in which she was divinely favoured as 'sacred Mary' and as a 'good princess', and emphasised that, while she might still be England's queen and was thus set apart from other women, she continued to adhere to contemporary feminine ideals, in speaking to her army 'with exceptional kindness'.[85] The providential interpretation of Mary's queenship presented by Wingfield was widely shared by her contemporaries well into her reign. In 1557 the Venetian ambassador Giovanni Michiel, for example, described how, during Edward VI's reign:

> her [Mary's] life having then been often in danger, she subsequently, on his [Edward's] death, saw herself excluded from the succession by the act of one of her own subjects, that no less daring than impious Duke of Northumberland, she being also abandoned by everybody, and miserably put to flight, together with her forces, her enemies intending to annihilate her completely; and, last of all, after her coronation from the insurrections to which during three years she has several times been exposed, it is evident that from the commencement of her life until now she has never been free since sorrows and dangers, against which it seems impossible for her to have been able to struggle had she not been assisted by some great favour from God, and by some especial care which He has of her innocence.[86]

Mary issued a letter informing the Council that she was the rightful queen of England and demanded their allegiance to her. The imperial ambassadors notified the emperor:

that when the letters arrived the Council were at table, and were greatly astonished and troubled. The Duchesses of Suffolk and Northumberland, it is said, began to lament and weep, whereat the Council commanded my Lord Grey to go and bring in the Lady Mary. He is to start to-morrow, with a good number of horse.[87]

Mary's bid for the throne was met with an outpouring of public support and Jane's regime collapsed within days. Despite the letters issued by Jane as queen, her claim never received popular support, largely because her father-in-law – widely blamed for Jane's elevation to the throne – was 'so hated for his tyranny and ambition'.[88] It was reported that 'my Lady Mary is loved throughout the kingdom, and that the people are aware of their [the Council's] wicked complaisance in allowing the Duke to cheat her of her right', while 'the general suspicion that he [Northumberland] poisoned the King in order to bring the Crown into his family has turned the people away from him'.[89]

Northumberland assigned Jane's father leadership of the army sent against Mary, but Jane countermanded his order and insisted that Northumberland himself should lead it. He duly departed from London with four of his sons.[90] Northumberland's attempt to intercept and defeat Mary's forces in East Anglia met with resounding failure and, as a result, the Council in London proclaimed Mary queen of England. On 19 July, it was reported that:

the Earls of Pembroke and Shrewsbury, the Lord Privy Seal, the Earl of Arundel, (Sir John) Mason, the three secretaries and Paget, whom they had called to the Council, together with the Treasurer, whom they knew to be of their opinion, had been persuaded that the Lady Mary was rightful Queen, and had decided to proclaim her as such this very day.[91]

When the public learned that Mary had been proclaimed queen, they celebrated with 'cries and acclamations', and 'such bonfires were made that it was a sight to see, and that night the people supped in the streets, with great rejoicing and music'.[92]

Learning of Mary's triumph, the duke of Suffolk 'made the same proclamation in the Tower unrestrained, [and] being commanded to come out without arms, to go to the house of the Lord Treasurer, he was obedient'.[93] Suffolk 'came himselfe out of the Towere, and comaunded his men to leave their wepones behinde them, sayenge that hee him selfe was but one man, and himselfe proclaymed my lady Maryes grace queene on the Towere hille'.[94] He then made his way to his daughter's lodgings 'and tore down the canopy [of estate], saying no more than that it was not for her to use it, for her position permitted her not to do so'.[95] The canopy had served as a symbol of Jane's queenship[96] and the duke's action of tearing it down publicly marked the dissolution of his daughter's sovereignty. The imperial ambassadors claimed that:

> when the Lady Jane heard of the Council's determination, she replied that she would give it [the royal dignity] up as gladly as she had accepted it; she knew that the right belonged to Queen Mary, and the part she had played had been prepared for her without her knowledge.[97]

Following the collapse of her regime, Jane was lodged in the house of the gentleman gaoler Nathaniel Partridge on Tower Green. Guildford was moved to the Beauchamp Tower.[98] It was reported that 'The other Queen has renounced all her honours, and has been shut up in the Tower with her husband and the Duke's wife, though all the rest are outside.'[99] Katherine's reaction to the news of her sister's deposition is unrecorded, but her own troubles – namely, the dissolution of her brief marriage – may have overridden the fear and despair that she surely felt regarding Jane's plight.

When Mary was proclaimed queen, the earl of Pembroke returned with his son and daughter-in-law from the Tower to Baynard's Castle, where he acknowledged Mary as the lawful queen and had his son's marriage to Katherine annulled.[100] Both Katherine and her husband protested – surely falsely, given their ages – that their union had been consummated. From Pembroke's perspective, the marriage was no longer welcome given the failure of Northumberland (and, by extension, Katherine's father) to secure Jane's succession. It was naturally inadvisable for Pembroke to be allied with a family tarnished by the crime of treason. In the seventeenth century, Heylyn reported that 'seasonably apprehending how unsafe it was to marry into that family which had given so much trouble to the Queen, [Pembroke] took the advantage of the time, and found some means to procure a sentence of divorce'.[101] Fuller claimed that 'the politick old Earl, perceiving the case altered, and what was the Highway to Honour, turned into the ready Road to Ruin, got pardon from Queen Mary, and brake the marriage quite off'.[102]

The marriage having been repudiated, Katherine 'was seldome seen with dry eyes for some years together, sighing out her sorrowful condition; so that though the Roses in her cheeks looked very wan and pale, it was not for want of watering'.[103] Similarly, in the nineteenth century, Agnes Strickland alleged that 'Poor forlorn Lady Katharine was in evil case.'[104] Katherine moved from Baynard's Castle to the Charterhouse following the collapse of her sister's regime and the annulment of her marriage to Henry Herbert.[105] Whether Katherine and her husband had developed feelings of affection towards each other during so short a period is unknown, despite later accounts of Katherine's melancholy, but evidence from Elizabeth I's reign – in the midst of an even greater crisis involving Katherine – seems to suggest that they had, and may have, on some level, continued to do so. During the 1560s, those who objected to Katherine's claim to the succession reported that the dissolution of Katherine's marriage to Herbert was 'agyinst both the Parties Wills as most manifestly appeeryd, not onely by their greate unwillingnesse unto it then, but also by their affectionate and willinge manner of lyving', which continued afterwards and so 'cannot be of eny force to breake the sayd Matrimony'.[106]

On 28 July, 'the Duke of Suffolke and Sir John Cheeke were had to the Tower'.[107] The following day, Frances, duchess of Suffolk, had an audience with the new queen at Beaulieu. The two cousins had long enjoyed a close relationship, and Frances surely hoped that the affection between them would ensure that her husband and eldest daughter received clemency from the queen. The duchess emphasised that her family had been the victims of Northumberland's ambition and claimed that her husband's illness was the result of having been poisoned by Northumberland.[108] Mary graciously granted the duke of Suffolk a pardon but did not extend one to Jane, despite her reported desire to be merciful. Indeed, if the duchess did not seek a pardon for her daughter, it may have been because of reports that Mary already intended to grant one to Jane. The imperial ambassadors stated that:

> three days before they went to fetch her [Jane] from Sion House to take her to the Tower and make her entry into the town as usurping Queen, she knew nothing of it, nor was she ever a party nor did she ever give her consent to the Duke's intrigues and plots.[109]

As a result, Mary 'could not be induced to consent that she should die' and 'would not permit her to have her put to death', despite the advice of the imperial envoys, who regarded Jane as too dangerous to be permitted to live.[110] If she heard of these rumours, then it is reasonable to assume that Katherine felt hopeful about the prospect of her sister being released from the Tower, while the knowledge that her father had been pardoned could only have cheered her. In the meantime, the new queen had other pressing considerations, namely the question of her marriage.

On 2 August, the imperial ambassadors wrote to the emperor reporting that Mary had been informed:

> that great part of the labour of government could with difficulty be undertaken by a woman, and was not within woman's province, and also that it was important that the Queen should be assisted,

protected and comforted in the discharge of those duties. Your Majesty [the emperor] therefore considered that she would do well to entertain the idea of marriage, and to fix on some suitable match as soon as possible.

In response, Mary:

declared she had never thought of wedding before she was Queen, and called God to witness that as a private individual she would never have desired it, but preferred to end her days in chastity. As she now occupied a public position, however, and well understood the reasons that moved your Majesty to mention the matter to her, she was determined to follow your advice, and choose whomsoever you might recommend; for after God she desired to obey none but your Majesty, whom she regarded as a father. She felt confident you would remember that she was 37 years of age, and would not urge her to come to a decision before having seen the person and heard him speak, for as she was marrying against her private inclination she trusted your Majesty would give her a suitable match.[III]

As would become apparent, Mary already had a husband in mind. The following day, 3 August, she made her formal entry into London and arrived at the Tower. The printer and historian Grafton recorded that:

At her entrie into the Tower, there were presented to her certaine Prisoners, namely Thomas Duke of Norffolke, who in the last yere of King Henry the eyght (as you haue heard) was supposed to be attainted of treason: But in the Parliament holden in this first yere of Queene Marye, the saide supposed attayndor was by the auethoritie and act of parliament for good and apparaunt causes alleaged in the sayde acte, declared to be vtterly frustrate and voyde. Also Edward Courtney sonne and heire of Henrie Marques of Excester Cosyn Germaine to king Henry the eyght, and Cutbert Tonstall Byshop of Durham with other persons of great calling: But specially Stephen Gardyner

Byshop of Wynchester, whome shee not onely released of imprisonment, but also immediatly aduaunced and preferred to be Lorde
Chauncelor of Englande, restoring him also to his former estate and
Byshoprick, and remoued from the same one Doctor Poynet, who a
little before was placed therein by the gift of king Edwarde the sixt.
And touching Edwarde Courtney, she not onely aduaunced him to
the Erledome of Deuonshire, but also to so much of his fathers possession as there remayned in her handes, whereby it was then thought
of many, that she bare affection to him by way of mariage, but it came
not so to passe (for what cause I cannot geue any reason) but surely
the subiectes of Englande were most desirous thereof.[112]

All of those who were released from the Tower had been disgraced during
the reigns of Henry VIII and Edward VI. As the queen's lady-in-waiting
and favourite Jane Dormer, duchess of Feria, remembered, Mary:

> was a great justicier, yet withal how merciful she was appeared
> manifestly by her gracious compassion to the Duchess of Somerset,
> to Sir John Cheke, Sir Edward Montague, Chief Justice, Sir John
> Cholmeley, the Marquis of Northampton, Sir Henry Dudley, Sir
> Francis Gates, the Lord Robert Dudley, and to the Duke of Suffolk;
> all of them her professed enemies and most of them attainted, all
> adverse to her religion and no friends to her title; and yet she released
> them all out of the Tower, where they were prisoners.[113]

It seems likely that Mary shared Frances' belief that Northumberland
was responsible for the treasonous activities in which the Greys were
implicated and, on 22 August – a day later than originally intended due
to the duke's desire to convert to Catholicism, probably in a desperate attempt to win a reprieve from the queen – Northumberland was
executed on Tower Hill. A contemporary remarked that, 'although
his treasons were many and notorious, his end was that of a true and
catholic Christian, and he took his death most patiently'.[114] His trial had
taken place on the 18th at Westminster Hall, where 'a great stage was

erected ... very majestic and richly tapestried, and in the midst of it a rich canopy, and under this a bench with rich cushions, and carpets at its foot'.[115] When the duke was escorted into the room, he showed 'a good and intrepid countenance, full of humility and gravity'.[116] Wriothesley recorded that:

> Fryday the 18 of August 1553 Sir John Dudley, Duke of Northumberland, and his eldest sonne [John] Earle of Warwick, [with] Sir William Parre, Marques of Northampton, were arraigned at Westminster hall, which after there enditements read confessed their endytements of treason, without passinge of any jurye of their Peeres, and so had iudgment to be drawne, hanged, and quartered: The Lord Thomas Howard, Duke of Norfolke, sitting under the cloth of estate, and gaue judgment.[117]

The queen graciously commuted the duke's sentence to decapitation, while both his eldest son and Parr were pardoned. Sir John Gates and Sir Thomas Palmer, who had been implicated in the attempt to place Jane on the throne, were also beheaded 'at the tower hill' that day.[118] When dining at Mr Partridge's house in the Tower, Jane thundered that Northumberland 'hathe brought me and our stocke [family] in most myserable callamyty and mysery by his exceeding ambicion'. She declared that his 'life was odyous to all men' and 'wicked and full of dissimulacion'.[119] It is likely that Katherine shared her sister's view of the duke.

On 1 October, an historic event took place at Westminster Abbey: the first coronation of a queen regnant of England. The coronation ceremonies represented the queen as a female warrior, in which she was likened to classical and biblical figures including Judith and Pallas Athene. This theme was reiterated throughout the early years of Mary's reign. As a case in point, in his *An Ave Maria in Commendation of our most Vertuous Queene*, published shortly after the 1553 coup, Leonard Stopes represented Mary as 'Our iewell, our ioye, our Iudeth, doutlesse, / The great Holofernes of hell to withstande', and compared her to 'Hester, that vertuous Quene; / The enuious Hamon to kyll is her care, / And all wicked workers to wede them out clene.'[120] The decisiveness of her leadership during the summer meant that Mary was perceived as having transcended conventional understandings of gender roles while following the precedents established by her male predecessors in exercising authority as lawful sovereign. As a result, this encouraged representations of Mary as a warrior queen in the medium of print, where she was presented in the guise of classical and biblical female warriors.

According to the Tower chronicler, Mary was:

> sytting in a charret of tyssue, drawne with vj. horses, all betrapped with redd velvett. She sat in a gown of blew velvet, furred with powdered armyen, hangyng on hir heade a call of clothe of tynsell besett with perle and ston, and about the same apon her hed a rond circlet of gold, moche like a hooped garlande, besett so richely with many precyouse stones that the value therof was inestymable; the said call and circle being so massy and ponderous that she was fayn to beare uppe hir hedd with hir handes; and a canopy was borne over the char.[121]

When she was crowned, she wore 'a gown of blew velvett, lyned with pouderyd armyn, having the same cyrclet on hir hedd with the whiche she cam thorough London the daye before'.[122] Mary, like earlier queen consorts, arrived for her coronation with her hair loose as a symbol of her virginity, an attribute traditionally prized in queens. Shortly before the coronation, Mary had carried out the traditional duty of the king in making Knights of the Bath, including the earl of Devon, the earl of Surrey, Lord Berkeley, Robert Rochester, Henry Jermingham and Edward Dormer.[123] In recording this activity, her contemporaries acknowledged that the queen regnant could effectively fulfil the duties traditionally associated with the king, especially when she was unmarried. It is tempting to speculate whether the thoughts of Katherine and her family were with Jane that day, so recently proclaimed queen of England but – unlike Mary – never crowned. Now she was a prisoner in the Tower and her fate uncertain.

4

'The Ruin of a Family so Illustrious'

As Jane endured imprisonment in the Tower, as yet uncertain as to whether the queen would order her release, her sisters and mother came to terms with a new regime and a future very different from that envisaged for the Grey family only a few months before. Mary's long-standing friendship with the duchess of Suffolk meant that Frances would some months later be in high favour at court – indeed, this royal favour may even have extended to Frances, on at least one occasion, being accorded precedence at court over the queen's half-sister Elizabeth.[1] For now, however, Frances' attention was surely focused on Jane, while her eldest daughter and son-in-law remained in the Tower.

It was in the family's interests to maintain a low profile. However, that autumn, despite having received a pardon, the duke of Suffolk was reportedly 'doing bad work in connexion with religion, and the Queen is angry with him for his manner of abusing her clemency and good nature'.[2] He had probably publicly voiced his dislike of Catholicism, which had reached the queen's attention.[3] A few weeks later, the imperial ambassador Simon Renard reported the queen's continuing irritation with Suffolk.[4] The duke's actions were to become increasingly reckless as autumn gave way to winter.

The dynastic significance of Katherine Grey and her sisters was recognised not only during the reigns of Edward VI and, especially,

Elizabeth I, but also during Mary I's brief queenship. As would later be the case during Elizabeth's reign, until such time as Queen Mary married and produced an heir of her body, the question of who would succeed her was controversial, given Mary's hostility to the notion of her half-sister Elizabeth succeeding her (as decreed by Henry VIII) alongside Catholic Europe's refusal to recognise Elizabeth as legitimate. For that reason, other candidates – including Katherine – attracted the attention of those with a vested interest in who would succeed Mary in the event of her dying childless. On 4 November, shortly before Jane Grey's trial for treason, Renard informed the emperor that:

> the Duke of Suffolk's children have been found to be bastards, because he had been betrothed *per verba de presenti* to the Earl of Arundel's sister [Lady Katherine Fitzalan] before taking the Lady Frances to wife. Therefore the right would go to the Queen of Scots, and the best thing to do in order to please nobles and commons would be to cause the next Parliament to confirm the Lady Elizabeth's right to succeed, on the condition that she marry Courtenay, and in case the Queen dies without heirs, in which event Elizabeth and her heirs should succeed, or, if she had none, Courtenay. Were the succession arranged in this wise all sides might be satisfied and all possible trouble avoided.[5]

The ambassador provided no further details to support his claim that Katherine and her sisters had been declared illegitimate. This is speculation, but Renard's belief that the Grey women were illegitimate and thus barred from the succession could have been based on gossip and hearsay at court. Alternatively, writing only days before Jane's trial, the ambassador may have based his claim on the reasonable assumption that a conviction for treason would prevent any of the Greys from inheriting the throne.

On 13 November, Katherine's sister went on trial for her life at London's Guildhall. Jane was only the second royal woman in the sixteenth century to be publicly tried on a charge of treason, and she would have been well aware of the fate of the first to have undergone this experience.[6] However, she could hope that the queen would show her mercy in view of her reported promises to do so. Jane was not the only person facing trial that day. She was accompanied by her husband, his brothers Ambrose and Henry, and Thomas Cranmer, archbishop of Canterbury. All of them 'were arrayned at the Guilde Hall in London of highe treason againste the Queene'.[7] Jane was dressed in 'a blacke gowne of cloth, tourned downe; the cappe lyned with fese velvett, and edget about with the same, in a French hoode, all black, with a black byllyment, a black velvet boke hanging before hir, and another boke in hir hande open'.[8] Her sombre black attire and her act of holding a book had the effect of testifying to her devout Protestant faith as well as sig- nalling her penitence and submission to the queen's justice.

At her trial, Jane was accused of having traitorously usurped the crown from Mary, evidence of which could be found in a number of documents that she had signed 'Jane the Quene'. The contempo- rary diarist Henry Machyn reported that all of those on trial that day 'wher cast for to dee'.[9] Jane was sentenced to be burnty alive on Tower Hill – the traditional penalty for women found guilty of treason – or beheaded, a decision to be made by the queen. It is impossible to know how Katherine responded to the news of her sister's sentence. Renard claimed after the trial that:

> three sons of the Duke of Northumberland, Jane of Suffolk and the Bishop of Canterbury were taken to the hall at Cheapside, and were there condemned to death. The only one of the Duke's sons who has not been condemned is now my Lord Robert. When execution is to take place is uncertain, for though the Queen is truly irritated against the Duke of Suffolk, it is believed that Jane will not die.[10]

A few days later, the ambassador reiterated, 'I am told that her life is safe.'[11] If these rumours reached her, then Katherine had every reason to hope that Jane's life would be spared. As has been noted, Mary's merciful conduct following her accession had been praised by her contemporar- ies, and if Renard is to be believed, she had no desire to order Jane's execution. In December, Jane was granted 'the liberty of the Tower', with the freedom to walk in the queen's garden.[12] Even as they continued to hope for Jane's release, however, it must have been an anxious and uncertain Christmas for Katherine and her family.

Meanwhile, the queen's attention was focused on the most important matter of her reign: the selection of a husband. After her coronation, Mary's councillors were chiefly occupied with the question of her marriage. Her release of Edward Courtenay, earl of Devon and a descendant of Edward IV, from the Tower in the summer of 1553, among other prisoners, was interpreted by some as evidence of her interest in marrying him, a point that relates to the much-vexed question of whom the queen should marry and the interest with which her contemporaries regarded the marriage question even in the early days of her reign. As the imperial ambassadors noted in July 1553, rumours circulated that Mary would marry Courtenay because he was of the 'blood royal'.[13]

While some favoured a union with Courtenay, the queen's preference was marriage to her cousin Philip of Spain. Rumours of an Anglo-Spanish marriage gave rise to unease both at court and in the kingdom at large. Edward VI had barred both Mary and Elizabeth from the succession partly because it was feared that they might marry foreign husbands who would subvert true religion and replace English laws with those of their own countries.[14] While the queen may have been influenced by the model of marriage between her grandparents Ferdinand of Aragon and Isabella of Castile, 'a classic example of a situation where status and office could transcend conventional gendered limitations',[15] her subjects struggled – and, throughout Mary's reign, would struggle – to separate her interests from those of her husband.

Fears that marriage to Philip would have the effect of transferring the English crown into foreign hands led to a conspiracy against the queen for, as Wingfield acknowledged, Mary's subjects 'were in such a tumult over the Spanish marriage'.[16] Wyatt's rebellion, which broke out in early 1554 and was named after one of its leaders Sir Thomas Wyatt (son of the poet), can be interpreted as the most serious threat to Mary's reign in that it explicitly aimed at removing her from the throne and replacing her with a Protestant ruler. Renard reported the rumour that the queen's half-sister Elizabeth was actively involved in the rebellion, 'levying troops in her part of the country and that some of the Council were in the plot'.[17] It was believed that the rebels intended to remove Mary from the throne and replace her with Elizabeth, who would marry Courtenay. Above all, the rebellion demonstrated the unpopularity of the Spanish marriage, with the rebels claiming that they sought:

> to protect the people's freedom and prevent the crown of the realm from falling into the hands of a foreigner, contrary to the ancient liberty and privileges of the kingdom, and the intention of the kings of England, her [Mary's] predecessors. They were determined to persevere in their rising unless the Queen renounced this match and married a nobleman of her own nation, giving them as hostages the Bishop of Winchester and my Lord Paget, who were foremost in counselling the Queen to accept the Spanish marriage.[18]

In the wake of the rebellion, the queen was presented as being 'desirous rather to quiete thys tumulte by mercie, then by iustice of the sword to vanquishe, whose most godly heart fraight with al mercie & clemencie, abhorred from al effusion of bloude'.[19] However, as she had in the summer of 1553, the queen acted decisively and bravely in the face of adversity. The scale of the threat presented by Wyatt's rebellion meant that it was necessary for her to assert her authority as a military leader, since she remained an unmarried queen regnant. She was required to portray herself as a courageous defender of the realm, while nonetheless signalling her dependence on her captains.

Wingfield's account of Mary's role in defeating the rebellion utilised gendered language to emphasise her courage and decisiveness, flouting the conventional understanding of women as weak and timid, while calling attention to her unique status as a queen regnant of England: her 'spirit was not broken enough for her to admit defeat or to dread these most wicked conspirators against her Highness; though only a woman, she showed the spirit of her ancestors in adverse circumstances and strove with all her might to reconstruct her army from stronger material'.[20] In this conceptualisation of royal authority, it is noteworthy that Wingfield stressed Mary's adherence to the customs of her male predecessors, while recognising her unprecedented status as a monarch who was 'only a woman'. Wingfield later reiterated that:

Now that the queen saw that all chance of peace had gone, she applied herself wholly to war, and to prevent the enemy striking while she was unprepared, she placed in control of the city of London, then wavering in its loyalty, William Howard, brother to the duke of Norfolk.[21]

She also 'gave the lieutenancy of her own army to the earl of Pembroke, a nobleman of especial courage and high spirit'.[22] In appointing her lieutenants, Mary was represented as acting as a king was expected to do in the circumstances of rebellion and as she was required to do as an unmarried queen regnant. Paulina Kewes related that, in Wingfield's narrative, Mary appears 'as in every way a model prince poised to fulfil the great mission with which God has entrusted her'.[23] The narrative probably circulated at court, perhaps as a celebration – as well as a vindication – of the queen's providentially ordained victory.[24] If it did circulate in court circles, ostensibly the purpose may have been to contribute to the growing sense that Mary was divinely favoured, as indicated successively in her overthrow of Northumberland's regime, her seizure of the throne and her defeat of Wyatt's rebellion.

In attempting to rally her supporters and suppress the rebellion, as part of her role as a courageous defender of the realm, Mary publicly delivered a speech at Guildhall on 1 February 1554. The queen's biographer John Edwards described this public oration as 'the speech of her life'.[25] It was subsequently represented in the medium of print as a decisive measure in ensuring that her cause was victorious. As had occurred during the coronation, the queen's royal authority was ceremonially symbolised by the presence of her regalia, arriving at Guildhall to show 'hare mynde un-to the mayer, aldermen, and the hole crafttes of London (in) are owne persone, with hare cepter in hare honde in tokyn of love and pes, and wente home agayne by watter at the Crane in the ventre'.[26] It is significant that the Greyfriars chronicler alluded to the queen's desire to show 'hare mynde' to the city officials, which had the effect of presenting her as acting decisively. The presence of the regalia seems to have been designed to emphasise her status as queen regnant on a public occasion when she needed to be seen to act with authority and defend her threatened sovereignty. Once inside Guildhall:

> she ... with her owne mowth declared to the audience there assembled the wicked pretence of the traytor Wyett, which was utterlie to deprive her of her crowne, and to spoyle the Cittie; which was so noblie and with so good spiritt declared, and with so lowde a voyce, that all the people might heare her Maiestie, and comfortinge their hartes with so sweet wordes that made them weepe for joye to heare her Majesty speake.[27]

The queen thus used the oration to call on the loyalty of her subjects, in direct opposition to the traitorous deeds and intentions of Wyatt and his followers. She also alluded to her proposed marriage to Philip of Spain by directly associating it with her marriage to the realm, assuring her subjects of her loyalty to them and promising that her marriage would not compromise it:

> What I am, loving subjects, yet know your Queen, to whom, at my coronation, ye promised allegiance and obedience, I was then wedded to the realm, and to the laws of the same, the spousal ring whereof I wear here on my finger, and it never has and never shall be left off.[28]

In relation to the marriage, she is said to have declared:

> I am neither so desirous of wedding, nor so precisely wedded to my will, that I needs must have a husband. Hitherto I have lived a

virgin, and I doubt not, with God's grace, to live still. But if, as my ancestors have done, it might please God that I should leave you a successor to be your governor, I trust you would rejoice thereat; also, I know it would be to your comfort. Yet, if I thought this marriage would endanger any of you, my loving subjects, or the royal estate of this English realm, I would never consent thereto, nor marry while I lived. On the word of a Queen I assure you, that if the marriage appear not before the court of Parliament, nobility and commons, for the singular benefit of the whole realm, then I will abstain not only from this, but from any other.[29]

Mary sought to assure the onlookers that she would only marry with their consent and with the approval of her Parliament, nobility and commons, despite having previously asserted that she would select her own spouse as her male predecessors had been accustomed to do and in spite of her councillors' opposition. She stressed that:

her action as to her marriage … had been advised by her Council as conducive to the welfare of the realm, and in no wise adopted in accordance with her own personal desires; if the reasons in favour of it had not been sufficiently understood, they might be repeated in Parliament.[30]

Her speech, like the later orations of Elizabeth, focused on the reciprocal fidelity and love between queen and subjects, in a bid to defeat the rebel army:[31]

Now, however, that Wyatt was nearing London, she wished to hear from her people whether they meant to behave like good subjects and defend her against this rebel, for if they did, she was minded to live and die with them and strain every nerve in their cause; for this time their fortunes, goods, honour, personal safety, wives and children were in the balance. If they bore themselves like good subjects she would be bound to stand by them, for they would deserve the care of their sovereign lady. And thus, with befitting persuasions, she urged them to take up arms.[32]

Following the queen's speech, those present 'cried out loudly that they would live and die in her service, and that Wyatt was a traitor; and they all threw up their caps to show their goodwill'.[33] Interestingly, Mary's oration was underpinned by references to her virginity, a trope that consistently featured in her supporters' narratives of her rule, including those produced by John Heywood and John Christopherson. In condemning Wyatt's rebellion, Christopherson celebrated the queen's virginity:

> But alas what harde hartes have those, that if she were but a private woman, being so gentle of nature, so vertuouse and so merciful, coulde drawe their sworde against her ... For albeit that all bloudeshedde is cruel and horrible in the sight of god, yet the shedding of so a pure virgins bloude, is of all other moste cruell and detestable.[34]

In utilising virginity as a literary trope, both Mary and her supporters explicitly addressed both her gender and her unmarried status, to emphasise her vulnerability – in alluding to the 'shedding' of her 'bloude' – and to establish a connection with the Virgin Mary, thus highlighting the queen's Catholic faith as well as presenting her as mother and protector of her realm. She was not 'a private woman' but a queen concerned with 'the singular benefit of the whole realm', and in her speech her royal authority was closely associated with both gender and precedent in an attempt to reassert her status and win the support of her audience in an atmosphere of rebellion and disorder. Mary's contemporaries believed that the successful defeat of the rebellion signified divine favour of the queen and her cause, for as Christopherson opined, 'if she [Mary] had been an adversarye of his [God's] truth, and of his holy word, as some folkes report her, he would never have so ayded her'.[35] Following the defeat of the rebellion and arrest of the rebels, 'all the Queens hoste came throughe London in goodlye araye, and Te

Deum was sunge in the Queens Chappell for ioye of the sayde victorie, and so fewe slayne'.[36]

For Katherine, Wyatt's rebellion culminated in tragedy, namely the executions of her father and sister for treason. Suffolk's disaffection the previous autumn had intensified to the extent that he was prepared to conspire against the queen. The evidence does not suggest that his actions were motivated by the desire to see Jane restored to the throne, but the establishment of a Catholic regime was undoubtedly anathema to the godly duke. Mary was aware of Suffolk's dissatisfaction and also appears to have been sceptical of his allegiance to her. The queen initially intended to send Suffolk to meet Wyatt's forces, perhaps as an opportunity for the duke to prove his loyalty.[37] The duke's refusal to command the royal forces in 1554 confirmed to Mary's councillors that he was conspiring against her regime.[38] On 25 January, the duke and his brother John 'fledd', Suffolk having been summoned to court by the queen's messenger from his house at Sheen where he was then in residence.[39] 'Yt is said that the same morning that he was going ther came a messenger to him from the quene, that he shulde come to the court.'[40] The duke allegedly protested that he was 'comyng to her grace' and was 'booted and spurred redy to ryde', but after offering the messenger refreshment, Suffolk 'departed himself, no man knoweth whither'.[41]

It was believed that the duke had plotted with the French to commit treason against the queen.[42] On 29 January, the imperial ambassadors informed the emperor, first, that 'the Duke of Suffolk and his brothers, Lord Thomas and Lord John (Grey), have gone off to the Duke's house some forty miles hence and have been proclaimed traitors' and, second, that 'the French ambassador had caused the Duke of Suffolk to fly by telling him that unless he did so the Council would have him arrested'.[43] The ambassadors recounted rumours spread by the rebels that Philip of Spain desired to marry Mary in order 'to conquer England' – in short, the same fear of foreign conquest espoused by Edward VI when justifying the exclusion of his half-sisters from the succession, and later reiterated by Jane Grey in the proclamation setting out her right to the throne – and also informed the emperor that the earl of Huntingdon, 'a mortal enemy of the Duke of Suffolk', had been granted permission by the queen to arrest the duke.[44] Having met his brothers at Lutterworth (St Albans was originally intended), Suffolk arrived with his men at Leicester on 29 January, where he was welcomed and received £500 from the bailiff of Kegworth in support, before later departing for Coventry.[45] As he approached, he learned that Huntingdon intended to arrest him and was informed that the city gates were bolted against him, leading him to flee.[46]

On 5 February, Cardinal Reginald Pole reported Suffolk's treason:

The city of London stood firm for the Queen, together with the rest of the nobility, except the Duke of Suffolk, father of that Jane whom the Duke of Northumberland had made his daughter-in-law and Queen; it being supposed that he had taken flight, from fear of being sent back to the Tower, seeing that this had been done to the Marquis of Northampton; and the Queen presupposing that Suffolk was gone into the province [Leicestershire] where he has his mansion and estate, her Majesty sent against him the Earl of Huntingdon, who has to wife the writer's niece [Katherine Pole], and has as many adherents and no less authority in that country than Suffolk himself, being of a rival family which is opposed to the Duke.[47]

The extent to which Katherine and her family were aware of Suffolk's hostility to the new regime is unknown, but Frances, at least, surely would have opposed her husband's actions in view of the precariousness of their situation. Having secured a pardon for her husband the previous July, the duchess would have been all too aware that the queen was unlikely to be merciful again. Jane remained in the Tower under sentence of death; having been convicted of treason, her execution could be sanctioned by Mary at a moment's notice. By engaging in treasonous activities, the duke placed not only himself but also his eldest daughter in grave danger; as events would prove, this decision to conspire against Mary was to have fatal consequences. Renard informed the emperor that:

the Earl of Huntingdon had routed the Duke of Suffolk, taken all his men prisoners, seized all his money and baggage, and forced him to fly with his two brothers accompanied only by five horse. Huntingdon is in pursuit, declaring Suffolk a traitor, and the Duke is making for Scotland. The people would not rise for him, and it is hoped that he will soon be a prisoner or forced to leave the realm.[48]

Renard also noted that one of the duke's servants had been hanged as a result of:

carrying a placard issued by the Duke to be published all over the country, to the effect that there were 12,000 Spaniards at Calais and as many more in the West Country, all ready to conquer England; so let the people rise up in arms against them and against the Chancellor and Paget, the Chancellor because of religion and Paget for his share in the match.[49]

By 6 February, it was known that Suffolk and his brother John had been arrested by Huntingdon.[50] They were captured at the family residence of Astley Castle in Warwickshire. 'The Duke was found in a hollow tree and John buried under some hay; and the Duke was discovered by a dog.'[51] The earl had learned that 'the Duke, being himself nearly two days without having eaten, and almost dead of hunger, and of cold, had left the woods, and come to the house of the worker, and warmed himself'.[52]

Suffolk, John and their brother Thomas were indicted at Leicester on 10 February. Following his capture, Suffolk wrote and signed a confession:

in which he owns that irritation at his arrest, the small esteem in which the Council held him, his alarm when [Edward] Warner was arrested, and the conversation of Carew and Crofts, who had plotted, together with many others, to set the Lady Elizabeth on the throne, moved him to leave the Queen's party and join the rebels. His brother,

Thomas, he says, specially strove to persuade him, and also tried to win over Pembroke, who refused to listen.[53]

The duke seems to have assigned responsibility for his actions to his brother Thomas, indicating that the latter was the dominant personality. As Loades has suggested, Thomas Grey may have been 'the real leader of the family', as well as 'the inspirer of his brother's [Henry's] foolish move'.[54] The duke was tried before his peers and on 17 February he was 'caried to Westminster ... by the clerke of the cheke and all the garde almoste'. He pleaded not guilty to the crime of levying war against the queen, declaring 'that yt was no treason for a pere of the realme as he was to raise his power and make proclamacion onely to avoyde strangers out of the realme', although he did acknowledge that he had met Huntingdon 'in arms'.[55] Suffolk was found guilty and escorted to the Tower, landing 'at the water gate with a countenance very heavy and pensyfe, desyring all men to praye for him'.[56]

As Wingfield wrote at the time, in rebelling against the queen, Suffolk was 'ungrateful for the favour he had received and the pardon he had obtained from his sovereign after Northumberland's sedition'.[57] The duke's treasonous activities effectively sealed his daughter's fate. Renard was adamant that Mary should not 'lose the opportunity of punishing the shameful infidelity of those who had conspired against her person and crown'.[58] While the queen had shown no desire to order Jane's execution, she did not now recoil from her duty, for 'God had shown her the grace of placing the exercise of justice in her hands'.[59] The reaction of Katherine and her family to news of Jane's death sentence is unrecorded, but their grief and despair were surely tempered by the realisation that Suffolk's actions against the Crown had placed the queen in an impossible situation. Wyatt's rebellion and the duke's role as a leader in the conspiracy fatally changed Jane's situation, for the queen, previously merciful, was now 'resolved to let justice have its course, as her clemency has already been abused'.[60]

As a result, Katherine and her family were faced with the horrifying reality that the 17-year-old Jane was to be executed for treason. On

11 February, Bishop Gardiner preached a sermon at court beseeching Mary to 'be merciful to the body of the commonwealth and conservation thereof, which could not be unless the rotten and hurtful members thereof were cut off and consumed'.[61] The martyrologist John Foxe printed a letter said to have been written by Jane to her father shortly before her execution. It reads as follows:

Father, although it hath pleased God to hasten my death by you, by whom my life should rather have been lengthened; yet can I so patiently take it, as I yield God more hearty thanks for shortening my woful days, than if all the world had been given unto my possession, with life lengthened at my own will. And albeit I am well assured of your impatient dolours, redoubled manifold ways, both in bewailing your own woe, and especially as I hear, my unfortunate state; yet, my dear father (if I may without offence rejoice in my own mishaps), meseems in this I may account myself blessed, that washing my hands with the innocency of my fact, my guiltless blood may cry before the Lord, Mercy to the innocent! And yet, though I must needs acknowledge, that being constrained, and as you wot well enough, continually assayed, in taking upon me I seemed to consent, and therein grievously offended the queen and her laws: yet do I assuredly trust, that this my offence towards God is so much the less, (in that being in so royal estate as I was) mine enforced honour blended never with mine innocent heart. And thus, good father, I have opened unto you the state wherein I at present stand; whose death at hand, although to you perhaps it may seem right woful, to me there is nothing that can be more welcome, than from this vale of misery to aspire to that heavenly throne of all joy and pleasure with Christ our Saviour. In whose steadfast faith (if it may be lawful for the daughter so to write to the father), the Lord that hitherto hath strengthened you, so continue you, that at the last we may meet in heaven with the Father, the Son, and the Holy Ghost.[62]

Modern historians have questioned the authenticity of this letter. Ives noted that it only appeared at least a decade after Jane's death, when it was included in the second edition of Foxe's *Acts and Monuments* (1570). 'The letter ... seems less a private message to a father than an early exercise in imaginative reconstruction.'[63] However, Jane did write a letter to the duke in the prayer book that she carried with her to the scaffold on 12 February:

> The lorde comforte youre grace and that in his worde whearin all creatures onlye are to be comforted and thoughe it hathe pleased god to take awaye ii of youre children yet thincke not I moste humblye beseche youre grace that you hauee loste them but truste that we by leauing thys mortall life haue wunne an imortal life and I for my parte as I haue honoured youre grace in thys life will praye for you in another life. [y]oure gracys humble daughter Jane Duddley[64]

In her preparations for her death, Jane's mind also turned to her younger sister. On the eve of her execution, she wrote a letter to Katherine in her Greek New Testament.[65] Katherine was then residing at the family property of the Charterhouse with her sister and mother. Historians have offered alternative interpretations of this letter. In the nineteenth century, Strickland viewed it as a 'beautiful farewell letter'.[66] By contrast, Chapman regarded the letter as 'a stern directive from a strongminded guide to a backward pupil'.[67] The content of the letter might seem to support Chapman's interpretation, but it may be more effective to approach it alongside, first, the letters that Jane had signed in her brief queenship and, second, her reported speech on the scaffold, all of which testified to the devout Protestantism at the core of her identity. These beliefs had developed in childhood, in a household in which her father was celebrated by European reformers for his godly beliefs and his hatred of Catholicism. As she grew to maturity, Jane's piety became the guiding force of her ultimately short life and it was this sense of purpose, this definition of self, which Jane sought to impress upon her sister on the eve of death and the beginning of eternal life. Her words extol the spiritual benefits of dying and express sentiments that would be echoed by the seventeenth-century Puritan preacher Thomas Adams in a sermon: 'Our death is not a perishing but a parting ... The soul is not lost to the body, but only sent before it to joy ... Death cannot be eventually hurtful to the good, for it no sooner takes away the temporal life but Christ gives eternal life in the room of it.'[68] Here is the letter:

I have here sent you, good sister Katherine, a book, which, although it be not outwardly trimmed with gold, yet inwardly it is more worth than precious stones. It is the book, dear sister, of the law of the Lord. It is his testament and last will, which he bequeathed unto us wretches; which shall lead you to the path of eternal joy: and, if you with a good mind read it, and with an earnest mind do purpose to follow it, it shall bring you to an immortal and everlasting life. It shall teach you to live, and learn you to die. It shall win you more than you should have gained by the possession of your woful father's lands. For as, if God had prospered him, you should have inherited his lands; so, if you apply diligently to this book, seeking to direct your life after it, you shall be an inheritor of such riches, as neither the covetous shall withdraw from you, neither thief shall steal, neither yet the moths corrupt. Desire with David, good sister, to understand the law of the Lord God. Live still to die, that you by death may purchase eternal life. And trust not that the tenderness of your age shall lengthen your life; for as soon (if God call) goeth the young as the old: and labour always to learn to die. Defy the world, deny the devil, and despise the flesh, and delight yourself only in the Lord. Be penitent for your sins, and yet despair not: be strong in faith, and yet presume not; and desire, with St. Paul, to be dissolved and to be with Christ, with whom even in death there is life. Be like the good servant, and even at midnight be waking, lest, when death cometh and stealeth upon you as a thief in the night, you be, with the evil servant, found sleeping; and lest, for lack of oil, you be found like the five foolish women; and like him that had not on the wedding garment, and then ye be cast out from the marriage. Rejoice in Christ, as I do. Follow the steps of your Master Christ, and take up your cross: lay your sins on his back, and always embrace him. And as touching my death, rejoice as

I do, good sister, that I shall be delivered of this corruption, and put on incorruption. For I am assured, that I shall, for losing of a mortal life, win an immortal life, the which I pray God grant you, and send you of his grace to live in his fear, and to die in the true christian faith, from the which (in God's name), I exhort you, that you never swerve, neither for hope of life, nor for fear of death. For if you will deny his truth for to lengthen your life, God will deny you, and yet shorten your days. And if you will cleave unto him, he will prolong your days, to your comfort and his glory: to the which glory God bring me now, and you hereafter, when it pleaseth him to call you. Fare you well, good sister, and put your only trust in God, who only must help you.[69]

Jane's letter to Katherine offered her spiritual advice, namely hope of eternal salvation, alongside a warning not to love the world, as Jane would confess in her scaffold speech to having done. Evangelical women of the period described themselves as heiresses to the spiritual inheritance that awaited believers, thus accounting for Jane's view that, while their father's lands had been taken away, 'their heavenly legacy could not be stolen by thieves or corrupted by moths'.[70]

Recent scholarship, however, has provided a more complex reading of Jane's letter alongside the other religious writings published post-humously under her name. Noting that these texts have uncritically 'been read as the authentic, and unmediated, voice of England's nine-day queen', Louise Horton argued that Jane's writings should be placed within the Edwardian evangelical establishment in view of the 'shared vocabulary' between Jane and reformers including Thomas Becon, John Bale and Miles Coverdale.[71] Horton further related that, while Jane's letter to her sister is often viewed as evidence of her religious steadfast-ness, 'the textual concordance' between the letter and Becon's work, namely a 'shared central conceit of a gift of scripture suggests that the letter is not a spontaneous bequest to Katherine Grey'.[72] Specifically, Jane's letter contains fifteen biblical allusions from Coverdale's Bible, while 'the resonance of the opening line, echoes the words of Becon on a further five occasions'.[73] Thus, for Horton, the similarities between the letter and Becon's earlier work 'challenge the perception of the letter being the uniquely personal words of [Jane] Grey to her sister'.[74]

Jennifer Richards has also noted that there is doubt over Jane's authorship of the texts attributed to her in the Tower, on the basis that her manuscripts have not survived, so what she actually wrote is unclear.[75] Both Horton and Richards suggested that Jane's texts should 'best [be] understood as collaborations' with Protestant clerics and the evangelical printer John Day in the creation of Jane's canon, with a view to shaping her identity as a Protestant martyr.[76] It is possible that Frances delivered to the printer, John Day, Jane's letters addressed to her former tutor Harding and her sister, alongside an account of her conversation with John Feckenham, abbot of Westminster (sent by the queen – unsuccessfully – to convert Jane to Catholicism prior to her execution).[77] Alternatively, Day may have obtained the texts as a result of his affinity with the Grey sisters' step-grandmother Katherine Brandon, dowager duchess of Suffolk, who had sponsored Day's printing of other reformist texts.[78] This theory is based on the suggestion that Jane's writing was 'formed within a community that had the means to publish and was conscious, especially through the examples of Katherine Parr and Anne Askew, of the power that writing and print gave reformist women to spread the Word', and her texts 'were ... subsequently transmitted in the nexus of [Katherine] Willoughby's patronage network'.[79]

Assuming that she did come into possession of the letter, we have no way of knowing how Katherine responded to Jane's letter on a personal level. Jane's relatives, irrespective of their grief and suffering, would have been well aware that the tarnishing of the Grey family with the crime of treason necessitated a public display of their loyalty to Queen Mary, with no hint of scandal further sullying their name. However, it is plausible that Katherine and her family revered Jane's memory in private. Certainly, there is nothing linking the Greys with the claim of a mid-sixteenth-century Mantuan visitor to England that 'many persons, members of whose families have been hanged and quartered, are accustomed to boast of it'.[80] In his study of attitudes to death in early modern England, Peter Marshall put forward the insightful suggestion that, after the Reformation, 'the act of remembering still involved negotiating an intricate nexus of emotional and social responses, private grief and public duty'.[81] Contemporary accounts of Katherine's demise in 1568 indicate that she had proven receptive to Jane's admonition that she 'learn ... to die', for, like her sister, her performance of death stressed her Protestant faith and belief that she died in God's grace.

In her study of noble executions in the sixteenth century, Maria Hayward noted that the clothing of the convicted 'allowed these individuals to demonstrate compliance or defiance, while bolstering their confidence, so allowing them to deport themselves well, make a good death and be remembered favourably'.[82] Her research also revealed that the condemned usually favoured one of three choices of colour on the scaffold: black, red or a neutral colour such as grey.[83] The choice of colour of attire was an issue infused with political and religious significance, and a means by which the condemned could make a final, powerful statement to those observing their end. Mary, Queen of Scots, for example, chose to wear red on the scaffold in 1587 because it was the liturgical colour of martyrdom in the Catholic Church and thus emphasised her belief that she died as a martyr to the Catholic faith. Jane's choice of black clothing made a similarly powerful symbolic statement about her devout religious beliefs, visually proclaiming her Protestant faith to accompany the godly words in her scaffold speech.

Jane's execution followed that of her husband Guildford Dudley on Tower Hill, which took place around ten o'clock in the morning.[84] Renard confirmed that Guildford 'suffered in public'.[85] Unaccompanied by a priest, Guildford was executed with one stroke of the axe, 'his carcas throwne into a carre, and his hed in a cloth, he was brought into the chappell within the Tower'.[86] Jane's beheading took place immediately after her husband's, on 'the greene ouer against the white tower'.[87] Before her journey to the scaffold, from her lodgings she witnessed Guildford's corpse being removed from the cart and taken into the Tower chapel of St Peter ad Vincula to be interred, but she was 'nothing at all abashed'.[88] Having mounted the scaffold, Jane made the following speech:

> Good people, I am come hether to die, and by a lawe I am condemned to the same. The facte, in dede, against the quenes highnesse was unlawfull, and the consenting thereunto by me: but touching the procurement and desyre therof by me or on my halfe, I doo wash my handes thereof in innocencie, before God, and the face of you, good Christian people, this day ... I pray you all, good Christian people, to beare me witness that I dye a true Christian woman, and that I looke to be saved by none other meane, but only by the mercy of God in the merites of the blood of his only sonne Jesus Christ: and I confesse, when I dyd know the word of God I neglected the same, loved my selfe and the world, and therefore this plague or punyshment is happely and worthely happened unto me for my sins; and yet I thank God of his goodnesse that he hath thus geven me a tyme and respet to repent. And now, good people, while I am alyve, I pray you to assyst me with your prayers.[89]

Jane's recorded speech provides evidence of Frances Dolan's suggestion that death on the scaffold could be embraced with the anticipation of salvation.[90] Jane's words, in which she clarified that she had not sought the crown but nonetheless accepted her fate as divine punishment for her sins, also illustrate how those condemned to execution typically confessed a much broader guilt; even where they were innocent of the crime for which they were to die, they resigned themselves to their fate as the just deserts of more general wickedness.[91]

Following her speech, Jane removed her gloves and handkerchief and passed them to her attendant and her book to the lieutenant's brother. Her two female attendants helped her to remove her gown, before she knelt, blindfolded, at the block. Feeling for the block, she cried: 'What shall I do? Where is it?' before one of the observers, mercifully, guided her towards it. Laying her head upon the block, Jane stretched her body forwards and proclaimed: 'Lord, into thy hands

I commend my spirit!'[92] Her remains were interred at the chapel of St Peter ad Vincula, joining those of two other decapitated queens: Anne Boleyn and Katherine Howard.

Jane and Guildford were regarded with pity both at the time and in the years after their executions. Many accounts stressed how the ambition of their families had led directly to the bloody events of that February morning. Grafton, who had printed the proclamation of Jane's accession in July 1553, described Jane as a 'gentle yong Ladie endued with singuler gifts both of learning and knowledge', while her husband was 'a very comely tall Gentlemen'.[93] Both Jane and Guildford 'suffered ignorantly for that, which their parentes & other had vnhappily brought about to the vtter subuersio of them & their famelies'.[94] The Elizabethan chronicler Raphael Holinshed, likewise, characterised the couple as 'two innocents ... they did but ignorantlie accept that which the others had willinglie deuised, and by open proclamation consented to take from others, and giue to them'.[95] Their 'deaths were the more hastened for feare of further troubles and sturs for hir [Jane's] title, like as hir father [Suffolk] had attempted'.[96]

In the seventeenth century, Fuller declared that Guildford was 'a goodly, and ... a godly Gentleman, whose worst fault was, that he was Son to an ambitious Father'.[97] Heylyn similarly proclaimed that Jane was 'brought unwillingly upon the stage, thereon to act the part of a Queen of England'.[98] Poets, too, related in their verses that 'BY Parents too ambitious Pride, / The Scaffold shall with Blood be Di'de. / A Vertuous Lady then shall die, / For being raised up too High'.[99] Jane was a 'poore innocent', the victim of others' 'dissimulacion', 'perswasions' and 'Couert craftynes', and her 'vtter vndoyng' was caused by others' 'pride and pevyshe presumpcion'.[100] By contrast, immediately after their deaths, Renard celebrated the executions of Jane and Guildford as necessary for the queen's safety and anticipated the further ruin of their relatives: 'the whole house of Suffolk would be obliterated by the execution of the three brothers now prisoners, whose death, as they were heretics, would contribute to the firm reestablishment of religion'.[101]

The death of Jane would be followed by that of her father, the duke of Suffolk, less than two weeks later. On 23 February, the duke was executed on Tower Hill. His execution that morning took place 'betwyn ix and x of the cloke afore none'.[102] On the eve of the duke's execution, the queen had sent two priests to the Tower in an attempt to convert him to Catholicism, but 'they were in no wise able to move him'.[103] Suffolk was unwillingly accompanied to the scaffold by the queen's chaplain Dr Hugh Weston, dean of Westminster:

For when the duke went vp the scaffold, the said Weston being on his left hand, pressed to go vp with him. The duke with his left hand put him downe againe off the staires, and Weston taking hold of the duke forced him downe likewise. And as they ascended the second time, the duke againe put him downe. Then Weston said, that it was the queenes pleasure he should so doo: wherewith the duke casting his hands abrode, ascended vp the scaffold, and paused a prettie while after

before making his speech.[104] The Tower chronicler reported that:

His wourdes at the comyng on the scaffolde were theis followeing, or moche like: 'Good people, this daie I am come hether to dye, being one whom the lawe hathe justlie condempned, and one who hathe no lesse deserved for my dysobedyence against the quenes highenes, of whom I do moste humbly axe forgevenes, and I truste she dothe and will forgyve me.' Then maister Weston, his confessor, standing by, saide, 'My lord, hir grace hathe allredy forgeven and praieth for you.' Then saide the duke, 'I beseche you all, goode people, to lett me be an example to you all for obedyence to the quene and the majestrates, for the contrarie therof hath brought me [to this end]. And also I shall most hartely desire you all to beare me witnes that I do dye a faythefull and true christian, beleving to be saved by non other but onely by allmightie God, thoroughe the passion of his son Jesus Christ. And nowe I pray you to praie with me.' Then he kneled downe, and

Weston with him, and saide the sallme of '*Miserere mei Deus*,' and '*In te, Domine, speravi*,' the duke one verse and Weston an other. Which don, he dyd put of his gown and his doblet. Then kniting the kercheve himself about his eyes, helde uppe his handes to heaven, and after laie downe along, with his hedd apon the blocke, whiche at one stroke was striken of by the hangman.[105]

The speeches of both the duke and his eldest daughter proclaimed their Protestant beliefs, namely the rejection of good works as being necessary for eternal salvation. In doing so, they vocally rejected the Catholic practices being restored by the government to the realm. Renard noted that Suffolk 'has refused to be converted to the old religion'.[106] At his execution, Suffolk 'would not acknowledge any other atonement than that which was perfected by the death of Christ: by this faith he supported himself, and in this faith he at length ended his life'.[107]

In the reign of Elizabeth I, the duke was described as having been:

a man of high nobilitie by birth, and of nature to his friend gentle and courteous, more easie in deed to be led than was thought expedient, of stomach neuerthelesse stout and hardie, hastie and soone kindled, but pacified streight againe, and sorie if in his heat ought had passed him otherwise than reason might seeme to beare, vpright and plaine in his priuate dealings, no dissembler, nor well able to beare iniuries, but yet forgiuing and forgetting the same, if the partie would seeme but to acknowlege his fault, and seeke reconcilement. Bountifull he was and verie liberall, somwhat learned himselfe, and a great fauourer of those that were learned, so that to manie he shewed himselfe a verie Mecoenas: as free from couetousnesse, as void of pride and disdainefull hautinesse of mind, more regarding plaine meaning men, than clawbacke flatterers. And this vertue he had, he could patientlie heare his faults told him, by those whome he had in credit for their wisdome and faithfull meaning toward him, although sometime he had the hap to reforme himselfe thereafter. Concerning his last offense for the which he died, it is to be supposed, he rather tooke in hand that

vnlawfull enterprise through others persuasions, than of his owne
motion for any malicious ambition in himselfe.[108]

Reformers lamented the demise of Jane and Henry Grey, observing
that 'this family is now overthrown and almost extinct, on account of
their saving profession of our Saviour, and the cause of the gospel'.[109]
There was 'reason to mourn over the ruin of a family so illustrious'[110]
because the Greys had shared a 'love of godliness' at odds with the 'tyranny of the papists by which she [England] is now oppressed'.[111] The
bloodshed did not end there: on 27 April, 'Lord Thomas Grey, brother
to the Duke of Suffolke, was beheaded at the Tower hill'.[112]

Jane's execution had serious dynastic consequences for Katherine:
until such time as Mary married and produced an heir, she was second
in line to the throne after Elizabeth, and given the queen's reputed
antipathy to her half-sister, it was by no means certain that Elizabeth
would succeed Mary should the queen die childless. Some months shy
of her fourteenth birthday, Katherine was left without a father and
elder sister, and with a future that had never appeared so uncertain. It
is impossible to know what Katherine thought of the brutal and shock-
ing deaths of her father and sister, but her later actions suggest that she
failed to learn lessons from their downfalls and executions. The demise
of Jane and the tarnishing of the Greys with treason ought to have been
a lesson to Katherine of the dangers of offending the monarch, which
could involve imprisonment, condemnation and execution. Instead,
her reckless decision to embark on a clandestine love affair and marriage
without securing royal permission ensured that her fate was every much
as tragic and bleak as Jane's.

5

At the Court of Mary I

In the aftermath of the executions of her father and sister, Katherine was faced with both coming to terms with their brutal fates and looking to the future. Irrespective of their private emotions, it was essential for Katherine and her family to demonstrate publicly their loyalty to Queen Mary. As has previously been noted, Frances was on good terms with the queen and this was shown by Mary graciously inviting the duchess to attend her at court a few months after the executions of Jane and the duke. In April 1554, former Grey manors in Leicestershire were returned to Frances' possession and in July she was appointed to Mary's Privy Chamber.[1] She was certainly joined there by Katherine, but whether the youngest daughter Mary also attended court, and in what capacity, is uncertain, for she would have been too young to serve in the queen's Privy Chamber. Erroneously, some have suggested that both Katherine and Mary served the queen at court as maidens of honour.[2]

During her residence at court, Katherine acquired a stepfather. The date of Frances' second marriage, to Adrian Stokes, her Master of the Horse, has proven somewhat controversial. Traditionally, it was believed that she remarried with indecent haste only weeks after the duke of Suffolk's execution. Strickland, for example, condemned Frances as follows: 'instead of wasting her precious time in tears and lamentations for the husband of her youth and the father of her children, and shrouding herself in dismal weeds, she assumed bridal garments' and remarried in the spring of 1554.[3] The Elizabethan historian William Camden believed that Frances, 'forgetting the Nobility of her Lineage, had married Adrian Stokes, a mean Gentleman, to her Dishonour, but yet for her Security'.[4] Interestingly, in his discussion of Edward Courtenay, earl of Devon (initially suggested as a husband for Mary I), the imperial ambassador reported in April 1555 that:

> it has been proposed that Courtenay might be married to the widow of the last Duke of Suffolk, who comes next to the daughter of Scotland in line of succession to the crown. If this is done, it will make Elizabeth very jealous, and would give rise to much dissention in the kingdom if the Queen died without issue.[5]

If true, then the proposed match did not take place. It has more recently been argued that Frances' second marriage only took place in the spring of 1555, rather than the year before as traditionally believed.[6] However, the traditional date of 1554 is confirmed by an inquisition post mortem of 1600 concerning Frances' estates. It records that the duchess married Adrian Stokes on 9 March 1554 and that date is seemingly further confirmed by the birth of a daughter in July 1555, indicating that Frances conceived in October 1554.[7] It is unnecessary to condemn Frances for the speed of her remarriage or to infer from it that she did not love her late husband. Rather, as Camden's account suggests, Frances took as her second husband 'a mean Gentleman' to obtain 'Security' and to avoid being matched with an ambitious nobleman, including Courtenay, who could assert a claim to the throne on her behalf. That Renard was unaware of Frances' remarriage indicates that it was very low-key, even secret. After her marriage, the duchess retired from court and may have endured a number of failed pregnancies, although evidence for these is lacking.[8] The last few years of her life are obscure, although the records show that she wrote to the earl of Rutland on 9 April 1557 from Islington, asking if she could have the use of his house at Holywell for six weeks or two months, but she did not specify for what reason.[9]

While they outwardly demonstrated their loyalty to the new queen, in private it is likely that Katherine, her sister and mother revered the memory of Henry and Jane after their deaths. Several scholars have noted that, in later life, Mary Grey owned a two-volume edition of John Foxe's *Acts and Monuments*, which depicted 'this virtuous lady' Jane as a Protestant martyr.[10] A month after Jane's execution, John Banks explained in a letter to Bullinger that Jane had refuted the opinions of the 'clever and crafty papist' Abbot John Feckenham, who had been sent by the queen in an attempt to convert Jane to the Catholic faith. Banks reported that 'it may be seen how her truly admirable mind was illuminated by the light of God's word, by two letters, one of which she herself wrote to the lady Catharine, her sister, a most noble virgin, to inspire her with a love of the sacred writings'.[11] He went on to note that the duke of Suffolk, like his daughter, died in the Protestant faith: 'in this faith he at length ended his life.'[12] In the course of honouring their memory, Katherine surely would have admired the piety and courage displayed by both Henry and Jane on the scaffold. Yet, with a Catholic queen on the throne determined to restore papal authority to the realm, it was imperative for Katherine and her surviving relatives to convey their religious conformity, irrespective of their private beliefs and practices.

In 1557, the Venetian ambassador Giovanni Michiel described the first Tudor queen as follows:

> She is of low rather than of middling stature, but, although short, she has no personal defect in her limbs, nor is any part of her body deformed. She is of spare and delicate frame, quite unlike her father, who was tall and stout; nor does she resemble her mother, who, if not tall, was nevertheless bulky. Her face is well formed, as shown by her features and lineaments, and as seen by her portraits. When younger she was considered, not merely tolerably handsome, but of beauty exceeding mediocrity. At present, with the exception of

some wrinkles, caused more by anxieties than by age, which make her appear some years older, her aspect, for the rest, is very grave. Her eyes are so piercing that they inspire, not only respect, but fear, in those on whom she fixes them, although she is very short-sighted, being unable to read or do anything else unless she has her sight quite close to what she wishes to peruse or to see distinctly. Her voice is rough and loud, almost like a man's, so that when she speaks she is always heard a long way off. In short, she is a seemly woman, and never to be loathed for ugliness, even at her present age, without considering her degree of queen. But whatever may be the amount deducted from her physical endowments, as much more may with truth, and without flattery, be added to those of her mind, as, besides the facility and quickness of her understanding, which comprehends whatever is intelligible to others, even to those who are not of her own sex (a marvellous gift for a woman), she is skilled in five languages, not merely understanding, but speaking four of them fluently, viz., English, Latin, French, Spanish, and Italian, in which last, however, she does not venture to converse, although it is well known to her; but the replies she gives in Latin, and her very intelligent remarks made in that tongue surprise everybody. Besides woman's work, such as embroidery of every sort with the needle, she also practises music, playing especially on the claricorde and on the lute so excellently that, when intent on it (though now she plays rarely), she surprised the best performers, both by the rapidity of her hand and by her style of playing. Such are her virtues and external accomplishments. Internally, with the exception of certain trifles, in which, to say the truth, she is like other women, being sudden and passionate, and close and miserly, rather more so than would become a bountiful and generous queen, she in other respects has no notable imperfections; whilst in certain things she is singular and without an equal, for not only is she brave and valiant, unlike other timid and spiritless women, but so courageous and resolute that neither in adversity nor peril did she ever even display or commit any act of cowardice or pusillanimity, maintaining always, on the contrary, a wonderful grandeur and dignity, knowing what became the dignity of a sovereign as well as any of the most consummate statesmen in her service; so that from her way of proceeding, and from the method observed by her (and in which she still perseveres), it cannot be denied that she shows herself to have been born of truly royal lineage. Of her humility, piety, and religion it is unnecessary to speak, or bear witness to them, as they are not only universally acknowledged, but recently blazoned by proofs and facts which fell little short of martyrdom, by reason of the persecutions she endured; so that it may be said of her, as Cardinal Pole says with truth, that in the darkness and obscurity of that kingdom she remained precisely like a feeble light buffetted by raging winds for its utter extinction, but always kept burning and defended by her innocence and lively faith, that it might shine in the world as it now does shine. It is certain that few women in the world (I do not speak of princesses or of queens, but of private women) are known to be more assiduous at their prayers than she is, never choosing to suspend them for any impediment whatever, going at the canonical hours with her chaplains either to church in public or to her private chapel, doing the like with regard to the communions and fast days, and, finally, to all other Christian works, precisely like a nun and a religious.[13]

Katherine would have been aware that the queen expected her attendants to behave virtuously and modestly. In 1537, when Anne Basset secured an appointment to the household of Queen Jane Seymour, her mother's agent in London, John Husee, advised Lady Lisle that Anne should 'be sober, sad, wise and discreet and lowly above all things', 'and to serve God and be virtuous'.[14] Such conduct was necessary, given that 'the Court is full of pride, envy, indignation and mocking, scorning and derision'.[15] Oliver Mallick noted, in relation to the household of Anne of Austria, that a queen's reputation was enhanced by selecting only virtuous persons to serve her,[16] a custom that surely also prevailed at Mary I's court. Indeed, female attendants fulfilled an iconographical function of mirroring their mistress' virtues.[17]

It seems likely that Katherine enjoyed a warm relationship with the new queen.[18] In the spring of 1559, contrasting Mary's attitude towards her with the treatment she was then receiving at Elizabeth I's hands, Katherine informed the imperial ambassador Gómez Suárez de Figueroa y Córdoba, count (later duke) of Feria, that she had served 'in the privy-chamber of the late Queen [Mary], who showed her much favour'.[19] Whether she felt any animosity towards Mary as a result of the executions of her father and sister is unknown, but the queen evidently bore no ill will towards Frances and her daughters. Katherine outwardly conformed to the Marian religious settlement, leading to the suggestion that Mary may have considered nominating her as her successor.[20] However, evidence for this is lacking. The restoration of Catholicism took place in stages but quickly gained momentum. After the coup of 1553, Mary publicised her desire for religious conformity, as recorded by the Tower chronicler who, as a London citizen, would have been aware of proclamations circulating in the city. One such was issued, stating:

> that she willed all men to embrace that religion which all men knew she had of long tyme observed, and ment, God willing, to contynue the same; willing all men to be quiet and not call men the names of heretyk or pa(pi)st, but eche man to live after the religyon he thought best untyll further order wer taken conceryng the same.[21]

In her wish to maintain stability in the realm, Mary ensured that she was represented as desirous of outward conformity in religion as a means of attaining allegiance to her regime, which was understandable in view of the circumstances that had led to her taking the throne amid the threat of civil war. Mary and her councillors may well have believed that the realm at large would welcome the restoration of papal authority. Two initiatives played a crucial part in the Catholic restoration: the queen's marriage and the appointment of Cardinal Reginald Pole as archbishop of Canterbury. The polemicist Nicholas Sander noted that, after her accession, Mary 'rejected the title of the profane ecclesiastical supremacy and resolved to restore the ancient rights and reverence due to the Apostolic See, which she had always honoured even at the risk of her life in the days of her father and brother, and sent for Cardinal Pole', and married Philip of Spain so that he could assist her 'in bringing the kingdom back again to the faith and obedience of the Church'.[22]

It was with this ambition in mind that Mary selected Philip as her spouse, despite it being 'the great wish of the country that she should marry Lord Courtenay whose noble descent entitled him to a prefer-ence over any other native, everybody being above all desirous that she should marry an Englishman, and by no means a foreigner', for 'there were no better means for reforming the religion than through the sup-port of so great a Prince, who, being very Catholic, would and could convert the English from their false doctrines'.[23] In spite of popular hos-tility, the wedding took place at Winchester Cathedral on 25 July 1554. It is entirely possible, even probable, that Katherine was present. Philip's perceptions of England were surely coloured by the dreary weather, for 'it rained, without ceasing so much as an hour' in the days leading up to the nuptials.[24] The day before the wedding, Mary met Philip 'in a great low hall accompanied by her ladies, not beautiful but very numer-ous, all dressed in purple velvet with their sleeves lined with brocade'.[25] Philip and Mary 'kissed and walked through two or three rooms, and then stood talking for a long time', before Philip spoke with Mary's ladies; afterwards, he departed to hear vespers in Winchester Cathedral and the queen made her way to her chapel.[26] It is interesting to speculate whether Katherine may have been one of the ladies who attended Mary that afternoon.

Although the queen may privately have been disinclined to renounce her unmarried state, as conveyed in her alleged promise to 'abstain from marriage while I live' if her spouse proved unpopular with her subjects,[27] it was recognised that she had a duty to marry and produce an heir to secure the succession, especially in view of what had happened during the previous reign. Cardinal Pole, by contrast, had argued that Mary should remain unwed, 'leaving the affairs of the succession of the realm to take their course'.[28] Marriage to Philip raised questions about whether Mary's sovereignty overrode that of her husband, who was not honoured with a coronation and was effectively relegated to the role of king consort during his residency in England.

The ceremonies of the wedding itself conveyed the ambiguity of the couple's respective standing. As Alexander Samson noted, the placing of Philip on the left side and Mary on the right 'underlined Philip's anomalous occupation of the place traditionally reserved for a royal consort in relation to a king'.[29] 'Their respective statuses as encoded in the physical space of the cathedral reversed traditional gender hierarchies.'[30] Shortly after the wedding, the royal couple departed for London and Mary's position on the journey was again represented as hierarchically superior to that of her husband, for as the Tower chronicler reported, 'the quene [was] of the right hande, and the king of the left'.[31] This placing was necessary in order to demonstrate that the royal marriage had not transferred the English crown into foreign hands, a concern that repeatedly arose over the course of the reign and which was perhaps most graphically evidenced in the outbreak of Wyatt's rebellion as a result of the 'tumult over the Spanish marriage'.[32]

By the end of 1554, Cardinal Pole had been appointed to the archbishopric of Canterbury and England had been reconciled with Rome, meaning that the hope that 'heresie' and 'falsehead' would be expelled from the realm to the 'glorie' of God was a seemingly achievable aim. In the spring of 1555, Mary met with her Council and informed them of her wishes concerning her religious settlement:

> You are here of our councell, and we haue willed you to be called to vs, to the intent yee might heare of me my conscience, and the resolution of my mind, concerning the lands and possessions as well of monasteries, as other churches whatsoeuer being now presentlie in my possession. First, I doo consider, that the said lands were taken awaie from the churches aforesaid, in time of schisme, and that by vnlawfull means, such as are contrarie both to the law of God and of the church.[33]

Several months after that meeting a parliament was held at Westminster, where:

> amongst other things the queene being persuaded by the cardinall [Pole] (and other of hir clergy) that she could not prosper, so long as she kept in hir hands any possessions of the church, did franklie and freelie resigne and render vnto them all of those reuenues ecclesiasticall, which by the authoritie of parlement, in the time of king Henrie, had beene annexed to the crowne, called the first fruits and tenths of all bishoprickes, benefices and ecclesiasticall promotions. The resignation whereof was a great diminution of the reuenues of the crowne.[34]

In her role as benefactress, Mary restored lands to the Church that remained in crown hands and forfeited the right of the Crown to most fees from the Church.[35] As the chronicler Wriothesley recorded, in 1556 Mary restored to the abbot of Westminster 'all suche landes as remayned that day in her handes suppressed and taken by King Henry the 8 for euer'.[36] In the spring of 1555, the king and queen rebuked Edmund Bonner, bishop of London, and his colleagues, demanding that heresy should be punished more harshly. They had discovered 'to our no lytle maruayle' that many heretics:

> being by the Iustices of the peace for their contempt & obstinacye, brought to the Ordinaries ... are eyther refused to be receiued at their hands, or if they be receiued, are neyther so trauayled wyth, as Christian charity requireth, nor yet proceeded wyth all according to the order of Iustice, but are suffred to continue in their errours, to the dishonor of almighty God, and daungerous example of others.

Bonner and the bishops were commanded:

> to haue in thys behalfe suche regarde henceforth to the office of a good Pastor and byshop, as when any such offenders shalbe by the

sayde officers or Iustices of peace broughte vnto you, you do vse your good wisdome and discretion in procuring to remoue them from their errours if it it may be, or els in proceding against them (if they shal continue obstinate) according to the order of the lawes.[37]

In calling for the harsher punishment of heretics, Philip and Mary portrayed themselves as united co-partners in a shared Catholic monarchy, showing that their shared religious aims were concerned with the safeguarding of Catholicism from the dangers of heresy, and that they were determined to maintain godliness and adherence to 'the lawes'.

Katherine's attitude to these religious developments was unrecorded but, given the godly household in which she and her sisters had grown up, she surely cannot have approved of the government's increasingly aggressive rejection of the Protestant faith. That rejection went hand in hand with the restoration of the medieval heresy laws and the imposition of death by burning for those found guilty of heretical practices. The first burnings took place in February 1555 and ended only with the queen's death in 1558. It would be interesting to know if, in private, Katherine pondered her sister Jane's instruction to 'live still to die, that you by death may purchase eternal life', and her warning that 'if you will deny his truth for to lengthen your life, God will deny you, and yet shorten your days'.[38] Obeying that instruction by practising a faith deemed to be heretical by the queen's government, however, brought with it very real, and potentially fatal, risks. Katherine's outward conformity would thus appear to have been entirely understandable, especially given that members of her family had so recently been condemned and executed for treason. Indeed, the queen's half-sister Elizabeth had chosen conformity as the safest course of action and 'has adapted herself to the will of her Majesty' in matters of religion.[39]

Other events at court surely would have been of greater interest to Katherine. In February 1555, jousts were held to celebrate the wedding of Katherine's cousin Margaret Clifford to Lord Strange, son of the earl of Derby, which took place in the Chapel Royal of Whitehall

Palace.[40] It is possible that Katherine attended her cousin's wedding and the accompanying entertainments. On 31 March, Katherine acted as godmother to Elizabeth, daughter of Sir William Cavendish.[41] Her friendship with Lady Jane Seymour, daughter of the executed duke of Somerset, was undoubtedly also a source of joy at this time.[42] In addition to these activities, she was almost certainly a close witness to the development of the queen's pregnancy that spring.

After her marriage to Philip, Mary was expected to produce an heir to ensure a Catholic succession. She would have been aware that a successful childbirth would seem to provide evidence of divine favour, thus vindicating her decision to proceed with an unpopular marriage that, as Wingfield reported, caused 'tumult'. At the end of 1554, the queen's pregnancy was made public. As early as 18 September, Renard had reported that:

> one of the Queen's physicians has told me that she is very probably with child; and if it is true everything will calm down and go smoothly here. As soon as I know for certain I will inform your Majesty, and I have already caused a rumour to be started for the purpose of keeping the malcontents within bounds.[43]

The following day, the duke of Savoy's ambassador, Count Giovan Tommaso Langosco di Stroppiana, wrote to the bishop of Arras that:

> the Queen is with child. I have personal reason to believe it, as I have noticed her feeling sick (or seen her being sick), besides which her doctor has given me positive assurance, saying that if it were not true all the signs described by physicians would prove to be fallacious. I can therefore give the news as certain. The Queen was saved and preserved through many great dangers and raised to the throne almost by a miracle, and for the peace and good of the kingdom it was ardently to be hoped that she might bear children to establish and make safe the success of the undertaking to which she has set her hand, namely, the restoration of the catholic religion and faith.[44]

A number of ballads were published celebrating the pregnancy, including the anonymously penned 'Nowe singe, nowe springe, our care is exil'd, Oure vertuous Quene is quickned with child'. The providential emphasis on Mary's pregnancy formed a central theme in the ballad: 'Nowe englande is happie, and happie in dede, / That god of his goodnes doth prospir here sede.'[45] It is noteworthy that the ballad reiterated popular motifs found in other Marian ballads, including likening the queen to a 'swet marigold', a theme utilised by the priest and poet William Forrest in his 'A newe ballade of the Marigolde', while describing the queen's accession and pregnancy as deliverances from 'greate thraldomes', 'wrongynge' and 'sorowes' expressed sentiments similar to those put forward in other contemporary ballads.[46] While acknowledging that Mary's marriage to Philip had been 'lamented' by many of her subjects, a sentiment that echoes the 'tumult' recorded by chroniclers, the ballad expressed hope that the queen would be divinely favoured 'with joye to deliuer, that when she is lighte / Both she & her people maie Ioye without flight'.[47]

Thus the outcome of the queen's pregnancy was closely associated with the 'joye' and welfare of her subjects, reiterating the suggestion that it provided further evidence of the divine favour that was manifested in her providentially sanctioned accession. As has been noted, Mary's accession was widely perceived as a restoration of the natural order.[48] The providential emphasis underpinning William Forrest's ballad, and others, as a literary technique and as a motif can be understood in the light of Alexandra Walsham's contention that 'providentialism was not a marginal feature of the religious culture of early modern England, but part of the mainstream, a cluster of presuppositions which enjoyed near universal acceptance'.[49] Indeed, it may plausibly be suggested that the providentialism that underlay literary representations of Mary's royal authority was intended to enhance her status as queen by presenting her in the guise of God's anointed on earth, while seeking to invite 'near universal acceptance' of her rule in an often uneasy atmosphere of disorder and rebellion.

Whether Katherine attended Mary for the duration of her apparent pregnancy is uncertain, given that information about her appointment at court is sketchy. A report from the Venetian ambassador in 1557 (referred to later in this chapter) may indicate that Katherine did not permanently reside at court. She may have lived with her mother intermittently during Mary's queenship at intervals when the duchess of Suffolk was not suffering from bouts of ill health.[50] Evidence pertaining to Katherine's relationship with Edward Seymour, earl of Hertford, demonstrates Katherine's closeness to both her mother and her stepfather. The Venetian ambassador reported in August 1554 that Katherine's cousin Margaret Clifford 'holds place in the Queen's privy chamber'.[51] As Katherine would later inform the imperial ambassador, she too held office there. Assuming that she attended the queen in that capacity in late 1554 and in the spring of 1555, she would have observed at close hand the progression of Mary's reputed pregnancy, an issue that would have been of interest to both Katherine and her family as its outcome had significant dynastic implications, especially given the queen's reluctance to name her half-sister Elizabeth as her successor should Mary die childless. Indeed, Mary's pregnancy attracted international attention in view of the hope of Catholic Europe that her providentially sanctioned queenship – in which she had delivered England from the evils of heresy through the restoration of the true faith – would be further blessed by the delivery of a healthy male heir.

It was this hope that accounts for the intense interest in the subject in the correspondence of foreign diplomats, both at Mary's court and abroad. Initially, the pregnancy appeared to be progressing positively. On 6 November, Renard informed the emperor that 'there is no doubt that the Queen is with child, for her stomach clearly shows it and her dresses no longer fit her'.[52] Luis Vanegas reported on 14 November that 'the Queen is in excellent health and three months with child. She is fatter and has a better colour than when she was married, a sign that she is happier, and indeed she is said to be very happy.'[53] On 23 November, Renard claimed that Mary 'is veritably with child, for she has felt the babe, and there are other likely and customary symptoms, such as the state of the breasts',[54] and the following day, the queen felt the baby move again when she and her husband met Cardinal Pole 'in the gallery looking over the river' upon his arrival at court.[55]

Shortly afterwards, practical steps were taken as a result of the queen's pregnancy. In December, it was proposed in Parliament that Philip act as guardian for his child, as:

> no more faithful or affectionate guardian than your Majesty could be appointed, for you would be the heirs' father and had shown such great love and regard for the realm, and would be certain to ward off all the misfortunes associated with the names of other protectors of recent memory.[56]

Renard reported in April 1555 that:

> The Queen has withdrawn, and no one enters her apartments except the women who serve her and who have the same duties as the court officials. This is an ancient custom in England whenever a princess is about to be confined: to remain in retirement forty days before and forty days after. However, it is believed that she will be delivered before the ninth day of next month. She would have liked to go to Windsor, but as that place is far from London, it was thought preferable that she should stay at Hampton Court.[57]

Once the queen had selected Hampton Court as the residence in which she would give birth to England's heir, she summoned her half-sister Elizabeth to the palace, 'where the Queen had taken her chamber to be delyvered of childe'.[58] Early modern pregnancy was a process that was 'fraught with obstacles and dangers from beginning to end'.[59] In view of this, expectant mothers responded by preparing for death: they wrote their wills, divided their property and acknowledged that they might not survive the ordeal. While they were admittedly unclear, the signs of pregnancy were of the utmost importance in allowing a woman to prepare for what could be a perilous enterprise. *Aristotle's Master-Piece* explained that 'There is a Necessity that Women should be instructed in the Knowledge of Conception, that the Parent, as well as the Child, might be saved from Danger.'[60] This advice is explicable in the context of the ambiguity of pregnancy, in which the signs of pregnancy were both ambivalent and open to interpretation.[61] Mary's age and constitution may have fuelled concerns about the pregnancy and its outcome, for it had been reported only the year before that 'her age [was] on the decline' and 'she is not of a strong constitution'.[62]

Not all of Mary's subjects rejoiced at the news of her pregnancy. Gossip and speculation about the queen's pregnancy involved numerous wild stories, some of which were hostile. In London, it was rumoured in March that 'The Quenes grace is not with childe and that another lady shuld be with childe and that ladies childe when she is brought in bedde shold be named the Quenes childe', while one individual in Hereford declared two months later that 'Now that there is a prince borne his father will bringe into this realme his owne nation, and putt out the Englishe nation'.[63] Similarly, in late March, Renard reported discontent in England and noted that an aim of the rumoured conspirators was:

> to publish that the Queen is not with child, but that there was a plan to pass off another child as her own. The purpose was to stir up a revolt among the people, arms in hand, it being supposed that all these points are very telling, as indeed they are, the whole plan proceeding from much invention and malice aforethought.[64]

Such contradictory statements and indications of political unrest arose, in part, from increasing uncertainty about Mary's pregnancy as the months passed. These reports also provide insights into the sense of unease felt by contemporaries towards the issue of the succession when it appeared to be unsettled; this restlessness would, of course, reverberate throughout the long reign of Elizabeth I.

The contradictory reports of the queen's pregnancy during the spring of 1555 point to a heightened sense of anxiety about its outcome. In April, the diarist Henry Machyn reported that:

The xxx day of Aprell and the last day of Aprell thydynges cam to London that the Quen('s) grace was delevered of a prynce, and so ther was grett ryngyng thrugh London, and dyvers plases *Te Deum laudamus* songe; and the morow after yt was tornyd odurways to the plesur of God! But yt shall be when yt plesse God, for I trust God that he wyll remembur ys tru servands that putt ther trust in hym, when that they calle on hym.[65]

The news that Mary had given birth to a son reached the Continent weeks later. By 17 May, Joanna of Austria, princess dowager of Portugal, was writing to Philip II congratulating him on the birth:

A servant of the Infanta Doña Maria who is on his way to Portugal and who left Flanders on the 3rd inst., brought a letter from Secretary Eraso saying that God had been pleased to deliver my sister, the Queen of England, of a boy, and that both her Highness and the child were well. I am very happy about this for the sakes of the Emperor and your Highness. May God give you long lives so that you may rejoice over this child and others who may be granted to you.[66]

However, the report was false and, shortly afterwards, doubt and uncertainty crept into the diplomatic correspondence concerning Mary's condition. On 23 May, Giacomo Soranzo, Venetian ambassador at the French court, wrote to the Doge and Senate with the news that:

the Queen of England had not yet brought forth, which began to surprise everybody, but that the ambassador resident here had told him lately that she could not go beyond the 20th of this month; and although some persons chose to disbelieve her pregnancy, and an individual who had seen her Majesty asserted that her body bore no signs whereby any one could vouch for it, yet nevertheless, knowing women's ways, his most Christian Majesty was of opinion that she was pregnant, but exceeded her time, as they often do, but that at any rate the matter will soon be very manifest to everybody.[67]

By June, it was being reported that 'the Queen was very heavy with child, and all the physicians agreed that her deliverance should take place by 6 June'.[68] However, on the 8th, Ruy Gómez de Silva wrote to Francisco de Eraso with the news that:

> the deliverance of the Queen is not expected until St. John's day [24 June], at the soonest. They say that the calculations got mixed up when they saw her with a girth greater than that of Gutierre López. All this makes me doubt whether she is with child at all, greatly as I desire to see the thing happily over.[69]

The atmosphere at court surely became increasingly tense and uncertain as the weeks passed with no sign of a child. Contrary to Gómez de Silva's belief, 24 June came and went with no delivery of an heir, and that day Renard wrote to the emperor:

> Everything in this kingdom depends on the Queen's safe deliverance. Her doctors and ladies have proved to be out in their calculations by about two months, and it now appears that she will not be delivered before eight or ten days from now. This is the reason why I have not written oftener to your Majesty. If God is pleased to grant her a child, things will take a turn for the better. If not, I foresee trouble on so great a scale that the pen can hardly set it down. Certain it is that the order of succession has been so badly decided that the Lady Elizabeth comes next, and that means heresy again, and the true religion overthrown. The English are inclined to favour the French, and will forget the friendly feelings for our side which they have latterly been pretending to harbour. Churchmen will be wronged, catholics persecuted; there will be more acts of vengeance than heretofore, and I do not know whether the King and his Court will be in safety among these people. A calamitous tragedy will lie ahead. It is almost incredible how the delay in the Queen's deliverance encourages the heretics to slander and put about false rumours; some say that she is not with child at all, but that a suppositious child is going to be

presented as hers, and that if a suitable one had been found this would already have been done. The expressions worn on people's faces are strange; folk have a more masked appearance than I have ever seen in the past. Those whom we have trusted inspire me with the most misgivings as to their loyalty. Nothing appears to be certain, and I am more disturbed by what I see going on than ever before. The nations do not get on well together. There is no justice and order, but an increasing amount of boldness and evil intentions. There is a widening split in the Council, as the French found out at the last session. The longer things go on as they do at present, the more urgent it appears to devise some remedy and carefully to consider the moment when the King had better cross over to your Majesty. Although I am sure your Majesty will have been informed of all this, I hope I may be forgiven for repeating it.[70]

Renard's report makes clear that, from the perspective of Mary's supporters, a successful outcome to the queen's pregnancy was crucial to prevent a Protestant succession.

While the queen's attention was focused on the deliverance of an heir to ensure a Catholic succession, another pregnancy surely occupied Katherine's mind: her mother's. The duchess conceived in October 1554 and gave birth to a daughter, Elizabeth, by her second husband on 16 July 1555 in Knebworth, Hertfordshire.[71] Tragically, Elizabeth died only months later, on 7 February 1556.[72] The birth of a daughter to Frances stood in stark contrast with the queen's failed pregnancy, which had not resulted in the much-longed for male heir and meant that the advantages of the Spanish union remained questionable to some, at least, of her subjects. By 14 August, it was reported 'that the Queen had dismissed the greater part of the Court and withdrawn to Oatlands, and that she herself admitted she was not pregnant, and that of this his Majesty had been assured by a person to whom she had confessed the fact with her own lips'.[73] The following month, the emperor informed Don Luis Sarmiento de Mendoza that 'the Queen was well also, although there is no longer any hope of her being with child'.[74]

Two circumstances – the queen's childlessness and her known antipa-thy to her half-sister Elizabeth – meant that the question of Katherine's place in the succession remained relevant, if ambiguous. In May 1557, the Venetian ambassador Giovanni Michiel reported that Katherine and Mary Grey 'are living with their mother the Duchess of Suffolk, and on the death of Queen Mary they, like their eldest sister, who was assisted by her husband or by others who had followers, would lay claim to the succession, in preference even to my Lady Elizabeth'.[75] The ambassa-dor also alluded to the claim of Katherine's cousin Margaret Clifford (daughter of Eleanor Brandon):

first cousin to the daughters of Frances, whose house being convicted of treason on account of Jane who was beheaded, her sisters likewise, being themselves reproached with the same crime, are consequently excluded from the succession; so that Margaret Lady Strange is the nearest of all to the blood royal, and to her the succession belongs.[76]

Foreshadowing the issues that would occupy centre stage during Elizabeth I's reign, Michiel emphasised the importance of settling the succession:

On this topic it merely remains for me to add that in like manner as the danger about the succession would be very great by reason of the disturbances and riots which might take place both at home and abroad were it delayed until the Queen's death, or if the decision were protracted; so on the contrary, by announcing it speedily, with the consent of the people, that is to say by an Act of Parliament, the country would be safe from any sedition, because, with the authority of the Queen in person, the successor might make himself known, and by many ways obtain the love and respect of the king-dom, so that on the Queen's death neither the English themselves would dare to stir, nor would foreigners think of doing so on seeing the country so united.[77]

The reign of the first English queen regnant was, in many respects, a troubled one. In 1556, a plot against Mary organised by Sir Henry Dudley – a first cousin of Katherine's father – aimed to 'deprive Mary of her state' and use her 'as she used Queen Jane', namely by deposing her and replacing her with Elizabeth.[78] The following spring, a conspiracy masterminded by Sir Thomas Stafford threatened the queen's security. Stafford was the son of Henry Stafford, 1st Baron Stafford and Ursula Pole, and was thus a descendant of George Plantagenet, duke of Clarence via his mother. He had been implicated in Wyatt's rebellion of 1554 and, three years later, his discontent showed no signs of abating. Hostility to the Spanish marriage led Stafford to rebel, for he believed that Mary had forfeited her right to rule as a result of 'marriage with a stranger, and for favouring and maintaining Spaniards, and putting castles into their hands, to the destruction of the English nation'.[79] The queen's lady-in-waiting Jane Dormer believed that Elizabeth 'had intelligence with Mr. Thomas Stafford', who planned to usurp the throne from Mary, reign as king and marry Elizabeth.[80] In April, Stafford 'tooke Scarboroughe Castle in the countie of Yorke; which came out of France and made proclamation there, naminge himselfe to be Protector of this realme, and the Queen to be unrightfull Queene'.[81] Fortunately, he 'was apprehended with the other his complices without effusion of bloude' and was imprisoned in the Tower.[82] On 28 May, Stafford was executed at Tower Hill 'by nine of the clock'.[83]

In addition to treasonable conspiracies, Mary was also faced with hostile foreign nations. That spring, 'continual disturbances' were reported 'between Scots and English'[84] and, by July, 'things in Scotland looked all towards war with England'[85] – but, by then, England was at war with another realm. On 7 June, a proclamation was issued declaring war on France. While Mary's decision to involve England in the Habsburg war against France has been attributed to marital solidarity, the proclamation noted that the French had aided the 'abominable treason' of Northumberland in 1553 and 'had secretly favoured' Wyatt's uprising the following year, while the French king had also supported more recent conspiracies against the queen, including that of Stafford by providing him with 'ships and supplies to seize our castle of Scarborough'.[86] Anglo-French relations from the spring of 1554 to the summer of 1557 had been complicated by the presence of English exiles in France hostile to Mary's regime.[87] That April, the queen had summoned her councillors and threatened them, 'some with death, others with the loss of their goods and estates, if they did not consent to the will of her husband' in regard to war.[88] After the proclamation of war was issued, 'the queene sent ouer an armie of men, ordeynynge the earle of Pembroke lorde general, which mette the king with his armie at a towne in France, called S. Quintins'.[89] Katherine's former husband Henry Herbert was among those who fought in Europe in the summer of 1557.[90] The war, however, did not end with an English victory, culminating infamously in the loss of Calais in January 1558. By the 10th of the month, 'heavy tidings' reached England of the loss of Calais, which had been the sole remaining English possession on the Continent – it was 'the dolefullest news, and the heaviest taken'.[91] Machyn explained that the loss was 'the hevest tydy[ngs to London] and to England that ever was hard of'.[92]

Privately, the queen might have comforted herself with her belief that she was with child. Having departed for Flanders in September 1555, Philip briefly returned to England in the spring of 1557 to obtain financial and military assistance for his foreign wars, and it was during this visit that Mary believed she had conceived a child. By the end of February, it was reported that 'it is quite certain that she is pregnant, although she tries to keep it a secret, and that she will be delivered some time this month or early in March'.[93] The rumour that Mary was pregnant raised questions about the succession. In March, the month in which Mary believed her child to be due, Renard addressed the subject in a letter to Philip:

The succession to the throne of England is a matter of such importance that your Majesty will certainly wish to examine the question in all its bearings, especially in view of the uncertainty and danger attending all developments in that country, on the assumption (which God forbid!) that the Queen will die without issue, in which case Elizabeth will be called to the throne in virtue of the will of Henry VIII, confirmed by Parliament in spite of the taint of illegitimacy. Now, Elizabeth was brought up in the doctrines of the new religion, she was formerly of the French faction, she hates the Queen and has many supporters who are suspect from the point-of-view of religion.[94]

Renard also noted that:

what ought to be done in the circumstances it is not so easy to say, nor is it easy to debar her from the succession. If it were attempted to induce Parliament to repeal the act by which Henry's will was confirmed, those who have espoused her cause would not consent. The religious factions would fight, Catholics against Protestants, with all the virulence customary among people of the same blood, to the prejudice of your Majesty's authority. If Parliament were to repeal the act, it could as easily vote it over again, once the Queen had died, as happened when she mounted the throne, displaying the inconstancy natural in these islanders, among whom nothing is ever securely established. Besides, repeal would altogether estrange Elizabeth's supporters from your Majesty and prove a fresh source of conspiracy, and of alliance among your adversaries. The Queen is hardly safe as it is; and unless my information and judgment are at fault, the leading men of the realm are leagued together to prevent repeal. They know that some months ago the Queen thought of having Elizabeth declared a bastard by Parliament and debarred from the succession. If that had been done the next of kin would have been the Queen of Scotland, and if she were ruled out as a foreigner, the wife of the Earl of Lennox or her children would come next, and then the daughters of the Duke of Suffolk. In none of these cases do I see the succession being firmly established. The realm would fall a prey to civil strife. And it is doubtful whether any of these persons would be more deserving of confidence than Elizabeth herself.[95]

If Renard is to be believed, then Mary's preferred successor was her cousin Lady Margaret Douglas, countess of Lennox, rather than Katherine or her sister Mary. Perhaps the queen considered that the treason of the Grey family disqualified them from the succession, but it is more likely that Mary was moved by considerations of primogeniture alongside Margaret's indisputable Catholicism. As early as November 1553, it was claimed that Mary:

> thought that if God were to call her without giving her heirs of her body, the Lady Margaret Douglas, wife of the Earl of Lennox, a Scotsman, and a daughter of Margaret, Queen Dowager of Scotland, by her marriage with the Earl of Angus, which took place after the death of King James (IV) of Scotland, would be the person best suited to succeed.[96]

In the same report, Renard reiterated his belief that neither Katherine nor her sister could inherit the throne, since 'the marriage of the said Frances with the Duke of Suffolk had been rather a concubinage than a marriage, because the Duke had formerly been affianced *per verba de præsenti* to the Earl of Arundel's sister'.[97] As has been noted, Henry Grey had been betrothed to Katherine Fitzalan, daughter of the 11th earl of Arundel, but he refused to honour the betrothal following his fourteenth birthday.[98] Irrespective of the ambassador's belief, there is no indication that the Grey sisters were illegitimate, although those who opposed Katherine's succession in the next decade argued that she was, in addition to putting forward other grounds for her exclusion. By contrast, evidence was marshalled by Katherine's supporters during Elizabeth I's reign to affirm her legitimacy. Given that Renard's report was written only two weeks after Jane Grey had been convicted of treason, it was in his interests for her sisters to be disqualified from the succession, irrespective of whether the grounds for doing so were compelling or not.

While she may not have selected Katherine as her heir, the suggestion that Mary favoured the middle Grey sister during her brief reign is interesting given that perhaps the best-known portrait of Katherine, the miniature attributed to Levina Teerlinc and held at the Victoria and Albert Museum in London, has been dated to *c*. 1555–60. Katherine would have been aged between 15 and 18 years old if she sat for this portrait during Mary's queenship, and the likeness undoubtedly supports the historical tradition of Katherine's beauty and physical charms. The paucity of extant documentation pertaining to Katherine's appearance means that it is helpful to have access to a portrait that sheds light on how she must have looked during a period in which she enjoyed royal favour and had no foresight of the turbulent years ahead.

A portrait said to date to 1562 has also been identified as a likeness of Katherine. In the portrait, painted by the Flemish artist Marcus Gheeraerts, the sitter, then in her twenty-second year, wears the fashionable costume of the day. Katherine's twentieth-century biographer Hester Chapman accepted the sitter as Katherine.[99] However, given that the artist only arrived in England six years later, in 1568, after fleeing persecution on account of his reformist beliefs, the image surely cannot be a portrait of Katherine. Dr J. Stephan Edwards has recently explored the possibility that the Berry-Hill portrait, identified as Elizabeth I, may actually represent Katherine.[100] The 'Berry-Hill Type' includes the Berry-Hill portrait itself, the Soule portrait, the Chawton portrait and the Syon portrait.[101] In his study of Jane Grey's portraiture, Edwards noted that Katherine's supporters produced portraits of her to advocate her claim to the throne. This 'groundswell of support' for Katherine during the early years of Elizabeth's reign may suggest that the Berry-Hill portrait (which was probably painted between 1558 and 1565) depicts Katherine.[102] Edwards' subsequent analysis, however, led him to conclude that the portrait is probably a likeness of Elizabeth and dates to 1555–63.[103]

The miniature held at the Victoria and Albert Museum serves as visual evidence that, in spite of the personal and political tragedies that had befallen Katherine and her family, she had developed into a striking and vivacious teenager who may have nurtured ambitions with regard to the succession but, equally, may have held hopes for a marriage that would offer her both political security and personal happiness. If the portrait was painted in the final year of Mary's reign, then it may have coincided with a romance that blossomed between Katherine and Edward Seymour, earl of Hertford. Prior to that, there are some indications that Katherine continued to feel affection for Henry Herbert and mourned the annulment of their marriage. In March 1559, de Feria informed Philip II that Katherine 'has been hitherto very willing to marry the earl of Pembroke's son'.[104] In the seventeenth century, Heylyn recorded a tradition that Katherine languished 'long under the disgrace of this rejection, none daring to make any particular addresses to her, for fear of being involved in the like calamities as had befallen her father and the rest of that family'.[105]

Tragically for the queen, it became apparent that, as in 1555, she was mistaken: she was not with child. During the summer of 1558, Katherine was not present at court because she had accompanied her friend, Lady Jane Seymour, to Jane's mother's house at Hanworth, Jane having fallen ill. Her illness occurred at a time when 'sicknesse was common that yere through all the realme and consumed a maruailous number', including members of the nobility and clergy.[106] Having departed from court, Katherine and her friend travelled to Hanworth in a litter alongside the mother of the queen's maids. Katherine would later admit that 'some good will' developed between Hertford and herself when she was residing at Hanworth with the earl's mother, the duchess of Somerset.[107] Likewise, Hertford explained that 'he first determined to be a Suter to the Lady Katherine in the tyme of Queene Mary'.[108] In this, the earl 'procured his saied sister' to speak to Katherine on his behalf on the subject of their marriage.[109] Irrespective of her reported affection for Herbert, it seems that Katherine fell in love with the 19-year-old earl that summer – somewhat ironically, given that he had been proposed some years before as a husband for her elder sister Jane. The duchess, observing the affection between her son and Katherine, advised him to abstain from Katherine's company, to which he responded, 'Young Folks meaninge well might well accompanie together and that both in that howse and alsoe in the Court he trusted he might use her

[Katherine's] company being not forbidden by the Quene's Highness expresse commandment.'[110] Hertford asked his sister Jane 'to break with the Lady Katherine touching marriage'.[111] For the moment, however, the relationship between the earl and Katherine progressed no further and, Jane having recovered, both women returned to court.

By October, it was evident that the queen was dying during an influenza epidemic that had claimed the lives of thousands. Indeed, it was reported that month that Mary 'was so dangerously ill that they feared for her life'.[112] As her health continued to worsen, in November Mary agreed that her half-sister would succeed her, irrespective of her private feelings on the subject, her councillors 'persuading her to make certain declarations in favour of the Lady Elizabeth concerning the succession'.[113]

The Venetian ambassador Michiel Surian claimed that, in the last days of the queen's life, 'many personages of the kingdom flocked to the house of "Miladi" Elizabeth, the crowd constantly increasing with great frequency'.[114] In view of her presence in the queen's Privy Chamber, it is unlikely that Katherine was one of them. Mary 'was moved to send two gentlemen' to her half-sister:

> to let her know that, as it had pleased the Lord God to end her days, she was content that she (Elizabeth) as her sister should become Queen, and prayed her to maintain the kingdom and the Catholic religion, in words replete with much affection; to which she sent a most gracious reply by two of her attendants, who visited the Queen in her name, condoling with her on her malady.[115]

Machyn recorded that, 'be-twyn v and vj in the mornyng' on 17 November at St James's Palace, 'ded quen Mare, the vj yere of here grace('s) rayne, the wyche Jhesu have mercy on her solle! Amen.'[116] Her cause of death is unknown, but V.C. Medvei has suggested that the queen may have died of a prolactinoma.[117] Other possibilities include influenza and uterine cancer. Alvise Priuli stated that Mary 'made her passage so tranquilly that had not a physician remarked it on its commencement, all the other persons present would have thought her better, and that she would fain sleep'.[118] The same day, 'the customary proclamation was made at Westminster and London'.[119]

Mary 'left orders that she was to be buried either at Windsor or Westminster, and that the body of Queen Katharine, her mother, should also be brought thither'.[120] Her remains were interred at Westminster Abbey on 14 December, but Elizabeth did not have those of Katherine of Aragon moved there from Peterborough. A contemporary account provides details of the late queen's burial:

> Tewsdaye, the xiiith of December, the corps of Queen Marie was honorablie caried from the mannor of St. James in the after-noone to the Abbaye in Westminster. Her picture lyeing on the coffin apparelled in her royall roabes, and a crowne of gould on the heade. And in the Abbay was a sumptuous and riche hearse made, under which the corps stood all night. And the morrowe beinge Weddensdaye, after the masse of Requiem, the corps were caried from thence to the new chappell, where King Henry VII. lieth, and there in the side chappell, on the left hand, her corps were buried for a tyme.[121]

The procession from St James's Palace to Westminster Abbey featured 'a grett compene of morners', alongside Mary's 'houshold servandes' and a host of gentlemen, squires, heralds, knights, 'pages of honor', monks and bishops.[122] Also present were 'lades rydyn, alle in blake, trapyd to the grond'.[123] On the following day, a mass for the deceased queen took place at the abbey, attended by lords, 'lades, knyghtes and gentyll women', all of whom made offerings.[124] After the mass, the bishop of Winchester delivered a sermon and Mary's remains were interred after her officers had broken their staffs of office and cast them into her grave to convey the end of their service.[125] Those present then attended a 'dener', or banquet, in the abbey.[126] In view of her appointment to Mary's Privy Chamber, Katherine would have been one of the 'lades' present at the funeral of England's first queen regnant. As a result of her royal blood and shared faith with Elizabeth, Katherine could reasonably have anticipated retaining her place in the new queen's Privy Chamber, but if she did, that hope was misguided.

Writing to Philip II, de Feria reported his belief that 'the more I think over this business, the more certain I am that everything depends upon the husband this woman [Elizabeth] may take',[127] thus foreshadowing an issue that was to occupy the minds of Elizabeth's statesmen for three decades. The question of the new queen's marriage was undoubtedly of interest to Katherine, since she was now heir presumptive to the throne according to Henry VIII's last will and testament. Like her contemporaries, Katherine had every reason to believe that Elizabeth would marry and produce an heir, but until such time as she did, Katherine could at least consider the possibility that she might one day be queen of England.

6

'The Next Heir to the Throne'

On 15 January 1559, Elizabeth I was crowned queen of England at Westminster Abbey. The coronation was the pinnacle of several days of glittering ceremonial in which Elizabeth's queenship was inaugurated. On 12 January, Elizabeth and her court left Whitehall Palace and travelled to the Tower by water. Customarily, monarchs stayed at the Tower before their coronations at Westminster Abbey. The queen was 'accompanied by many knights, barons, ladies, and by the whole Court'.[1] The procession passed under London Bridge, following which artillery was fired. On the morning of the 14th, Elizabeth made her state entry into London amid great public rejoicing. It was a freezing cold day and snow fell.[2] According to Il Schifanoya, a native of Mantua living in London, the queen travelled through the streets:

> in an open litter, trimmed down to the ground with gold brocade, with a raised pile, and carried by two very handsome mules covered with the same material, and surrounded by a multitude of footmen in crimson velvet jerkins, all studded with massive gilt silver, with the arms of a white and red rose on their breasts and backs, and laterally the letters E. R for *Elizabetta Regina* wrought in relief, the usual livery of this Crown, which makes a superb show.[3]

Elizabeth wore:

> a royal robe of very rich cloth of gold, with a double-raised stiff pile, and on her head over a coif of cloth of gold, beneath which was her hair, a plain gold crown without lace, as a princess, but covered with jewels, and nothing in her hands but gloves.[4]

The pageants that greeted the queen included a triumphal arch divided into three floors, on the first of which were depicted Henry VII and Elizabeth of York with white and red roses positioned in front of them. On the second floor, Elizabeth's parents were depicted seated with a white and red rose in front of Henry VIII and a pomegranate between them, while a white eagle with a gold crown on its head and a gilt sceptre in its right talon and the other resting on a hillock appeared before Anne Boleyn, with small branches of little roses and her coat of arms and device placed in front of her.[5] This represented something of a public – and symbolic – rehabilitation of Elizabeth's disgraced mother, affirming the lawfulness of Henry's marriage to Anne and the legitimacy of their only surviving child. It was also a strident rejection of the official acceptance of Anne's guilt during the previous three reigns. 'On the third floor above a Queen was seen in majesty, to represent the present one, who is descended from the aforesaid.'[6]

The Protestant schoolmaster Richard Mulcaster was commissioned to produce a pamphlet detailing the queen's coronation festivities, entitled *THE PASSAGE of our most drad Soueraigne Lady Quene Elyzabeth through the citie of London to Westminster the daye before her coronacion*. This commission was made by the London merchants who had paid for the coronation tableau, and the pamphlet appeared within a fortnight of the coronation.[7] The pamphlet proved to be popular and 'provided a prototype for Elizabethan public relations', for the medium of print acted as 'a powerful means of publicity'.[8] Mulcaster reported that, in response to the effusive welcome accorded her by the London citizens:

her grace by holding up her handes, and merie countenaunce to such as stode farre of, and most tender & gentle lāguage to those that stode nigh to her grace, did declare her selfe no lesse thankefullye to receiue her peoples good wyll, than they louingly offred it unto her. To all that wyshed her grace wel, she gaue heartie thankes, and to such as bade God save her grace, she sayde agayne god saue them all, and thanked them with all her heart. So that on eyther syde ther was nothing but gladnes, nothing but prayer: nothing but comfort. The Quenes maiestie reioysed marueilously to see, ye, so ecceadingly shewed towarde her grace, which all good princes haue euer desyred, I meane so earnest loue of subiectes, so euidently declared euen to her graces owne person being caried in the middest of them.[9]

Mulcaster described the queen's active engagement with the various pageants on her route to Westminster, in which she already demonstrated the common touch that would characterise her relations with her subjects throughout her reign. She displayed 'a perpetuall attentiuenes in her face' and 'reioysyng visage' that further endeared her to onlookers.[10]

On the day of the coronation itself, the queen arrived at Westminster Abbey, where mass was celebrated. She was:

received under the canopy by the Archbishop and another Bishop, they having previously perfumed her with incense, giving her the holy water and the pax, the choristers singing; then the Earl of Rutland followed her Majesty with a plain naked sword without any point, signifying Ireland, which has never been conquered; then came the Earl of Exeter with the second sword; the third was borne by Viscount Montagu; the Earl of Arundel, having been made Lord Steward and High Constable for that day, carried the sword of royal justice, with its gilt scabbard loaded with pearls. The orb was carried by the Duke of Norfolk, Lord Marshal, and in advance were knights clad in the ducal fashion, carrying the three crowns, they being the three Kings-at-arms; they bore the three sceptres, with their three crowns of iron, of silver, and of gold on their heads, and in their hands three naked iron swords, signifying the three titles of England, France, and Ireland.

In this way they proceeded to the church, the Queen's long train being carried by the Duchess of Norfolk, after whom followed the Lord Chamberlain, upon purple cloth spread on the ground; and as her Majesty passed, the cloth was cut away by those who could get it. Then followed the duchesses, marchionesses, countesses, etc., dragging their trains after them, going two by two, and being exquisitely dressed, with their coronets on their heads, and so handsome and beautiful that it was a marvellous sight.[11]

The people were asked whether they desired Elizabeth to be their crowned queen; they loudly responded 'Yes'.[12] Descending from the tribune between the high altar and the choir, Elizabeth seated herself under her canopy of estate and mass commenced again.[13] The coronation was undoubtedly an unforgettable day for the new queen, but once the festivities celebrating her coronation had come to an end, a number of important dynastic and political issues required Elizabeth's attention: chiefly, marriage and the succession.

Katherine's presence at the coronation and in the festivities leading up to that glittering occasion may have gone unrecorded,[14] but the foreign dignitaries, city officials and courtiers attending the coronation would have been well aware that the queen's most urgent duty was to marry and produce a male heir to perpetuate the Tudor dynasty. Until that dynastic goal was achieved, Katherine's claim to the throne was an undeniably relevant political issue that could not be ignored. Indeed, while Mary I had allegedly favoured the Catholic Lady Margaret Douglas as her successor, Katherine's Protestant background positioned her to Elizabeth's councillors as an attractive alternative candidate to the Catholic Mary, Queen of Scots, who had already publicly proclaimed herself the legitimate queen of England in a withering dismissal of Elizabeth's succession to the throne. Following the death of Mary I, the royal arms of the Scottish queen and her husband, the dauphin François, son of Henri II of France, were quartered with those of England. This aggressive act of asserting Mary's claim to the English throne would only have strengthened support for Katherine's succession rights among Elizabeth's Protestant councillors. While Mary's claim to succeed Elizabeth may have been stronger by right of heredity, the Grey claim was likely favoured by the English political elite because it promised to continue 'a clear and unchallenged Protestant line of succession to the English throne'.[15]

The queen was well aware of Katherine's claim to succeed her in the event she died childless. Modern awareness that Elizabeth was succeeded peacefully by James VI of Scotland in 1603 has arguably obscured the significance of Katherine's succession rights, especially given that she was, legally, the queen's heir presumptive according to Henry VIII's last will and testament. But James' inheritance of the English throne was neither inevitable nor predestined. As Retha Warnicke has argued, James' 'accession in England was definitely more complex than mere biological destiny', contrary to the beliefs of some of the biographers of Mary, Queen of Scots.[16] The succession remained unsettled during Elizabeth's long reign, with no certainty as to who would succeed her. By the mid-1590s, the Jesuit Robert Persons identified sixteen possible heirs to Elizabeth and, in 1601, the lawyer Thomas Wilson named twelve competitors for the throne.[17] During the first years of Elizabeth's reign, the queen's councillors had every reason to believe that she would marry and produce an heir, but until such time as that was achieved, Katherine was regarded by many of the queen's statesmen and courtiers as the candidate with the strongest claim to succeed Elizabeth, in view of her dynastic rights enshrined in Henry's last will and testament.

Prior to Elizabeth's reign, Katherine's presence in the contemporary records is fragmentary, with limited insights into her character. After 1558, however, she became a subject of national and international interest because of, first, her claim to succeed Elizabeth should the queen die childless and, second, the scandal of her secret marriage. The possibility of Katherine becoming queen was significant in view of the bearing her succession would have on the English religious settlement. To Elizabeth's Protestant councillors, including her chief adviser Sir William Cecil, Katherine was the most attractive successor, whereas Mary, Queen of Scots attracted Catholic support. With regard to Elizabeth's first decade as queen, Mortimer Levine has suggested that the early Elizabethan succession question 'was above all a question of whether the next wearer of the crown should come from the line of Stuart or that of Suffolk'.[18] For that reason, at the beginning of Elizabeth's reign the imperial ambassador made overtures to Katherine because of Spanish antipathy to the prospect of the French king's daughter-in-law Mary, Queen of Scots becoming queen of England. The ambassador's exchange with Katherine offers revealing insights into her dynastic ambitions and her resentment of the queen's treatment of her.

The count of Feria, then serving as ambassador at the English court, reported to Philip II on 24 March that:

lady Catherine, who is a friend of mine and speaks confidentially to me, told me that the Queen does not wish her to succeed, in case of her (the Queen's) death without heirs. She is dissatisfied and offended at this, and at the Queen's only making her one of the ladies of the presence, whereas she was in the privy-chamber of the late Queen [Mary], who showed her much favour. The present Queen probably bears her no goodwill. I try to keep lady Catherine very friendly, and she has promised me not to change her religion, nor to marry without my consent. She has been hitherto very willing to marry the earl of Pembroke's son, but she has ceased to talk about it as she used to.[19]

Katherine received Spanish support when she apparently promised the imperial ambassador that she would remain a Catholic and would not (re)marry Henry Herbert; instead, a Habsburg husband could be found for her.[20] The ambassador was evidently not aware of Katherine's romance with Hertford, but this exchange indicates Spanish interest in establishing Katherine as a rival heir to Mary, Queen of Scots, whose claim to the English throne was backed by France as a result of her marriage to the dauphin François (the couple became king and queen of France in 1559 following the death of Henri II). It was claimed that Elizabeth 'could not well abide the sight of her [Katherine]' and, in her frustration at her loss of royal favour, Katherine 'had spoken very arrogant and unseemly words in the hearing of the Queen and others standing by'.[21]

William Schutte has argued that, 'thrust suddenly into the limelight, she [Katherine] seems to have allowed her position as possible successor to go to her head'.[22] Certainly her comments were less than circumspect, but they surely resulted from what Katherine perceived to be an insulting snub from Elizabeth. As noted previously, Katherine had been favoured by Mary I with an appointment to the queen's Privy Chamber but, upon Elizabeth's accession, she was demoted from the Privy Chamber and placed in the new queen's Presence Chamber, an act that signified a lack of royal favour. Whether or not Elizabeth had grounds for her dislike of Katherine, the latter certainly had every reason to resent the queen's attitude towards her. From Elizabeth's perspective, however, she evidently had no desire to be seen to favour Katherine as her heir presumptive given that she had not yet reached a decision on the question of her marriage, the most important issue confronting her at the beginning of her reign.

Although Elizabeth has long been identified and celebrated as the Virgin Queen, the belief that she viewed herself as such from the beginning of her queenship is a misapprehension deriving from a retrospective view of her reign.[23] The evidence does not support the traditional belief that Elizabeth consciously decided at the beginning of her reign not to marry, whether because she was opposed to marriage or because she was determined to rule alone. This is an assumption based on William Camden's version of her speech to the 1559 parliament, but documents dating from Elizabeth's reign do not support this account of the speech.[24] As in Mary's reign, it was taken for granted by Elizabeth's statesmen that she would marry in order to produce an heir, especially given contemporary ambivalence – if not hostility – to female monarchy.

The Scottish reformer John Knox, whose *The First Blast of the Trumpet Against the Monstrous Regiment of Women* was published in the year of Elizabeth's accession, thundered that 'where women reigne or be in authoritie, that there must nedes vanitie be preferred to vertue, ambition and pride to temperancie and modestie, and finallie, that auarice the mother of all mischefe must nedes deuour equitie and iustice'.[25] According to law, 'women are remoued from all ciuile and publike office, so that they nether may be iudges, nether may they occupie the place of the magistrate, nether yet may they be speakers for others'.[26] Indeed, 'a naturall shamfastnes oght to be in womankind, whiche most certeinlie she loseth, when soeuer she taketh vpon her the office and estate of man'.[27]

These contemporary beliefs produced a dilemma: the innate qualities of a female monarch were viewed as a barrier to any attempt on her behalf to rule successfully, yet marriage to a foreign prince ran the risk of resulting in the queen's loss of authority and, by extension, subverting native laws and customs in favour of those of the husband's nation or, in the case of marriage to a subject, leading to factional strife at court. By contrast, the Grey sisters' former tutor John Aylmer (later bishop of London), in *An Harborowe for Faithful and Trew Subiectes* (1559), questioned the widespread assumption that a married queen regnant was duty-bound to subordinate herself to her husband:

> Yea say you, God hath appoynted her to be subject to her husband ... therefore she maye not be the heade. I graunte that, so farre as perteining to the bandes of mariage, and the offices of a wife, she must be a subiecte; but as a Magistrate she maye be her husbande's heade ... Whie may not the woman be the husbande's inferiour in matters of wedlock, and his head in the guiding of the commonwelth.[28]

Irrespective of whether they accepted female rule or not, Elizabeth's contemporaries unanimously agreed that it was her duty to marry and produce an heir to continue the Tudor dynasty. Indeed, Parliament's repeated petitions during Elizabeth's reign to persuade her to marry can be interpreted as an effort 'to fulfill its fundamental patriarchal responsibility – to preserve the social order by securing a husband for the queen and an heir to the crown'.[29] However, the choice of husband was a more controversial issue, especially in view of the 'tumult' caused by Mary I's selection of Philip of Spain as her spouse.

When the Commons petitioned Elizabeth to marry, the queen allegedly declared in response that 'I happily chose this kind of life, in the which I yet live: which, I assure you, for mine own part, hath best contented my self', and noted that, if the petition had limited 'place or person', she would 'have misliked it very much, and thought it in you a very great presumption, being unfitting and altogether unmeet for you to require them, that may command ... or to take upon you to draw my Love to your liking, or to frame my will to your fantasie'.[30] Mary I had referred to her male predecessors when she admonished her councillors for seeking to choose her husband and stressed that it was the sovereign's right, regardless of their sex, to select their spouse without the interference of councillors: 'I especially applaud you for encouraging me to marriage, which I both hope and believe is intended for me, but I do not applaud the idea that you should attempt to allot me a companion of my conjugal bed by your decision.'[31] When the parliament of 1559 beseeched Elizabeth to marry 'in order that the Royal House may not die out', the queen responded that:

> she could only tell them that the getting of children and successors of her blood was God's work, who would procure her a husband in His own good time. She proposed when the time was ripe to do as they desired, but would only wed a man who was not only King in name, but would also govern her Royal self and the whole Kingdom, and who should be agreeable to the Estates, but she must have time for consideration.[32]

Elizabeth's words in 1559 – and later in her reign – indicate that she shared her predecessor's attitude to the selection of a spouse.

In 1559, there was certainly no shortage of candidates for the queen's hand in marriage. Prospective husbands included a host of foreign suitors, such as the king of Sweden and the dukes of Ferrara, Holstein, Saxony, Savoy and Nemours, as well as English candidates such as the queen's favourite Robert Dudley, Sir William Pickering, the earls of Arundel and Westmorland, and the duke of Norfolk.[33] Initially, the leading candidate may have been the Archduke Charles, son of the Holy Roman Emperor Ferdinand I. From an imperial perspective, marriage to Elizabeth was a vital means of maintaining Catholicism in the realm. Emperor Ferdinand expressed concern in January 1559 that 'Her Grace, that Queen, is filled with the new views of the Christian Faith, and what is more, that under the rule of Her Majesty our Catholic religion has in her realm again totally broken down.' He therefore believed that his sons, the archdukes Ferdinand and Charles, would not wish to marry Elizabeth because of 'the danger of forfeiting ... eternal salvation'.[34] The queen wrote to Emperor Ferdinand on 5 June from Westminster, explaining that 'when however we reflect upon the question of this marriage [to a son of Ferdinand] and eagerly ask our heart, we find that we have no wish to give up solitude and our lonely life, but prefer with God's help to abide therein of our free determination'.[35] After an audience with Elizabeth, the Holy Roman Emperor's envoy Baron Breuner reported to Archduke Charles on 7 June that:

> she has not yet made up her mind to marry anyone in this world. She had, it is true, not forsworn marriage, as her mind might for various reasons change, but she could not at the moment come to any resolution and was also unwilling to bind herself for the future.[36]

He also divulged to Emperor Ferdinand that Elizabeth had revealed that 'she had been desired in marriage by many during and after her imprisonment. Her Council and her loyal subjects daily and hourly begged and exhorted her to marry whom she would, so that they might hope to have heirs for this Royal Crown of England.' Yet 'she to this hour had never set her heart upon, nor had come so far as to wish to marry, anyone in the whole world'. Elizabeth 'found the celibate life so agreeable, and was so accustomed to it, that she would rather go into a nunnery, or for that matter suffer death, than marry against her will', but had not 'forsworn marriage entirely, for she was but human and not insensible to human emotions and impulses, and when it became a question of the weal of her Kingdom, or it might be for other reasons, her heart and mind might change'.[37] By the summer, however, hostile relations with France led the queen and her ministers to favour an imperial alliance, while marriage to Charles:

> would rescue her [Elizabeth] and give the country peace and strength, but her religious feeling runs so high that she and her Councillors will never dare to trust his Highness. They think it would be taken as a sign that they had some secret understanding with my King both in religion and in other matters.[38]

The bishop of Aquila believed, however, that 'salvation can only come from a marriage with the Archduke'.[39]

Privately, Elizabeth may have desired to marry her childhood friend, Robert Dudley, who had been appointed as her Master of the Horse shortly after her accession. Katherine would have been well aware of Dudley's charms, for he was the brother of her sister Jane's husband Guildford. Three days before Elizabeth's accession, the imperial ambassador de Feria had included Dudley in a list of individuals with whom Elizabeth 'is on very good terms'.[40] The queen's intimacy with Dudley attracted considerable interest and it was not long before it became a source of scandal, both on account of the queen's unmarried status and because Dudley had a wife, Amy. De Feria informed Philip II in April that:

> during the last few days Lord Robert has come so much into favour that he does whatever he likes with affairs and it is even said that her Majesty visits him in his chamber day and night. People talk of this so freely that they go so far as to say that his wife has a malady in one of her breasts and the Queen is only waiting for her to die to marry Lord Robert.[41]

The following month, the Venetian ambassador noted that Dudley was 'in very great favour, and very intimate with her Majesty. On this subject I ought to report the opinion of many, but I doubt whether my letters may not miscarry, or be read; wherefore it is better to keep silence than to speak ill.'[42]

By August, Baron Breuner had launched an investigation on his master's behalf into 'the calumnies' circulating about the queen's relationship with her favourite, learning from the ladies of the bedchamber 'by all that is holy that her Majesty has most certainly never been forgetful of her honour'.[43] He did concede, however, that Elizabeth 'shows her liking for him [Dudley] more markedly than is consistent with her reputation and dignity'.[44] That month, Kat Astley – formerly Elizabeth's governess and now a Lady of the Bedchamber – fell on her knees before the queen and begged her to cease meeting with Dudley, for it 'occasioned much evil-speaking' and sullied Elizabeth's 'honour and dignity'.[45] If the queen's subjects became 'discontented' as a result, then she 'would thus be the cause of much bloodshed in this realm'; rather than have that happen, Kat 'would have strangled Her Majesty in the cradle'.[46] Elizabeth responded that 'she had had so much sorrow and tribulation and so little joy', and Dudley deserved her favour on account of 'his honourable nature and dealings'.[47] She also protested that her relations with him were not dishonourable, given that 'she was always surrounded by her ladies of the bedchamber and maids-of-honour'.[48] Nevertheless, Dudley's intimacy with the queen provoked such hostility that, by September, it was rumoured that a plot was afoot for both to be killed at a banquet given by the earl of Arundel.[49]

Meanwhile, a Spanish conspiracy developed with the goal of kidnapping Katherine and having her married to Don Carlos, son of Philip II. Katherine's co-operation in the scheme was taken for granted.[50] A number of individuals were suggested – including the countess of Feria, Lady Montague and Lady Hungerford – to arrange for Katherine to be 'enticed away' on board a ship to take her to Spain.[51] The extent of Katherine's involvement, if any, in this scheme remains open to question. She undoubtedly gave de Feria reason to believe that she was 'friendly' towards him, but it was unknown whether Katherine 'or any of the parties before rehearsed are privy to these practices, or whether they are only thought meetest by some on this side'.[52] Neither the imperial ambassador nor the Spanish king were aware of Katherine's blossoming relationship with Hertford. The imperial envoys were, however, undoubtedly cognisant of Katherine's claim to succeed Elizabeth and, for that reason, in November 1559 Baron Bruener wrote to Emperor Ferdinand that if Archduke Charles travelled to England, ostensibly to court the queen, he would likely 'see Catherine [Grey] who doubtless will succeed this Queen in the Kingdom'.[53] The following month, the baron wrote to the Archduke Maximilian, king of Bohemia, on the subject of the prospective marriage between Elizabeth and the Archduke Charles, noting that if Charles visited England, 'His Royal Highness [Charles] would also have seen Catherine (who, if the Queen die without heirs of her body) is the next heir to the throne, and would so have been providing against the future.'[54]

In the midst of these intrigues, Katherine's love affair gained momentum. Hertford's brother Henry and his sister Jane delivered tokens and messages between the earl and Katherine, who met privately 'as time might serve and as folk of those years of that sort will do'.[55] Hertford later revealed 'that he hath had secret talk treaty and conference divers tymes with the said Lady Catherine at Westminster' on the subject of their marriage.[56] When she was interrogated in February 1562, Katherine likewise recalled 'that at Westminster there hath been secret talk and meetinge betweene her and the said Edward Earl of Hartford the Lady Jane his sister allways being present concerninge matter of contract of matrimony'.[57] She would also reveal that there began to be 'good will' between the earl and herself during Mary's reign when she spent time at the duchess of Somerset's residence at Hanworth, and 'the love did againe renewe' between the couple during the first year of Elizabeth's reign.[58] For that reason, the couple agreed that it was necessary to seek the assistance of Katherine's mother, who could petition the queen on their behalf.

In October, 'when the Queenes Majestie came to Hampton Courte the Earle rode to the Lady Ffraunces Suffolke mother to the Lady Katherine', to request Frances' agreement for her daughter's marriage to Hertford.[59] She was then in residence at the Charterhouse at Sheen with her second husband, Adrian Stokes. There, Hertford 'moved her, the Lady Frances, to grant her good-will that he might marry the Lady Katharine, her daughter'. In response, Frances consulted with her husband. The duchess reportedly viewed Hertford as a 'fitt husband for her said daughter if it should so please the Queens Highness'.[60] Stokes advised Hertford to make suit to the queen and those of her councillors who favoured the earl. Stokes promised that:

> he would himself make all the interest he could for him and Katharine with those he knew of the council, and that the duchess Lady Frances should write to Queen Elizabeth for her Majesty's favour and good-will, and in very deed the Lady Frances required me to make a rough draft of a letter to that purpose.

Frances subsequently sent a message to the court requesting Katherine to ask leave of the queen to come and speak with her mother; upon doing so, Frances revealed Hertford's request to Katherine.[61] After the duchess 'brake the mater unto'[62] her daughter, Katherine confirmed her willingness to marry the earl. Stokes advised that Frances should write to the queen requesting 'her good will and consent to the sayed marry-adge'.[63] Unfortunately for Katherine, Frances was so ill that she never wrote the letter and died very soon afterwards.[64]

The couple's hopes of marrying were dealt a severe blow by the death of the duchess of Suffolk on 20 November at the age of 42. Her cause of death is unknown. It has been suggested that both Katherine and her sister Mary were at Frances' deathbed.[65] On 5 December, the duchess was buried at Westminster Abbey with full honours befitting a member of the royal family. Katherine, as Frances' eldest surviving daughter, officiated as chief mourner. There is no record of her response to her mother's death, but the fragmentary surviving evidence – namely that pertaining to Katherine's desire to involve her mother in the bid to marry Hertford — seems to suggest a close and loving relationship, the loss of which surely devastated the 19-year-old. John Jewel, consecrated as bishop of Salisbury the following January, delivered the sermon. Frances' remains were interred in a chapel on the south side of the choir.[66] The Clarencieux King of Arms proclaimed:

> Laud and praise be given to Almighty God, that it hath pleased him to call out of this transitory life unto his eternal glory, the most noble and excellent Princess the Lady Frances, late Dutchess of Suffolk, daughter to the right high and mighty Prince Charles Brandon, Duke of Suffolk, and of the most noble and excellent Princess Mary, the French Queen, daughter to the most illustrious Prince King Henry VII.[67]

The dean then began the service in English, as befitted the funeral's Protestant nature. The mourners, including Katherine, knelt on a cushion and a carpet before the altar, before two assistants made their way to the hearse and led Katherine away by the arm, with her train being carried by some of the other mourners.[68] Following the offering, Jewel delivered his sermon, after which the dean proceeded to communion, at which Katherine and Mary participated.[69] After the funeral, those present departed for the duchess' residence of the Charterhouse in a chariot.[70] The inscription on Frances' grave reads (in Latin):

> Nor grace, nor splendour, nor a royal name,
> Nor widespread fame can aught avail;
> All, all have vanished here.
> True worth alone Survives the funeral pyre and silent tomb

Spanish interest in Katherine's claim to the throne showed no signs of abating that autumn. Only a week before Frances' death, the ambassador, Álvaro de la Quadra, wrote to Philip II with the opinion that:

if the Archduke comes and makes the acquaintance and obtains the goodwill of these people, even if this marriage [to Elizabeth]—of which I have now no hope except by force—should fall through, and any disaster were to befall the Queen, such as may be feared from her bad government, the Archduke might be summoned to marry Lady Catherine to whom the kingdom falls if this woman dies. If the Archduke sees her (Catherine) he should so bear himself that she should understand this design, which in my opinion may be beneficial and even necessary.[71]

The queen had learned of the intrigues involving Katherine that summer when Thomas Chaloner wrote to Elizabeth from Flushing in August with the news that he had heard from 'oon Robert Hogyns an Inglishe gentilman here pentioner to the King', shortly before the death of Henri II of France, that there was a plot 'to sollicite and gett into their handes my Lady Katherin Graye, whom further, as events shuldfall owte, they might either mary with the Prince of Spayne, or with some other persone of lesse degre, if lesse depended on her'.[72] Katherine was reported 'to be of a discontented mynde, as not regarded or estemed of Your Highness or of her frends'.[73] Chaloner advised the queen: 'It is not difficult in myne opinion by some good meanes to know of my Lady Kartrin a yong gentilwoman if ever any body have made such a motion unto her.'[74] As a result of this intelligence, Elizabeth prudently decided that it was in her best interests to extend her favour to Katherine. De Quadra wrote to de Feria in January 1560 from London, reporting that:

the Queen calls Lady Catharine her daughter, although the feeling between them can hardly be that of mother and child, but the Queen has thought best to put her in her chamber and makes much of her in order to keep her quiet. She even talks about formally adopting her.[75]

Almost certainly this gesture was political in nature, to remind the French that there were other candidates for the English throne besides

Mary, Queen of Scots whom the queen could favour.[76] That Elizabeth did not intend by her action to signify that Katherine was her successor is suggested by Cecil's report to the ambassador 'that neither she nor any other woman will succeed in order to exclude also the Countess of Lennox, whose son if he were taken to France might disagree with their stomachs'.[77]

The court was rocked by scandal when Amy Dudley died in suspicious circumstances in September 1560. Although the queen's biographer William Camden recorded that Amy 'died of late by a Fall from a steep place',[78] the timing was perhaps rather convenient in view of the fact that some days earlier Elizabeth had predicted Amy's demise, alongside rumours that Dudley had long desired to marry the queen. The imperial ambassador claimed in September that Cecil had informed him that 'Robert was thinking of killing his wife, who was publicly announced to be ill', and also stated that 'the Queen told me as she returned from hunting that Robert's wife was dead or nearly so, and asked me not to say anything about it'.[79] As early as the previous November, de Quadra reported a rumour 'from a certain person' that Dudley 'has sent to poison his wife'.[80] Certainly, by March it was speculated that Dudley would divorce Amy in order to marry the queen.[81] The coroner's verdict at the inquest into Amy's death ruled that her death was an accident.[82]

Despite the circumstances of his wife's death, Dudley continued to hope that Elizabeth would marry him. In February 1561, he approached de Quadra and beseeched the ambassador to recommend him as a husband for Elizabeth with the support of Philip II, to which Elizabeth:

> did not deny that she had some affection for Lord Robert for the many good qualities he possessed, but she certainly had never decided to marry him or anyone else, although she daily saw more clearly the necessity for her marriage, and to satisfy the English humour that it was desirable that she should marry an Englishman, and she asked me to tell her what your Majesty would think if she married one of her servitors as the duchess of Suffolk and the duchess of Somerset had done.[83]

In December 1560, Sir Nicholas Throckmorton reported from France that he had been asked by the Spanish ambassador 'whether the Queen, my mistress, were not secretly married to the Lord Robert', for:

> whatsoever any man doth make your mistress believe, assure your-self there was never Princess so overseen if she do not give order in that matter betimes. The bruits of her doings, said he, be very strange in all Courts and countries. He said the Queen, your mistress, doth show that she hath honour but for a few in her realm, for no man will advise her to leave her folly; – with other things which were grievous for me to hear.[84]

As the years passed, rumours would continue to circulate that Elizabeth would marry Dudley. In June 1566, Marcantonio Barbaro, Venetian ambassador at the French court, claimed that while Elizabeth had alleg-edly promised to marry the Archduke Charles, 'I have been told by a person who is well advised about things in England, that the love her Majesty bears Lord Robert is such that she will either finally take him for husband, or will never take anyone else.'[85]

A few weeks after Amy Dudley's death, de Quadra related the news that Elizabeth's councillors 'fear that if the Queen were to die your Majesty [Philip II] would get the kingdom into your family by means of Lady Catharine', and Cecil informed the ambassador 'that it would be well to treat of a marriage between her and one of your Majesty's relatives'.[86] Cecil did, however, admit that Elizabeth would never name Katherine as her heir, since 'the English run after the heir to the Crown more than after the present wearer of it'.[87] In March of that year, Cecil had learned from John Middleton in Brussels 'that there is prac-tising for a marriage to be made betwixt the Prince of Spain and the Lady Katherine Grey, which is not of the best liked for divers respects, and by some hindered'.[88]

The strength of her claim to succeed Elizabeth, alongside the queen's failure to marry, gave rise to other suggested matches for Katherine in addition to Spanish interest in her hand in marriage.

Thomas Randolph, English ambassador in Scotland, reported to Cecil in September 1560 that Sarlabos, captain of Dunbar Castle, had claimed that Elizabeth's Privy Council favoured a marriage between Katherine and James Hamilton, third earl of Arran, who was a descendant of James II of Scotland. The councillors allegedly desired the match because Katherine, 'as ... an heir apparent of England so shall she be matched with an heir apparent of Scotland; so that if both those who are in possession of the crowns die without succession, the right shall come to them'.[89] Given the queen's attitude to the marriages of her royal relatives, it is questionable whether she would have assented to a union between the earl, who possessed a claim to the Scottish throne, and a cousin regarded by many of her councillors and courtiers as heir presumptive to the throne should Elizabeth die without producing heirs of her own. From Elizabeth's perspective, such a marriage could have endangered her political security, especially if Katherine's union with the earl resulted in offspring. In the seventeenth century, Fuller believed that 'Queen Elizabeth beheld her [Katherine] with a jealous eye, unwilling she should match either Forreign Prince or English Peer, but follow the pattern she set her of constant virginity'.[90] Katherine's own attitude to the rumoured match with Arran, if she learned of it, is unknown, but in view of her relationship with Hertford, she surely would not have welcomed this attention to the question of her marriage.

7

A Second Marriage

In November or December 1560, Katherine clandestinely married the earl of Hertford and, in doing so, incurred Elizabeth's lasting displeasure. Prior to her marriage, the evidence of Katherine's exchanges with the imperial ambassador indicates that she may have harboured ambitions to be recognised as Elizabeth's heir presumptive, but her relationship with Hertford seems at odds with this, since she was surely well aware of the need to secure royal permission to marry. Failure to do so could have weakened her claim to the succession if she were to suffer royal disfavour. Perhaps in Katherine's case – as with the queen's aunt, Mary Boleyn, in 1534 – 'love overcame reason'.[1] If so, both Katherine and her husband would pay a heavy price.

Historians have questioned Hertford's motives in marrying Katherine, with some believing that he may have had an ulterior motive of political ambition while others suggest that theirs was an all-consuming love match. Some of Katherine's friends feared that she was being exploited by the earl, who 'ment but only to mock her and that there woulde noe further good come thereof'.[2] As the son of an executed traitor, the earl had more reason than most to fear the consequences of royal disfavour and therefore his liaison with Katherine would seem to have been motivated by the recklessness of love, rather than political ambition. It has been argued that Hertford's love for Katherine is demonstrated by the fact that he gave orders to be buried alongside her, rather than alongside either of his two subsequent wives.[3]

The testimony of the couple indicates that they fell deeply in love with one another. When interrogated, Hertford noted 'that he hath had secret talk treaty and conference divers tymes with the said Lady Catherine at Westminster only not for any matter of incontinency but for marriage to be had with the said Lady Catherine as he saith'.[4] The death of Katherine's mother was a setback in view of her promise to approach Elizabeth regarding her daughter's marriage, but the couple pressed ahead with their plans regardless. The evidence suggests awareness at court of their relationship. Before the marriage took place, Cecil remarked to Hertford 'that it was said that there was goodwill between hym and the sayd Lady Catherine', which he denied.[5] When she was examined, Elizabeth Sentlow confessed 'that this two yeres paste or rather more ther hath been greate conversacyone and famylyaryty betwixt therlle of Hertford and the Lady Cateryne Gray soe as yt was thought by all ther conversantes that ther was gret love betwene theme'.[6]

The relationship was not all smooth sailing, however. Katherine quarrelled with Hertford because she believed that he bore good will towards Frances, daughter of Sir Peter Mewtas; to reassure her of his affections, the earl promised to marry Katherine if a convenient time could be found when the queen came to London.[7] Katherine remembered that it was at Hampton Court that 'she was movid by the Lady Jane [Seymour] for marryage to be had between her and the said Erle of Hertford upon which motion she told her that at the queen's Majesties repair to Westminster than next ensewinge she would make him further Answere'.[8] Hertford, who was then 'lying sick at his howse in Channon Rowe', had written to Jane 'prayinge her to sollicite and continewe his Sewte unto the saied Lady Catherine as she had begonne and to feele her disposicion for Marriadge with him'.[9] When Elizabeth went to Westminster, 'in the Closet within the Maidens Chamber the said Earl himself movid her for marryage', to which she responded 'that she boare her good will to have him to her husband, the said Lady

Jane being present'.[10] Later, in an attempt to ascertain whether their union was valid, the commissioners would question Katherine about 'the forme and wordes of the promise'.[11] The earl revealed to Katherine that 'he had born her good will of longe tyme' and promised that he did not intend to mock her. 'And she at the same tyme declared that she liked both him and his offer', following which 'they gave one to thother their hands'.[12]

Lady Jane and her manservant Glynne delivered tokens and messages between the earl and Katherine.[13] Hertford and Katherine agreed that they would marry 'when they could get oppertunity by the queens majestyes removinge or by her graces going in to the Parke a walking or otherwise', and planned for their wedding to take place 'at the said Erles howse' at Cannon Row.[14] Jane's assistance during both the court-ship and marriage was essential; without it, the couple would not have been able to marry. Katherine Howard's secret meetings with Thomas Culpeper in 1541 had demonstrated the necessity of at least one accom-plice to facilitate a clandestine liaison, and the failure of the Crown to accuse any of Anne Boleyn's female attendants of abetting her adulter-ies has led the majority of historians to view that queen as innocent of the crimes for which she was executed.[15] Although Katherine Grey was not herself a queen, the point demonstrates the lack of privacy at court and the necessity of assistance in conducting clandestine liaisons.

Katherine would later recall 'that upon a certaine day happenynge between Allhallow's tide and Christmas last was xij monthe beinge the same day that the queenes Majestie went from her graces palais of Westminster to Eltham', about an hour after the queen had departed, Katherine and Jane Seymour 'went alone without any other compa-nye by the sands at a low water to the said Earls Howse'.[16] Katherine had been excused attending the queen after claiming to have a swell-ing in her face.[17] When interrogated, neither Katherine nor Hertford could recall the exact date. On the day of the wedding, the earl asked his gentleman ushers Penne and Fortescue, his body servants Barnaby and Jenkin, and his groom of the chamber Cripps to take the day off, returning in the afternoon. Barnaby was asked to go to a goldsmith's in Fleet Street with an important letter.[18] Later, William Powell was in the kitchen with Jenkin and 'saw the Lady Jane and the sayd Lady Catheryne comeinge in at the water gate of the sayd howse'.[19] He had seen Katherine at the house several times before.[20] Upon Katherine's arrival, 'there seeinge no body nor cumpany at her entrye she went with the said Lady Jane into a chamber within the said howse', at which point Jane left to fetch a priest, 'which priest forthwith procedyd to solemnization of matrimony between her and the said Lord Edward Earle of Hartford'.[21] Katherine later confessed that she did not know the priest's name and had never met him before. The priest 'was a well complectioned man with an awbren beard, of a mean stature in a long gown' and the collar turned down. If she saw him again, she thought 'she could call hym to remembraunce'.[22] Katherine recalled that 'that there was noe Communion there ministred but she saied the Minister had a Booke of Common Service in his hand and such Prayers as concerned marriadge he redd'.[23] Hertford had commissioned a ring for Katherine that was described as being 'a Gold Ringe at the saied Marriadge of fyve lincks without any stone'[24] and was inscribed with the following verses:

As circles five, by art compact, show but one right in sight,
So trust uniteth faithful minds, with knot of secret might,
Whose force to break (but greedy death) no wight possesseth power,
As time and sequels well shall prove. My ring can say no more.

After the wedding, Katherine had 'carnall copulation with the said Earle divers tymes' in his house at Cannon Row.[25] Hertford confessed that 'he and the Ladie Catherine vnarrayed themselves and went to bedde noeboddie helpinge them but themselves' after they were wed.[26] At that time, Jane 'was from them in the saied howse'. Katherine later got dressed without anyone else assisting her.[27] Katherine and Jane remained in the house until dinner time, at which point they returned to court to sup with Sir Edward Rogers, comptroller of the queen's household. The earl accompanied Katherine to the water stairs of his house, kissed her and bid her farewell. None of the queen's gentlewomen knew that she had gone to the earl's house that day and none of them asked her any questions upon her return.[28] After their marriage, Jane and Glynne aided the couple's meetings both in the queen's palaces and at the earl's house at Cannon Row.

Whether Katherine and Hertford believed they could keep their marriage a secret, and for how long, is unknown but matters were complicated by the death of Jane Seymour, which coincided with Katherine's suspicion that she was pregnant. Before Jane's death, Katherine reckoned herself to be with child, to which the earl replied: 'We must abide by it, and trust to the Queen's mercy.'[29] Jane died in March 1561 at the age of 19.[30] The diarist Machyn recorded that on the 26th:

at after-none at Westmynster [was brought] from the quen('s) armere[31] my lade Jane Semer, with [all the quire] of the abbay, with ijC. of (the) quen('s) cowrt, the wyche she was [one] of the quen('s) mayd(s) and in grett faver, and a iiijxx morners of [men and] women, of lordes and lades, and gentylmen and gentyllwomen, all in blake, be-syd odur[32] of the quen('s) preve chambur, and she [had] a grett baner of armes bornne, and master Clarenshux was the harold, and master Skameler the nuw byshope of Peterborow dyd pryche. [She was] bered in the sam chapell wher my lade of Suffoke was.[33]

Although they might not have realised it at the time, Jane's death was to prove disastrous for Hertford and Katherine because it meant that she could not testify to their marriage as a witness.

After Jane's death, Katherine met with Hertford with the assistance of her maid Mrs Leigh. Due to the death of her father, Leigh departed from Katherine's service at Westminster the day before Elizabeth Sentlow removed to Greenwich after the solemnisation of Katherine's marriage. Leigh had entered Katherine's service 'by the Lady Paston now wife to Mr Garrard'.[34] Elizabeth Sentlow would later recall that she did not know, after Jane's death, whether the earl repaired to Katherine's chamber or whether he met her in any other place, for 'the Lady Cateryne would sondrye tymes be absent from hyre chamber with only a mayde of hyre owne whose name was Leghe'.[35] Hertford would inform his examiners that he had 'carnall copulation' with Katherine, first at his house and subsequently 'in her chamber at the Courte'.[36]

That spring, the earl applied for a licence to travel to the Continent 'for the sight of other countries and commonwealths ... to come to knowledge of things [appropriate to] his estate'.[37] Hertford told Katherine that he had his passport and showed it to her in the orchard or garden at the court at Westminster, but she could not remember 'the certeyne tyme thereof'. Before his departure, the earl delivered Katherine a writing assuring her lands valued at £1,000 a year for her living, but she lost it 'with other writeinges at the removeinge in the progresse tyme'.[38] Another lost writing was 'a certeyne accompte or declaration of the prouffitts of her Landes', delivered to her by 'one Mr Newporte beinge her officer'.[39] The earl told Katherine that if she could confirm 'the certaintie' of her pregnancy, 'he wolde not longe tarrie from her'.[40] Katherine responded that she was still uncertain about her condition. While in France, Hertford intended to make stops at 'Orleans, Blois, Amboise, Tours, Angers, and sundry fair castles and houses situated upon the Loire'.[41] He arrived in Paris on 13 May and attended Charles IX's coronation at Rheims two days later.[42] Sir Nicholas Throckmorton, English ambassador at the French court, had advised the earl to remain in France until September before travelling to Italy.[43]

After the earl's departure abroad, Cecil spoke to Katherine at Greenwich and 'dyd advise to take good heed how she proceeded in familiarity with the said Erle without making the queenes majesty privye thereunto'.[44] Similarly, the marchioness of Northampton and Lady Clinton 'dyd seriously advertyse her to beware the cumpany and familiarity with the said Erle', but she denied to both Cecil and the women 'that there was any such matter'.[45] Cecil had also previously warned Hertford about the risks of pursuing Katherine, echoing the attitude of the duchess of Somerset. It has been convincingly argued that Katherine's 'claim was strongly supported by Cecil who worked tirelessly behind the scenes to promote it'.[46] For that reason, it was in

Cecil's interests to ensure that Katherine did nothing to jeopardise her claim to succeed Elizabeth. He was determined to prevent Mary, Queen of Scots from being recognised as heir presumptive to the English throne, in contrast with his royal mistress' seeming receptivity to Mary's claim and unceasing hostility to Katherine's candidacy.

Katherine wrote letters to the earl but received no response, leading her to doubt his intentions. She received no letters or tokens from Hertford during his time abroad, aside from a pair of bracelets delivered to her by Hertford's brother Henry at Havering; the earl also sent tokens to a number of ladies and gentlemen at court.[47] One of Katherine's letters to him that was delivered to Glynne at the Charterhouse at the beginning of the court's progress informed him that she 'was quick with childe'.[48]

By then, Katherine was presented with problems of an entirely unexpected, and unwelcome, nature. In June, the earl of Pembroke approached Katherine with a view to arranging her remarriage to his son Henry Herbert. Pembroke was undoubtedly attracted to Katherine's position as heir presumptive according to Henry VIII's last will and testament, but she rejected his suggestion: 'The earl of Pembroke cannot yet bring his purpose to pass, for the Lady Catherine will not have his son.'[49] However, she soon changed her mind: the evidence suggests that Katherine, at that time, doubted Hertford's commitment to her and began hedging her bets. She was unaware that Hertford intended to remain in Paris for another six weeks before moving on to Italy in September.[50] Katherine may have feared that the earl would fail to acknowledge their marriage and paternity of her child when the time came to do so.[51] As a result of Hertford's silence, Katherine almost certainly looked to Herbert as a protector, someone who could provide her with a measure of security.

It may have been the couple's anticipated remarriage at this time that fuelled the later belief that Katherine and Herbert continued 'in mutuall Love testified by sondrey means, meny Tokens, Messingers, and other signes of the same, [which] cannot be of eny force to breake the sayd Matrimony'.[52] The anonymous author may have learned of

Herbert's gift giving in the expectation of remarrying Katherine. Even as she pondered Herbert's attentions, Katherine would have become aware of the queen's hostility for, as Sir Henry Neville informed Throckmorton, 'whatsoever is the cause I know not, but the Queen has entered into a great misliking with her'.[53] It is possible that Elizabeth had heard rumours of Katherine's liaison with Hertford, although, if she had, she did not then act on her suspicions. That summer, Katherine accompanied the court on Elizabeth's summer progress: she could not have known it, but it was the last summer of her life in which she would enjoy freedom.

On 10 July, the queen travelled to the Tower by water to visit the Royal Mint and then departed for the Charterhouse, where she resided for three days; on the final day she supped at a dinner arranged by Cecil at the Savoy Palace.[54] On the 14th, the court made its way into Essex.[55] By that time, Herbert's attitude to Katherine had changed completely. Although he had begun courting Katherine in the expectation of their remarriage, he soon learned of her pregnancy and wrote insultingly to her:

I perceive your mind to keep my tokens back, but if I can not have them at your hands, I will seek them at that companion's hands … by whose practise to cover your whoredom and his own knavery and adultery you went about to abuse me … Having hitherto led a virtuous life I will not now begin with loss of honour to lead the rest of my life with a whore that almost everyman talks of. You claim promise madam of me when I was young, and since confirmed as you say at lawful years, but you know I was lawfully divorced from you a good while ago. And if through the enticement of your whoredom and the practise and devise of those you hold so dear, you sought to entrap me with some poisoned bait under the colour of sugared friendship; yet (I thank God) I am so clear that I am not to be further touched than with a few tokens that were by cunning slight got out of my hands both to cover your abomination and his likewise.[56]

Sir William Petre entertained the queen and her court for four days at Ingatestone at a cost of £136, and she also stayed with the earl of Oxford at Hedingham for six days at the cost of £273.[57] At Beaulieu, Herbert wrote a second letter to Katherine:

> Like as a good while ago I was your friend madam, so your deserts now … makes me right sorry for that which is past of my part … Wherefore, without delay I require you madam to send me, by this bearer, those letters and tokens with my tablature and picture that I sent you … or else, to be plain with you, I will make you as well known to all the world as your whoredom is now, I thank God, known to me and spied by many scores more.[58]

Katherine's response to this threatening missive is not recorded, but her inner turmoil can only be imagined in view of Hertford's continuing silence. The court reached Suffolk in August. During her visit to Ipswich, Elizabeth observed that 'in Cathedrals and Colleges there were so many wives, and widows and children seen', which she attempted to rectify by issuing an injunction banning females from clerical lodgings.[59]

For Katherine, time was running out by then, for there was only so much she could do to conceal her pregnancy. Sixteenth-century women did not possess separate maternity clothes; instead, when pregnant, expectant mothers added stomachers to their gowns, which were then removed after childbirth.[60] Any attempt by Katherine to keep her condition a secret soon proved futile, with it becoming a subject of scandal and gossip. At a communion service in Ipswich, Katherine realised by 'the secret talk she saw amongst men and women that her being with child was known and spied out'.[61] As a result, Katherine had no choice but to reveal her marriage and pregnancy. She approached Elizabeth Sentlow for assistance. When interrogated later, Katherine revealed that:

> after she heard by the brute in the Courte that she should be with Childe thereupon the Saturday next before she was commytted to

the Tower she dyd disclose to Mrs Seyntlow of the prevey Chamber both that she was marryed to therle of Hertford and that she was with Childe.[62]

Elizabeth Sentlow's response would hardly have comforted Katherine. She 'thereupon wept and declared that she was very sorry because that she had not made the queenes majestye prevye thereunto'.[63] The following day, in desperation, Katherine sought the assistance of the queen's favourite, Robert Dudley. Katherine visited Dudley's chamber in Ipswich and 'declared the same to my Lord Robert at night by his bed side requireinge him to be a meane to the queenes highnes for her'.[64] Although he agreed to intercede on her behalf, neither party can have anticipated Elizabeth's reaction. She ordered Katherine to be arrested and incarcerated in the Tower, while also sending messengers to France commanding Hertford's return.

Katherine's lodgings in the Tower[65] were furnished with footstools and velvet cushions that had belonged to her great-uncle Henry VIII, alongside six pieces of tapestry, a bed of damask, two Turkey carpets, a chair of cloth of gold and a cushion of purple velvet.[66] Her sister had been executed at the Tower seven years earlier for treason; now, Katherine shared Jane's prison and must have wondered whether she would suffer a similar fate as a result of incurring royal displeasure. On 17 August, Elizabeth instructed Sir Edward Warner, Lieutenant of the Tower, to examine Katherine:

> very streightly, how many hath bene pryvee to the Love betwixt the Erle of Hertford and hir from the begynning; and lett hir certenly understand that she shall have no Manner of Favor, except she will shew the truth, not only what Ladyes or Gentillwomen of this Court wer therto privee, but also what Lords and Gentillmen: For it doth now appere that sondry Personages have delt herin; and when it shall appeare more manifestly, it shall increase our Indignation ageynst hir, if she will forbeare to utter it.[67]

1. Lady Katherine Grey.

2. Lady Jane Grey.

3. Lady Mary Grey.

4. Bradgate Park.

5. Henry VIII.

6. Mary Tudor, queen of France and duchess of Suffolk.

7. Edward VI.

8. Mary I.

9.   Elizabeth I.

10.   Edward Seymour, earl of Hertford.

11. Hampton Court Palace.

12. Tower of London.

13. John Hales, *A Declaration of the Succession of the Crowne Imperiall of Ingland* (1563).

14. Mary, Queen of Scots.

15. James VI of Scotland and I of England.

16. Salisbury Cathedral.

17. Tomb of Lady Katherine Grey and Edward Seymour, earl of Hertford, Salisbury Cathedral.

She also requested Warner to send for Elizabeth Sentlow and 'deale with hir, that she may confess to you all hir Knowledg in the same matters'.[68] Although Katherine was interrogated on 22 August, Warner conceded that 'she will confess nothing'.[69] Elizabeth Sentlow was incarcerated in the Tower for six months as a result of failing to disclose her knowledge of Katherine's clandestine marriage.[70]

Upon receiving a letter from Elizabeth ordering Hertford's return to England, Throckmorton:

> resorted to the Earl of Hertford's lodging, and declared her pleasure for his immediate return, who answered that he was sick in bed of a fever, and was grieved that he could not with all diligence perform her commandment, and trusted that she would not interpret the worse if he delayed his setting forward for three or four days.[71]

Throckmorton subsequently informed Cecil that the earl intended to return to England 'as soon as possible' and gave the impression of being 'very ignorant' as to why the queen had requested his return.[72] When Elizabeth's summons was issued, it was initially believed:

> that the Queen intended no evil to him or Lady Catherine, but on her own account desired to have him in England, in order that it might be decided by law that the Lady Catherine was his wife, whom he had married for his pleasure, and therefore that she [the queen] might legally marry the Lord Robert for her's

because she had no desire to marry anyone else.[73] This interpretation was to prove misguided, for Elizabeth had no intention of marrying Dudley, or permitting Hertford and Katherine to live as man and wife.

Upon Hertford's return from France, having been arrested at Dover, 'he was examined and cast into the Tower'.[74] Machyn noted that, on 5 September, 'was browth to the Towre the yonge yerle of Harford from the cowrte, a-bowtt ij of the cloke at afternone he cam in-to the Towre'.[75] Incarcerated in the Tower, both Hertford and Katherine were at the mercy of the queen. Following his imprisonment, the earl was questioned about the marriage. Writing to Throckmorton on 21 September, Peter Osborne believed that no marriage would be proven to have taken place since Katherine and Hertford 'agree not in the circumstances'.[76]

The scandal of Katherine's marriage attracted international attention. On 26 September, the papal nuncio John Francis Commendone wrote to Charles Borromeo, archbishop of Milan:

> the Earl of Hertford, who married Mylady Catherine [Grey], that was afterwards taken and clapt in the Tower, returned of his own accord from France to England, and forthwith was made prisoner, and that it is thought his life is in peril, as also his wife's; which perchance may give occasion for more consideration of what I wrote on the 4th [*sic*, 5th] touching the Queen of Scotland, because this Mylady Catherine is of the house of Suffolk, and stands next to the Queen of Scotland in succession to the throne.[77]

The following day, Commendone wrote to the cardinal of Mantua, reporting:

> that the Earl of Harfort [*sic*], who married Mylady Catherine, sister of the late Mylady Joan [*sic*], that was proclaimed Queen of England in opposition to Queen Mary [I], has returned from France to England, and has forthwith been put in prison, and that both the Countess's own life and her husband's are in jeopardy.[78]

Although her marriage was now a cause célèbre, Katherine was unaware of gossip about it 'bycause she hath long been and now is a close prisoner in the tower of London'.[79]

The secrecy of the Hertford–Grey marriage led to questions about its validity. Diana O'Hara has noted that 'in purely clandestine unions the element of dishonesty and secrecy implied in such conduct exposed the parties to criticism, and by implication extended to compromise the honesty of those involved'.[80] Elizabeth's belief that Katherine's marriage threatened her security as queen is explicable given that clandestine marriages 'created possibilities for political maneuvering, allowing members of noble families to strengthen their claims to the throne through intermarriage'.[81] When Katherine and Hertford were interrogated, the queen's commissioners asked a number of questions to ascertain whether their marriage was valid. For example, the couple were asked at what place and time they first agreed to marry; where their wedding took place, on what day and at what time; what manner of person the priest was; what book he used when officiating; whether communion took place or not; whether any prayers were said; what part of the chamber Jane stood in; and what apparel was worn by the earl, Katherine and Jane. They were also questioned about the circumstances in which they agreed to marry, including the places and times in which Hertford had discussed marrying Katherine with her friends and family. More intimate questions focused on who went first to bed; which side of the bed each party had lain on and who was first to rise out of bed; what Katherine had worn upon her head when they were in bed; and who helped both parties to undress.[82] In addition, Hertford's servants were interrogated about their knowledge of the marriage, while Katherine's stepfather Adrian Stokes and Hertford's brother Henry were also questioned.

The irregular nature of the marriage was reflected in the dispensing of the calling of banns, which usually required a licence. The public process of matrimony was initiated by calling for the banns to be read.[83] In 1576, Archbishop Grindal would note that an irregular marriage could involve the following: 'privy or secret contracts; any that have married or contracted themselves without the consent of their parents, tutors, or governors; any that have married without banns thrice solemnly asked.'[84] Aware that the validity of her union with Hertford was in doubt, Katherine showed the examiners the wedding ring that the earl had given her as evidence that the marriage had taken place. Ultimately, Katherine and Hertford's efforts to establish the validity of their marriage were unsuccessful because the officiating priest could not be located, while Jane's death meant that she could not testify as a witness. As de Quadra reported:

> the Queen claims that the marriage is not to be considered valid as there was no witness, although both Catharine and the Earl (Hertford) declare they are married. If they do not like to say, however, who were the witnesses, or that any other persons know of the marriage the act will be held illegal.[85]

Laura Gowing has suggested that, in early modern England, 'pregnancy was perceived as the natural punishment of whoredom: one frequent insult was "if she is not with child, she has deserved to be so"'.[86] Katherine's dishonourable behaviour – namely, her clandestine marriage and pregnancy – may well have served to highlight her unsuitability to be Elizabeth's successor, especially as she would receive most of the blame for her liaison with Hertford. As Gowing further noted, 'women were at the pivotal centre of the circulation of blame and dishonour for sex: responsibility was channelled entirely through them'.[87] Martin Luther himself had warned that:

> girls, too, are aware of this evil [lust] and if they spend time in the company of young men, they turn the hearts of these young men in various directions to entice them to love, especially if the youths are outstanding because of their good looks and strength of body. Therefore it is often more difficult for the latter to withstand such enticements than to resist their own lusts.[88]

Those who favoured the claim of Mary, Queen of Scots to the English succession and opposed Katherine's candidacy utilised these contemporary perceptions of female sexuality to argue for Katherine's exclusion from the succession on the grounds of her 'greate wickednes' and 'Whordome'. Her supporters, therefore, ignored the problematic circumstances of her clandestine marriage and instead drew attention to the birth of two healthy Protestant sons as proof of her suitability to succeed Elizabeth.

Turning away from the succession debate and to the immediate context, the Treason Act of 1536 had made it a treasonable offence to marry or 'deflower' a member of the royal family without the monarch's permission. Thus, given that Katherine and Hertford had broken the law, the queen was justified in ordering their arrest and incarceration. Moreover, Katherine's behaviour dishonoured Elizabeth because of the contemporary stipulation, noted earlier in this book, that a queen should only select virtuous attendants to serve her, because of the role these women played in mirroring the queen's virtues. In 1549 Sir John Cheke, who served as tutor to Edward VI, advised that 'chastititie, shamefastnes, and temperaunce, are the more peculier vertues of women, and the greater shame for women to offend therin'.[89] This contemporary expectation was especially pertinent to Elizabeth's household because of her unmarried state. Sara Mendelson and Patricia Crawford have argued that 'virginity conferred special status only upon extraordinary women, as the example of Queen Elizabeth shows', for Elizabeth's 'virginity served as a potent symbol of female power, enhancing the magical and religious aura that surrounded her'.[90] As queen regnant, moreover, Elizabeth also acted as governor of her household – a microcosm of the kingdom – and was thus responsible for maintaining a godly and virtuous establishment. Authors of contemporary prescriptive literature, such as the reformer and cleric Thomas Becon, advised guardians to ensure 'that there be no whoring nor uncleanness of body, no, not so much as a filthy word used in his house; but all cleanness and purity of life'.[91] Becon explained that 'a virtuous matron' should 'look unto her house' and 'be an example of all godliness and honesty to her household; to reprove vice sharply in her servants, and to commend virtue'.[92]

In marrying Hertford, Katherine was surely aware that it could lead to a loss of royal favour as a result of failing to secure the queen's permission to marry, and could end her chances of being recognised as heir presumptive. Perhaps she reasoned that love mattered more to her than political ambition. If that were the case, then her choice was to have painful consequences.

8

The Queen's Displeasure

The atmosphere at court was tense as the official investigation into the Hertford–Grey marriage got under way, especially since seasoned courtiers would have been well aware of the potentially fatal consequences of incurring royal disfavour. By contemporary standards, the queen's response to Katherine's unwelcome news was entirely reasonable. As has been noted, the Treason Act of 1536 had ruled that 'It shall be high treason for any man to espouse, marry or take to his wife' a relative of the monarch 'or to deflower any of them being unmarried' without having been granted 'the King's licence … under the great seal', and the Act also held that 'the woman so offending shall incur the like danger'.[1] Moreover, Elizabeth regarded herself as the guardian of her female attendants; thus, sexual immorality on their part reflected badly on her because her sexual reputation was affected by any stain on the reputation of a maiden of honour who lived in close proximity to the queen.[2]

Aside from the succession question and how it was affected by the unwelcome news of Katherine's marriage, there were two closely linked reasons for Elizabeth's fury. First, for political reasons, it was imperative that Elizabeth control the sexual activity of her courtiers, as an early modern patriarch was required to control the behaviour of their dependants in order to claim their own authority.[3] Other monarchs had reacted similarly to clandestine liaisons at court for this exact reason. Thus, when Henry Percy, heir to the earldom of Northumberland, was rumoured to be precontracted in 1523 to Anne Boleyn, 'a foolish girl yonder in the court',[4] Henry VIII swiftly instructed Cardinal Wolsey to have their betrothal terminated. Second, the scandalous nature of the queen's relationship with Robert Dudley – which had given rise to 'calumnies' about Elizabeth and was regarded by foreign ambassadors as not being 'consistent with her reputation and dignity'[5] – had already invited questions about Elizabeth's suitability as a monarch. Given that her political enemies at home and abroad regarded her as both illegitimate and heretical, accusations of sexual immorality only served further to weaken Elizabeth's authority. Such accusations only intensified following the suspicious death of Dudley's wife, Amy, in September 1560 and, the same year, lurid rumours of illegitimate children resulting from Elizabeth's affair with Dudley were in circulation.[6] As Martin Ingram noted, the criticism of Elizabeth's conduct perhaps explains 'the vigour with which she disciplined prominent members of her court who flouted the conventions of sexual decorum'.[7]

The revelation of Katherine's marriage occurred only three years after the publication of Knox's *The First Blast of the Trumpet Against the Monstruous Regiment of Women*, which had warned that 'wher soeuer women beare dominion, there must nedes the people be disordered, liuinge and abounding in all intemperancie, geuen to pride, excesse, and vanitie. And finallie in the end, that they must nedes come to confusion and ruine.'[8] Knox's views were shared by many of his contemporaries. By secretly marrying without royal permission, Katherine's actions raised major questions about whether Elizabeth was able to govern her household and, by extension, the kingdom effectively, especially in a political climate that was already marked by ambivalence to the concept of female monarchy. It was this challenge to her authority as queen, and what she feared to be a conspiracy to install Katherine as queen, that explains the vehemence of Elizabeth's response.

Additionally, the unsettled nature of the succession in 1561 accounts for Elizabeth's harsh actions, as the birth of a son to Katherine that

September arguably created an alternative royal heir. It is entirely possible that the queen had not yet reached a decision about her own marriage or whether she had a successor in mind should she die childless. In September, Elizabeth had an audience with William Maitland of Lethington, ambassador of Mary, Queen of Scots. The queen acknowledged that Mary 'is of the blood of England, my cousin, and next kinswoman, so that nature must bind me to love her duly, all which I … confess to be true'.[9] 'If her right be good she may be sure I will never hurt her',[10] but when Maitland asked Elizabeth to name the Queen of Scots as her heir, she confided that she:

> abhorred to draw in question the title of the crown, so many disputes have been already touching it in the mouths of men … when I am dead, they shall succeed that has most right. If the queen your sovereign be that person, I shall never hurt her; if another have better right, it were not reasonable to require me to do a manifest injury. If there be any law against her (as I protest unto you I know none, for I am not curious to inquire of that purpose), but if any be, I am sworn when I was married to the realm not to alter the laws of it.[11]

She asked Maitland whether 'I could love my winding-sheet? Princes cannot like their own children, those that should succeed unto them.'[12] Elizabeth confided that:

> I know the inconstancy of the people of England, how they ever mislike the present government and have their eyes fixed upon that person that is next to succeed … I have good experience of myself in my sister's time, how desirous men were that I should be in place, and earnest to set me up.[13]

While she refused to recognise Mary as her heir presumptive, the queen explicitly ruled out the possibility that Katherine would succeed her, explaining that while some of her possible successors have 'made declaration to the world that they are more worthy of it [the succession] than either she [Mary] or I, by experience that they are not barren but able to have children', nonetheless, neither Katherine nor her sister could 'succeed to the crown by reason of their father's forfeiture'.[14]

Elizabeth feared that Katherine's marriage was part of a wider conspiracy to depose her. Regarding the investigation into the Hertford–Grey marriage, Cecil reported: 'nobody can appear privy to the marriage, nor to the love, but maids, or women going for maidens. The Queen's Majesty thinketh, and so do others with her, that some greater drift was in this; but for my part I can find none such.'[15] Some suspected that the marriage had been arranged with the connivance of several gentlemen, including the earl of Arundel.[16] The earl of Bedford and the bishop of Salisbury were also rumoured to have been involved. De Quadra claimed that the marriage was arranged a year before, after the death of Amy Dudley, and implicated Cecil in it due to his enmity towards Dudley. The ambassador reported:

> that both Lady Catharine's marriage and the bringing over of the king of Sweden were arranged a year ago, after the death of Robert's wife, and that Cecil (who was then in great disgrace with the Queen and at enmity with Robert) was at the bottom of it in the fear that, in accord with common belief, the Queen would marry Robert and restore religion to obtain your Majesty's favour.[17]

Since Cecil was back in Elizabeth's favour, he had 'gradually and cautiously separated himself from these negotiations, and is now endeavouring to hush up and amend the past'.[18] De Quadra revealed the toll that the stress was taking on Elizabeth's health: 'To all appearance she is falling away, and is extremely thin and the colour of a corpse.'[19]

When Katherine's marriage to Hertford became public knowledge, his mother, the duchess of Somerset, promised Cecil that she had not known of their clandestine union.[20] In April of that year, the duchess had informed Cecil that she was content for her son to travel abroad and hoped that the queen could arrange a marriage for him with a suitable noblewoman. She was unaware that he had secretly married Katherine the previous year.[21] Her letter to Cecil in August 1561, following the disclosure of the clandestine marriage, reads as follows:

> Good Master Secretary, – Hearing a great bruit that my Lady Katharine Gray is in the Tower, and also that she should say she is married already to my son, I could not choose but trouble you with my cares and sorrows thereof. And although I might, upon my son's earnest and often protesting unto me the contrary, desire you to be an humble suitor on my behalf, that her tales might not be credited before my son did answer, yet, instead thereof, my first and chief suit is that the queen's majesty will think and judge of me, in this matter, according to my desert and meaning. And if my son have so much forgotten her highness calling him to honour, and so much overshot his bounden duty, and so far abused her majesty's benignity, yet never was his mother privy or consenting thereunto. I will not fill my letter with how much I have schooled and persuaded him to the contrary, nor yet will desire that youth and fear may help, excuse, or lessen his fault; but only that her highness will have that opinion of me as of one that, neither for child nor friend, shall willingly neglect the duty of a faithful subject. And to conserve my credit with her majesty, good master Secretary, stand now my friend, that the wildness of mine unruly child do not minish her majesty's favour towards me. And thus so perplexed with this discomfortable rumour, I end, not knowing how to proceed nor what to do therein. Therefore, good master Secretary, let me understand some comfort of my grief from the queen's majesty, and some counsel from yourself, and so do leave you to God.
> Your assured friend to my power,
> Ann Somerset[22]

Anne Seymour, duchess of Somerset, has traditionally suffered from a poor reputation. Historians have utilised Catholic works hostile to the duchess to inform their perception of her as a haughty, arrogant and grasping woman. An unknown Spanish chronicler writing during the 1550s described Anne thus:

The Protector had a wife who was prouder than he was, and she ruled the Protector so completely that he did whatever she wished, and she, finding herself in such great state, became more presumptuous than Lucifer. She thought that as her husband ruled the kingdom she ought to be more considered than the Queen [Katherine Parr], and claimed to take precedence of her.[23]

This latter claim was later embroidered by historians, including Katherine Parr's biographer Anthony Martienssen, to accuse the duchess of physically pushing Katherine out of her place at the head of entrances and exits at court.[24] None of Anne's contemporaries made such an absurd allegation against her, but it has proven enduring in informing subsequent perceptions of her character. In the nineteenth century, Strickland, for example, characterised the duchess as 'offensive and arrogant', and 'haughty' in having 'jostled a queen for precedency'.[25] In the twentieth century, Anne was condemned for being 'an intolerable woman whose pride was monstrous, a termagant who exercised much influence over her weaker husband by the lash of her tongue'.[26] Another historian repeated the myth of her rivalry with Katherine Parr: 'a proud, domineering woman, with a passion for precedence and an overwhelming interest in personal aggrandizement', Anne 'had never liked Katherine Parr ... her hatred became almost paranoiac'.[27]

However, recent scholarship has drawn attention to her extensive religious patronage, while recognising that Anne's 'reputation as an aggressively proud woman, who greatly influenced the governmental policies of the lord protector is largely a myth'.[28] This scholarship has also demonstrated that the duchess almost certainly did not encourage her husband, the Lord Protector, to have his brother, the Lord Admiral, executed in 1549, notwithstanding the Spanish chronicler's belief that 'he certainly would have been spared if it had not been for the wife of the Protector, who pressed the matter forward, and said to her husband, "My lord, I tell you that if your brother does not die he will be your death."'[29] Although she had known of her son's infatuation, she had attempted to dissuade his pursuit of Katherine but to no avail.

Elizabeth's fury towards the couple would hardly have lessened upon hearing that Katherine had given birth to a son on 24 September at the Tower. On 27 September, de Quadra wrote to the duchess of Parma explaining that 'Lady Catherine was delivered of a boy three days ago', while also confiding that the couple's failure to name any witnesses would likely result in their marriage being invalidated: 'Notwithstanding this, the Queen is not without anxiety about it.'[30] Commendone believed that 'the Queen is taking steps to have Mylady Catherine's son declared a bastard by Parliament'.[31] The child was named Edward, probably for his father, and was baptised in the Tower chapel of St Peter ad Vincula.[32] On 26 September, John Somer reported the birth of Katherine's son but noted the difficulties facing the couple:

> Lord Hertford and she agree upon the time, place, and company of their marriage, but cannot bring either witness or minister. They must either find out the minister, or determine what the law will say if it be a marriage or no. The matter lies chiefly, notwithstanding all determination, in the Queen's mercy.[33]

Katherine's contemporaries were well aware that the birth of a son that autumn only served to strengthen her claim to the throne, especially if it could be proven that her marriage was valid. Writing on 7 February 1562, Bishop John Jewel noted that, if Katherine's marriage to Hertford was valid, then their son 'will be brought up with the hope of succeeding to the crown'.[34] The queen was aware that Katherine 'has many supporters, among them, it is said, even Cecil, the Queen's first secretary, who governs all the state'.[35] As Victoria de la Torre related, Katherine's already strong claim to succeed Elizabeth according to Henry VIII's last will and testament was only strengthened by the birth of a Protestant male heir.[36] Indeed, Katherine's claim attracted support because of her evident fertility and because she was 'subsumed in her noble, virile Protestant husband'.[37] Hertford was the son of the Lord Protector Somerset, regarded by Protestants as having preserved England's imperial crown and godly faith during Edward VI's reign and, for this reason, London reportedly favoured the earl on the grounds of religion.[38]

The play *Gorboduc*, written by Thomas Sackville and Thomas Norton, was performed by the gentlemen of the Inner Temple before Elizabeth at Whitehall on 18 January 1562 and made reference to the contemporary succession question, with the accession of Mary, Queen of Scots being implied to subject England to the 'unnatural thraldom of stranger's reign'.[39] The play implied that Katherine was the rightful successor, as she was from a 'native line' and her claim was based on Henry VIII's will that was authorised by 'former law'.[40] The queen's response to the play is unknown, but she would not have taken kindly to its implied criticism of the possibility of Mary, Queen of Scots becoming queen of England, on account of her desire to maintain cordial relations with the Scottish queen.

Elizabeth's severe attitude towards Katherine is explicable given that Elizabeth favoured Mary's claim to the succession and she was also aware of the threat posed by Mary to her own security, in view of her French Catholic support.[41] Mary could have perceived the recognition of the legality of Katherine's marriage as a threat to her own claim; furthermore, Elizabeth was also then hoping to arrange a marriage between Mary and Dudley.[42] While some historians have doubted Elizabeth's sincerity in offering her favourite as a husband for the Scottish queen, Mary herself was initially receptive to the marriage because she hoped that marriage to Dudley would result in the official confirmation of her right to succeed Elizabeth.[43] In spite of the queen's opposition to the prospect of Katherine being named as her successor, however, many of her statesmen were determined to prevent a Catholic succession. De Quadra reported in January that William Rastell, a justice of the Queen's Bench, had travelled to Flanders 'to avoid signing an opinion which seven or eight lawyers are to give on the succession to the crown, declaring as it is suspected that there is no certain heir. All this is to exclude the Scotch Queen and Lady Margaret [Douglas].'[44]

On 10 February, Elizabeth wrote to Warner instructing him to escort both Katherine and Hertford to the archbishop of Canterbury's palace at Lambeth to answer questions about their wedding, as part of the 'Comission to examyn, inquire, and judge of the infamose Conversacion, and pretended Mariage betwixt the Ladye Katheryn Grey, and the Erle of Hertford'.[45] The queen explained that 'our Will is to have Justice'.[46] In that, she was not to be disappointed. The commission ruled that the Hertford–Grey marriage was unlawful and their offspring illegitimate. On 8 June, Sir Henry Sidney informed Throckmorton that 'the match between my Lord of Hertford and my Lady Katherine as I hear is judged advoutry, and the punishment thereof left to the Queen, as chief governor of ecclesiastical matters'.[47] On the same day, Cecil reported to Thomas Chaloner that 'judgment is given that the child born of the Lady Katherine was not legitimate, and the parents adjudged for penance to such fine as the Queen shall assess; but as yet they remain secure in the Tower, and the fine is not declared'.[48] The responses of Katherine and Hertford to the commission's verdict were not recorded.

In the seventeenth century, William Camden noted that Katherine 'was (as many thought) sharply handled'.[49] In the Tower, the couple contrived to meet, 'they having corrupted their Keepers'.[50] That Katherine and Hertford were permitted to meet indicates sympathy on the part of their jailers.[51] The Lieutenant of the Tower later acknowledged 'that he had admitted the Earl and Countess of Hertford to visit one another once on being over persuaded, and afterwards thought it was of no use keeping them apart'.[52] Hertford visited Katherine's rooms on the night of 25 May and again on the 29th, the earl having successfully bribed the guards George and Dalton to permit him to visit her; on both occasions, they made love.[53] When they attempted to meet on a third night, they were prevented by Katherine's rooms being locked by the guards.[54]

By the summer of 1562, Katherine would have been aware that she was pregnant with her second child. Hertford was summoned before the Court of Star Chamber for his 'threefold Crime: that he had deflowred a Virgin of the Bloud Royal in the Queen's House; that he had broken Prison; and that he had ravished her the second time'.[55]

The earl protested that 'he had lawfully contracted Marriage with' Katherine and had visited her in prison 'to comfort her, who mourned for the Sentence pronounced, and had payed his Marriage-debt'.[56] Hertford was punished by being fined the exorbitant sum of £15,000, although he was not required to pay all of it, as he would note in a statement in 1573:

For Mr. Secretary Walsingham, who desired a Note of the somme already paid in.

The somme set upon me in the Star-chamber was fivetyne thousand pounds, my land never being distreined therfore, tyll a litle before my coming to the Tower. At what tyme her Majesty released ten thousand pounds of the fyvetyne thowsand. After, when I was at Tower, and made sute for the release of my poore Tenants pitifully distreined for the remain demaunded, wch was fyve thowsand pownds, her Majesty sayd she would have one thowsand payd afore she would releaze any part of the sayd five thowsand pounds. Whereupon was payd in, one thowsand one hundred, fourscore and seven pounds (£1187). Shortly after, her Majesty cut off one thowsand pownds more. So as ther remaineth to be payd tow thowsand eight hundred and thirtyne pownds (£2813) which my trust is her Ma'ty will eyther wholy cut off or at the lest, the greatest part; if it may please her Ma'ty to remember the whole somme was first set but for terror, as also my humble retourne out of France upon the first cawll, my patient abiding her Maty's heavy displeasure in prison ten years lacking one moneth, my sondry grete losses in the sayd space, by my officers, and lastly, sithense her Maty's most happy favor restored, my diligent attendaunce and arredinesse these full six years, to do any service commaunded which I shall be more able to perfourme when I may find some frute of her Maty's favorable speaches and good opinion; her Maty's gratious dealing in this behaulf being more worth unto me then ten tymes the valew of the remain. Otherwise contrary to my owne disposition I shallbe enforced to leave her Maty's comfortable presence by renewing my sute of travel, wherby, in letting my land to most advantage, abating my maintenance, I may take order to pay my credit at home and at my retourne be able to serve her Maty, whear now for want I can not shew my affectionate mind if her Maty should any wayes employ me.[57]

Despite her loss of royal favour, Katherine's cause continued to attract the attention of councillors, courtiers and diplomats in view of Elizabeth's ongoing failure to resolve the succession question. The medium of portraiture testifies to this interest in the countess of Hertford and her claim to the succession during the early and mid-1560s. Portraiture was utilised by Katherine's supporters in an attempt to secure her recognition as heir presumptive.

During the period of her imprisonment, a miniature of Katherine with her eldest son Edward, Lord Beauchamp, was painted by the Flemish miniaturist Levina Teerlinc, who served as a painter at Elizabeth's court. It is held at Belvoir Castle, residence of the duke of Rutland. Full-sized versions of the miniature are held at Syon House, Audley End, Petworth House, Warwick Castle and Hever Castle. The timing of the portrait's creation – 1562/63 – is significant, occurring as it did after the queen had ordered the ecclesiastical commission to declare Katherine's marriage to Hertford invalid. The image depicts the mother as Madonna carrying the Lord's anointed, the future king of England, and copies of the portrait were made, probably to strengthen Katherine's claim to the throne.[58] As Martin Spies has highlighted, the miniature features Katherine in the roles of wife and mother by drawing attention to the white cap covering her hair, her husband's miniature and her rings, all of which indicate her married status.[59] It proclaims the validity of Katherine's marriage and rejects the bastardisation of her son, with the countess presented as transmitting her dynastic claim to Edward according to Henry VIII's will.[60] The miniature was commissioned to commemorate the couple's union, their offspring and the consequences of the marriage for the line of succession, and can be viewed as 'a legitimation strategy campaigning for the validation of her controversial marriage and the recognition of her son as the lawful heir to her place in the line of succession as the senior representative of the House of Suffolk'.[61] That John Hales published his tract arguing for Katherine's dynastic claim to the throne in 1563, at the same time or shortly after the creation of the miniature, only served to strengthen Katherine's claim to succeed Elizabeth. It is significant that full-sized versions of the Belvoir miniature were created during the seventeenth century, which testifies to the determination of Katherine's descendants to honour and remember her claim to the throne of England.

In spite of her disgrace, Katherine's claim to succeed Elizabeth became an increasingly contentious issue during the early and mid-1560s. In the autumn of 1562, Elizabeth fell ill with smallpox and rumours of her imminent death plunged the succession into crisis in view of its unsettled state. De Quadra reported on 16 October that:

> the Queen has been ill of fever at Kingston, and the malady has now turned to small-pox. The eruption cannot come out and she is in great danger. Cecil was hastily summoned from London at midnight. If the Queen die it will be very soon, within a few days at latest, and now all the talk is who is to be her successor.[62]

The ambassador alluded to the lack of agreement among the queen's councillors about which claimant had the most right to succeed Elizabeth if she were suddenly to die:

> her Council was almost as much troubled as she, for out of the 15 or 16 of them that there are there were nearly as many different opinions about the succession to the Crown. It would be impossible to please them all, but I am sure in the end they would form two or three parties and that the Catholic party would have on its side a majority of the county, although I do not know whether the Catholics themselves would be able to agree, as some would like the queen of Scots and others Lady Margaret, who is considered devout and sensible.[63]

On 25 October, de Quadra imparted that, in the midst of crisis talks about the succession at Hampton Court:

> the Council discussed the succession twice, and I am told there were three different opinions. Some wished King Henry's will to be followed and Lady Catharine declared heiress. Others who found flaws in the will were in favour of the earl of Huntingdon. Lord Robert, the earl of Bedford, the earl of Pembroke, and the duke of Norfolk with others of the lower rank were in favour of this. The most moderate and sensible tried to dissuade the others from being in such a furious hurry, and said they would divide and ruin the country unless they summoned jurists of the greatest standing in the country to examine the rights of the claimants, and in accordance with this decision the Council should then unanimously take such steps as might be best in the interests of justice and the good of the country.[64]

The ambassador's report indicates that Katherine's claim to succeed the queen continued to enjoy support from some of Elizabeth's councillors, but it also suggests the grounds on which others viewed her claim as problematic. Some councillors argued that Henry VIII's will was fraudulent as it had not been signed with the king's own hand but instead endorsed with a dry stamp, thus barring Katherine from succeeding.[65] In his study of the early Elizabethan succession question, Levine suggested that 'who possessed the prior right to the succession was dependent upon whether or not the will of Henry VIII was valid'.[66] The anti-Suffolk succession tracts alleged that the will had to be signed with the king's own hand in order for it to be valid, and claimed that the will had merely been stamped after Henry VIII's death rather than having been signed by him.[67] Maitland viewed the king's will as a 'dissembled and forged signed testament', and argued that 'the publishing of so many exemplifications of King Henries supposed will' were 'not of so great force in lawe as to serve for the recoverye of any thing, ether reall or personall'.[68] However, if – as Katherine's supporters claimed

– the king's will was authentic, then Katherine had the best claim to succeed Elizabeth.[69]

Those who favoured Katherine's claim had to consider whether the marriage between her grandparents Charles Brandon and Mary Tudor was valid, in terms of whether the duke's marriage to Margaret Mortimer had been annulled.[70] John Hales claimed that Brandon had obtained an annulment on the grounds of his pre-contract to Anne Browne, whereas supporters of Mary, Queen of Scots argued that he had not been pre-contracted to Anne or had carnal copulation with her at the time of marrying Margaret; however, Clement VII had issued a bull in 1528 affirming that Brandon had obtained an annulment from Margaret on grounds of affinity and consanguinity, granted by the archdeacon of London, and also held that Brandon's children with both Anne Browne and Mary Tudor were legitimate.[71]

That Elizabeth's imminent death was anticipated in the autumn of 1562 is suggested by the actions of conspirators with regard to the succession. At this time, a plot led by Arthur Pole came to light that planned for Mary, Queen of Scots to marry one of Pole's brothers and for her to ennoble him as duke of Clarence, perhaps with a view to placing Mary on the English throne.[72] On 17 October, de Quadra reported that 'Arthur Pole with two of his brothers and his brother-in-law Fortescue, were taken on trying to escape to France, and it is likely to go hard with them'.[73] The previous month, Pole intended 'to leave England on pretext of religion, but the truth is that he is going to try his fortune and pretend to the Crown with the help of the Catholics here'[74] for, as a descendant of George, duke of Clarence, Pole could stake a claim to the English throne. He unsuccessfully attempted to win support from both the Spanish and French ambassadors, before he and his brother Edmund applied for aid from the duke of Guise, uncle of Mary, Queen of Scots.[75] In October, Pole and his brother were arrested; some months later, they were convicted of treason and imprisoned in the Tower. In the following century, it would be remembered that:

God was pleased in a very good time to discover this Plot. For had they gone thither and discovered their intents, it had (if God had not powerfully opposed it) not only animated the Guises to have seconded them, and furnished them with Men and Money, but having returned into Wales, they would have gathered great Forces to augment their Numbers, and put the Queen to the incomparable Trouble and Danger of a Civil War.[76]

Even after the queen's recovery from illness, the climate of anxiety regarding the succession continued to linger. In November, a meeting took place at the earl of Arundel's residence, attended by the duke of Norfolk and others. They were reported to favour Katherine as the queen's successor, Norfolk 'perhaps with the idea that one of his little daughters may in time be married to Lady Catharine's son'.[77] When she learned of the meeting, Elizabeth 'wept with rage' and rebuked Arundel. The earl 'told her that if she wanted to govern the country by passion he could assure her that the nobles would not allow her to do so'.[78]

In response, the queen took steps to weaken support for Katherine's claim. The earl of Lennox – husband to Lady Margaret Douglas, niece of Henry VIII – was released from the Tower, having been imprisoned for what Elizabeth viewed as a treasonous attempt to match his son Henry, Lord Darnley, with the widowed Mary, Queen of Scots. His liberation:

has two objects, first, to hinder Lady Catharine by providing a competitor, and secondly, to give a little satisfaction to the catholics who are desperate at Lady Margaret's misery, and place all their hopes in the queen of Scots and the husband she may choose. By giving them some small hope that the succession may fall to Lady Margaret and her son they may cool somewhat towards the queen of Scots. All this is convenient for the Queen, who wants to have the power to declare her own successor when she likes.[79]

The possibility of Elizabeth's death that autumn only had the effect of increasing her councillors' determination to settle the succession. On 28 January 1563 the Commons petitioned the queen at Whitehall, speaking of how 'almighty God to our great terror and dreadful warning lately touched your highness with some danger of your most noble person by sickness', and beseeched her to marry and produce an heir to avoid 'certain and utter destruction' of the realm, namely:

> the great dangers, the unspeakable miseries of civil wars: the perilous intermeddlings of foreign princes with seditions, ambitions, and factious subjects at home; the waste of noble houses; the slaughter of people; subversion of towns; intermission of all things pertaining to the maintenance of the realm; unsurety of all men's possessions, lives, and estates; daily interchange of attainders and treasons.[80]

Thomas Norton's petition before assembled MPs alluded to the queen's recent illness and the dangers posed by a Catholic succession in the person of Mary, Queen of Scots.[81] In his speech for the House of Commons, Sir Ralph Sadler declared that while he 'cannot say who hath the best and most just title to succeede the Q. majestie in her imperiall crowne', he had 'a gret mislyking to be subject to a foreyn prynce, a prynce of a strange nacion' and protested that Mary's accession would be 'unnaturall', especially given that 'Englishmen hath alwayes so moche detested the regiment of straungers'.[82] Furthermore, Sadler believed that Mary was barred from succeeding because she was 'a straunger [and] by the lawes of the realme, as I understand, she cannot inherite in Englande'.[83]

English Protestants sought to exclude both Mary, Queen of Scots and Margaret Douglas, countess of Lennox, from the succession, but because there were as yet no legal grounds for excluding a claimant from the succession solely due to their religious affiliation, Protestant pamphleteers produced other arguments (namely, English laws of inheritance) to prove that neither woman could legally succeed to the throne.[84] Describing in his 1563 speech his experience in Scotland of attempting to arrange a marriage between Edward VI and the infant Mary, Queen of Scots, Sadler used Scottish ambivalence to the proposed marriage to conclude that, if the Scots would rather suffer 'the extremyte of the warres and force of England, then they wolde consent to have an Englishman to be their kyng', why then should the English 'yelde to their Scottishe superiority, or consent to establish a Scotte in succession to the crowne of this realm, contrary to the lawes of the realme, and therby to do so grate an injurye as to disinherite the next heire of our owne nacyon'?[85]

In response to her councillors' request, Elizabeth promised to consult on the matter of the succession, 'as cause of conference with the learned shall show me matter worthy utterance for your behoofs so shall I more gladly procure your good after my days than with my prayers whilst I live be mean to linger my living thread'.[86] On 7 February, de Quadra reported that:

the nobles are divided on the subject of the succession, as the enemies of Lord Robert see that she (the Queen) would really condescend to appoint Lord Huntingdon her successor, and that this would be opening the door to the marriage with Robert and put the kingdom in his hands, they have most of them met with the earl of Arundel and the majority are inclined to assist Lady Catharine. When the opportunity arrives I think they will confine themselves to excluding Huntingdon, and after that is done each one will follow his own bent.[87]

Elizabeth responded that:

the matter required further consideration, and, with that, turned her back on them and entered her own apartment. The lords afterwards went to her and proposed the same, whereat she was extremely angry with them, and told them that the marks they saw on her face were not wrinkles, but pits of small-pox, and that although she might be old God could send her children as He did to Saint Elizabeth, and they (the lords) had better consider well what they were asking, as, if she declared a successor, it would cost much blood to England. Notwithstanding all this, however, they pressed her still to do it, and she said she would consider the matter and they were to come to an agreement. I believe they wish to do this some day this week, but it is clear that she is determined not to nominate a successor, and she will not do so.[88]

The ambassador believed that 'there are so many antagonistic claims none of which can be satisfied without offending the others'.[89] By March, de Quadra had learned of a rumoured plan 'to reduce the succession to the crown to four lines or families in the kingdom, leaving to the Queen the nomination of the one that has to succeed her out of these four. It is a trick of Cecil's so that it shall fall where he wishes.'[90] He reported Cecil's support for Katherine's claim, noting that Cecil desired:

to give the crown to the earl of Hertford ... but the adherents to such a course will be weak in comparison to the Catholic party who favour the queen of Scotland, as some of the heretics side with Huntingdon and some have no fixed plan, but will follow the strongest.[91]

Towards the end of the 1563 parliamentary session, the MP John Hales wrote and circulated a tract entitled *A Declaration of the Succession of the Crowne Imperiall of Ingland*. He argued that, according to the will of Henry VIII, Katherine, 'the leading Protestant claimant', was Elizabeth's successor. Her claim was legally binding given that the king's will had been enacted into law.[92] *A Declaration*, more than any of the other succession tracts in circulation during the 1560s, went the furthest in arguing for the legality of Katherine's claim to succeed Elizabeth, endorsing it according to Henry VIII's will and 'the common Lawes of this Realme'. Hales criticised the findings of the original commission and proclaimed the validity of the Hertford–Grey marriage in line with 'the lawe of nature, Godd's lawe, and the common lawe', Lord John

Grey and Hales having sent Robert Beale abroad to consult learned men in Europe about the marriage.[93]

In his tract, Hales also argued that foreigners (namely, Mary, Queen of Scots and her heirs) were barred by common law from succeeding to the English throne. Hales, and other opponents of Mary, maintained that she could not succeed Elizabeth because she was Scottish and thus an alien; English law stipulated that a foreigner, or person born out of allegiance to the English monarch, could not inherit property within the realm.[94] As Hales explained, 'the Scottish Quene is not the Kinge of Ingland's child; nor was borne in the Kinge of Ingland's Alleigaunce; nor yet come of Father and Mother in the Faythe and Alleigaunce of the Kinge of Ingland; nor is a Free-Woman in Ingland', and so, by law, 'she can not inherite in this Realme'.[95] Thus 'the Scottishe Queene can make justly, by the Lawes of Ingland, no Clayme to the Crowne. Wherefore? bycause she hath no Right in Law, nor Reason.'[96] Hales put forward evidence to demonstrate that Henry VIII had made a will 'according to the Statute', thus barring 'all others' from succeeding.[97] Hales rejected attempts to discredit Henry's will by arguing:

Kinge H. made a Will; sith it appearethe by the Testimony and Subscription of the xj Witnesses, that it was signed with his owne Hand; sith it was so praeferred by the Executors; sith it was as his Will enrolled in the Chauncery, and published under the Great Seale of Ingland, wherein it was written, that it was signed with his owne Hand; sith the Particle, and the Record therof be without Order destroyed, and all the other Wills burnt; and sith there can come forth no suche Witness to disprove it, as the Law admitteth.[98]

In addition to setting out why Mary could not succeed to Elizabeth's throne, Hales explained that Margaret, countess of Lennox – allegedly favoured by Mary I as her successor – was also disqualified from the succession on account of her parentage (her father was Scottish, leaving her with divided loyalties) and because of her illegitimacy, since her father 'had another Wife livinge' when he married Margaret Tudor, dowager queen of Scots.[99] Hales viewed the rumour that Charles Brandon had been married to Margaret Mortimer when he wed Mary Tudor as 'a mere Slaunder, growen altogether upon Malice' and acknowledged that, even if it were true, it had no bearing on Katherine's place in the succession, for it concerned only the legitimacy of Charles' daughters Frances and Eleanor, neither of whom were named in Henry VIII's will as possible successors.[100] Hales believed that both of Charles' daughters were 'borne in lawfull Matrimony' and, as a result, that Katherine was Elizabeth's heir presumptive 'both by Kinge H. his Will, and also by the Common Lawes of this Realme'.[101]

When Elizabeth discovered the tract, she was incandescent with rage. As Cecil explained, Hales:

> had secretly made a book in the time of the last Parliament wherein he hath taken upon him to discuss no small matter, viz., the title to the Crown after the Queen's Majeste. Having confuted and rejected the line of the Scottish Queen, and made the line of the Lady Francis mother to the Lady Catherine only next and lawful. He is committed to the Fleet for this boldness, specially because he hath communicated it to sundry persons.[102]

Hales' tract endangered Elizabeth's plan to marry Mary, Queen of Scots to Dudley and ran the risk of worsening the queen's relations with Mary.[103] In many respects, in view of the publication of Hales' tract, the timing of Katherine's second pregnancy could not have been worse. This, coupled with the fact that her supporters had meddled in the succession debate, ended any hope of the queen reconciling with the countess of Hertford.[104]

In his diary, Machyn recorded the birth of Katherine's second son: 'The x day of Feybruary was browth a-bed within [the] Towre with a sune my lade Katheryn Harfford, wyff to the yerle of Harfford, and the god-fathers wher ij warders of the Towre, and ys name was callyd Thomas.'[105] From the perspective of her supporters, the birth of a second son strengthened Katherine's claim to succeed Elizabeth.

Despite the official ruling that the Hertford–Grey marriage was unlawful, Katherine remained an attractive candidate in view of the lack of
progress made with regard to the queen's marriage. Protestant reformation was linked across Europe with a drive to enthrone godly kings,
and by extension, to disallow female rule, and so this desire for a godly
king intensified during Elizabeth's reign, as her Protestant councillors
envisioned a godly male monarch ruling in tandem with his godly male
councillors.[106] On 14 July 1561, Cecil had written to Throckmorton
praying that 'God send our mistress a husband, and by him a son, that
we may hope our posterity shall have a masculine succession.'[107] Two
years later, such a hope had only become more pressing. Those who
favoured Katherine's claim did so on the basis that she was 'a Protestant
claimant whose blood claims to the crown were, in this context, vali-
dated by her marriage to a Protestant male of similar standing and by
her status as the mother of sons (virility married to fertility)'.[108]

The onset of plague in London in the summer of 1563 led the queen
to order the release of Hertford and Katherine from the Tower. Warner
informed Cecil in September that Katherine's pet monkeys and dogs
had damaged the furnishings in her accommodation.[109] Following her
removal from the Tower, Katherine and her younger son were placed
under house arrest in the custody of her uncle Lord John Grey at Pirgo
in Essex, while her husband was taken to his mother the duchess' house
at Hanworth with his elder son. Hertford gave Katherine a mourning
ring engraved with a death's head and the words 'While I lyved, yours'.
They never saw each other again.[110] The Privy Council issued a letter to
Lord John at the end of August informing him of Katherine's imminent
arrival in his household:

... the appointed removal of the Lady Catherine Grey from the
Tower to his custody is in consequence of Her Majesty's compassion-
ate desire to place her out of danger of the plague by which the Tower
is now environed, which privilege Her Majesty has upon much
humble suit also granted to the E[arl] of Hertford, meaning not that
she should be at any further liberty thereby, but only to be free from

the place of danger. Her Majesty thought it best, in respect that his Lordship is a nobleman and of grave consideration to regard any trust committed to him, and also the uncle of the said Lady Catherine, to commit her to his custody. Her Majesty's pleasure is further that the said lady shall remain with him and his wife as in custody during her Majesty's pleasure; nor is she to have conference with any person not being of his Lordship's household without their knowledge; which Her Majesty meaneth her to understand and observe as some part of her punishment, and therein Her Majesty meaneth to try her disposition towards obedience.[111]

The same letter also advised Lord John to ensure that his niece's:

demeanour in his Lordship's house is the same as if she were in the Tower until she may attain more favour of Her Majesty, for it is true that Her Majesty meant no more by this liberty than to remove her from the danger of the plague, and so they pray his Lordship to let her plainly understand.[112]

Katherine's correspondence with her husband after their release from the Tower and during the years that followed provides evidence of the deep love and affection that existed between the couple, while shedding light on the pain that both parties felt as a result of their enforced separation. When Katherine and Hertford were moved out of the Tower some months after the birth of their second son in 1563, Katherine wrote to her husband thus:[113]

No small joye, my Deare Lorde, is it to me the comfortable understanding of your mayntayned helth. I crave of God to let you susteine, as I doute not but he wyll; you neyther I havyng any thinge in thys moste lamentabyll tyme so much to comforte by pytyfull absense each other wyth, as the hearing, the seaking and contynuance thereof in us both. Though of late I have not byn well, yet now, I thank God, pretely well, and longe to be merry with you as you do to be with me.

… I say no more but be you merry as I was heavy when you the third time came to the door and it was locked. Do you thynke I forget old fore-past matters? No surely I can not, but bear in memory far many more than you think for. I have good leisure so to do when I call to mind what a husband I have of you and my great hard fate to miss the viewing of so good a one.[114]

She referred to him as 'my good Ned' and signed the letter as 'Your most lovyng and faithful wyfe during lyfe, Katharine Hartford'.[115] Following her release from the Tower, Katherine travelled to Pirgo with her younger son, his nurse, two manservants and three ladies-in-waiting.[116] Katherine's uncle wrote to Cecil upon her arrival:

Good cowsigne Cecill, what cawse all we have to thincke ourselves bounden and beholdinge unto you, the livelye facte of your great friendshipp in the delivery of my Nyece to my custodye are sufficient pledges and tokens for our bondage unto you duringe our lives; and althoughe I can justlye lament the cawse of her imprisonment, yet can I not lament thus far forth her beinge there, becawse I see yt hathe ben the onelye means wherebye she hath seen her selfe, knowen God, and her dewtye to the Quene; which when it shall farther please the Quenes Majestie to make triall of, I dowbt not but my sayinge and her doinges shall accorde; in which meane time I shall accordinge to my Lord Roberts [Dudley] lettre, and yours, directed unto me, se all thinges observed accordinglie. Assure your selfe (cowsigne Cecill) She is a penitent and a soroful woman for the Quenes displeassr and most humblye and heartelye desires you to fynishe that your frendshipp begonne, for the obteyninge of the Quenes favor in the full remission of her faulte. This with my wyves hearte commendatyons and myen to you and my good lady (ower cousen) your wyfe, I byd most heart-ely farewell. From Pyrgo the 29th of August, 1563.

By yor lovyng Cousine
and assured pouer frynd dowryng lyfe
John Grey[117]

Evidently, both John and Katherine believed in the necessity of stressing Katherine's recognition of the offence of her clandestine marriage, which transgressed from 'her dewtye to the Quene'. In emphasising Katherine's penitence and sorrow, both clearly hoped that the queen would look kindly on her. That autumn, Katherine wrote to Cecil herself in a bid to attain Elizabeth's forgiveness, while thanking him for securing her and her husband's release from the Tower. Days after her uncle had written the above letter, Katherine put pen to paper:

Good cosyne cecill: after my very hartye commendacions to my good cosyne your wyfe and yow, wyth lyke thanks for your greate frendship showed me in thys my lords delyvery, and myne, wyth the obtaynyng of the Queens Maiesties most gracious faour thus farforth extended towards us. I can not but acknowledg my selfe bounden and beholdyng unto yow therfore, and as I am sure yow dout not of myne owne deare lords good wyll for the requitall therof to the uttermost of hys power, so I besich yow, good cosyne cecill, make the lyke accompt of me duryng life to the uttermost of my power, besecheng your farther frendshyp for the obtayning of the Queens Maties most graceous pardon and faour towards me, wych wyth upstretched hands and downe bente knees, from the bottom of my hart, most humbly I craue. Thus restyng in prayer for the Queens Maties long raigne ouer us, the forgevnes of myne offence, the short enioying of my owne deare lord and husband, wyth assured hope throughe gods grace and yowr good helpe, and my lord Robert, for the enioying of the Queens hyghnes faour in that behalfe: I byd yow, my owne good cosyne, most hartely farewell, from pyrgo the thred of September.
    yowr assured frend and cosyne to my small power
    Katheryne Hartford[118]

Katherine's mood seems to have alternated between hope and despair, and these shifts of mood are reflected in her letters as the months passed. On 20 September, her uncle wrote to Cecil explaining that Katherine was pining away as a result of the queen's displeasure:

My good cowsigne Cecill, the onely desire and care that my ladye hath of the Queenes Majesties favour enforsethe these fewe lines, as nature bindeth me, to put you in remembrance, of your offered frendshipp and great good will, alredye showed, to the full perfectinge of the Queenes Majesties favour in my neece. I assure you cowsigne Cecill (as I have written unto my lorde Robert [Dudley]) the thought and care she takethe for the wante of her Highenes favour, pines her awaye: before God I speake it, if it come not the soner, she will not longe live thus, she eatethe not above six morselles in the meale. If I saie unto her, "Good madam, eate somewhat to compfort your selfe," she faules a wepinge and goethe upp to her chamber; if I aske her what the cause is she usethe her self in that sorte, she aunswers me, "alas Unckell, what a liffe is this, to me, thus to live in the Queenes displeasure; but for my lorde, and my childerne, I wolde to God I were buried." Good cowsigne Cecill, as time, places, and occasion maye serve, ease her of this woofull greiffe and sorrowe, and rid me of this liffe, which I assure you grevethe me even at the hearte rootes. Thus besceachinge God in this his visitacion, to preserve us with his stretched owt arme, and sende us, merely to meete, I salute you and my ladie with my wives most hartey commendacions and mine. From Pirgo, the xxth. of September,

    by your lovyng cousin
    and assured pouer
    frynd dowryng my lyfe
    John Grey.[119]

On 7 November, Katherine wrote again to Cecil, thanking him:

for yowr contynewall shewynge of yowr good wyll towarde my owne good lord and me we bothe accompt owr selues verye muche beholdyng to yow we praye yow styll to extende that fauor towarde owr case and state we can not thynke owr selues enoughe bounde unto yow good master Secretarye. All we can do is to beare yow owr assured good wyll, and to praye for yow, and to wyshe yow healthe agayne and thus I leaue committyng yow wyth my cousigne yowr wyffe to god, to whom I praye make my louyng commendacyons.[120]

That day, Lord John also wrote to Cecil, acknowledging his many favours to Katherine and desiring his opinion of the enclosed copy of her petition to Elizabeth, which would be delivered to the queen by her favourite Robert Dudley. Katherine's petition was signed 'Your Maiesties most humble bounden and obedient subiecte' and in it she dared not ask for a pardon from the queen on account of her disobedient act of marrying without Elizabeth's permission. She spoke of her 'miserye' and 'continuall greife' due to the grievousness of her fault and the forgetting of her duty to the queen, for which she suffered 'great torment of minde', but nonetheless hoped for forgiveness on account of Elizabeth's 'mercyfull nature' and 'princelye pittie'.[121] In December, the countess followed up her previous letter with the following missive, which provides insights into what must have been an increasingly anguished realisation that, perhaps, Elizabeth would not forgive her for her offence:

What the long want of the Queens Maiestys accoustumed fauor towards me hath breade in thys myserable and wreched body of myne, god only knoweth, as I dayly more and more, to the torment and wastyng therof, do otherwyse feale then well able to exprese: wych if it shuld any long tyme thus contynew, I rather wyshe of god shortly to be buryed in the fayth and feare of hym, then in thys contynuall agony to lyve; as I haue wryten unto my lord Robert, so good cousyne Cycell, do I unto yow. I must confese I neuer fealte what the want of my prynces faour was before now, wych by yowr good means and the rest of my very good Lords ons obtayned I shall not requyre any of yow, if it faull through my default, to be means for the restetucyon therof: so myndfull, god wyllyng, shall I be not to offend her hyghnes, ths desyryng the contynuance of yowr frendshyp I most hartely byd yow farewell, good cousyne Cecyll, prayng yow to make my harty commendacyons to my cousyne yowr wyfe. from pyrgo the xiij of desember.

yowr poore cousyne and assured
frend to my small power
Katheryne Hartford[122]

It is significant that, even as she pleaded with Elizabeth for mercy, Katherine referred to herself by her married name, a striking illustration of her refusal to accept the official verdict that her marriage to Hertford was null and void and their children illegitimate. In fact, signing herself in such a manner was an act of defiance and arguably one that the queen would not have taken kindly to.

Meanwhile, Lord John wrote to Cecil supplying a full inventory of Katherine's apparel. Upon her arrival at Pirgo she was poorly furnished and in such dire financial straits that, at New Year, 'she had nothing to send any friend ... which had induced Lady Clinton to give Lady Gray a pair of silk hose, to present to Lady Knowles in Lady Katharine's name, as if from her'.[123] The inventory included, for Katherine's younger son, velvet caps, a russet taffeta hat, two coats (one in russet damask and the other crimson velvet), white cloth and red cloth to make him petticoats, as well as black velvet, bound with sables, to make a gown for Katherine, russet velvet to make a gown and kirtle, damask to make a night gown, crimson satin to make a petticoat, a petticoat of crimson velvet, a velvet hood, two pairs of black silk hose, black cloth to make a cloak, cambrics to make ruffs and handkerchiefs, and linen to make smocks.[124]

Dudley and Cecil requested Hertford to send £114 to Pirgo to defray his wife's charges while in the custody of her uncle.[125] The earl sought Dudley's assistance in obtaining a pardon from the queen so 'that we may be unburdened of her highness's intolerable displeasure, the great weight whereof hath sufficiently taught us never again to offend so merciful a princess'.[126] Dudley responded that 'he had moved the queen's majesty in his behalf, but he did not find her in the mood, at present, to grant his prayer'.[127]

In March, Lord John approached Cecil again in the hope of securing mercy for Katherine in 'her miserable and compfortlesse estate':

It is a great while, me thinckethe, Cowsine Cecill, since I sent unto you, in my Neeces behalfe, albeit I knowe, (opportunitie so servinge) you are not unmindfull of her miserable and comfortlesse estate. For who, wantinge the Princes favor, maye compt him selfe to live in any Realme; and becawse this time of all others hathe been compted a time of mercie, and forgevenes, I cannot but recommende her woe-full liffe unto you. In faithe, I wolde I were the Queenes Confessor this Lent, that I might joine her in pennaunce to forgeve and forget; or otherwise able to steppe into the pulpett, to tell her Highnes, that God will not forgeve her, unleast she frelye forgeve all the worlde. Thus restinge in hope of her Majesties further favor, shortlie to be extended, towardes my Neece, I committ you to Almightie god. From Pirgo the sixthe of Marche 1563.

    By your lovyng cousin
    and assured frynd,
    John Grey[128]

For daring to suggest that Elizabeth ought to forgive the couple as her Christian duty, in addition to his involvement in Hales' scheme, Lord John was briefly incarcerated in the Tower.

Katherine and her younger son were moved to Ingatestone to be placed in the custody of Sir William Petre, and in November 1564 Lord John died, officially from 'thought', but more likely gout. Katherine's elder son Lord Beauchamp remained with the duchess of Somerset at Hanworth, while Hertford was placed in the custody of Sir John Mason.[129] In June 1565, the Privy Council recommended that 'some remission of her majesty's displeasure be showed' to Katherine, following the unwelcome news that the Scottish queen intended to marry Henry, Lord Darnley, eldest son of Margaret, countess of Lennox – a marriage that would only strengthen Mary's claim to succeed Elizabeth and thus lead to 'perils' for both the English queen and her realm.[130]

Elizabeth ignored her councillors' request and her dislike of the Grey family would hardly have lessened when she discovered Mary Grey's secret marriage shortly afterwards. Katherine undoubtedly learned of her younger sister's disgrace that summer. The youngest Grey daughter clandestinely wed Thomas Keyes, who served as Elizabeth's sergeant porter, on 16 July at Whitehall Palace, attended by three of her cousins.[131] On 21 August, Cecil wrote to Sir Thomas Smith: 'Here is a unhappy chance and monstruoos. The Serjeant Porter, being the biggest gentillman in this Court, hath marryed secretly the Lady Mary Grey; the lest of all the Court. They are committed to severall [separate] prisons. The offence is very great.'[132] Evidently, Mary had failed to learn from Katherine's example; like her sister, she was condemned to house imprisonment, separated from her husband.

The following May, Katherine was moved from Ingatestone to Gosfield Hall, residence of Sir John Wentworth. Wentworth had initially sought 'to be excused from that service'.[133] In October of that year, Katherine wrote to Hertford's servant Anthony Penne from Gosfield regarding his obtaining a gold chain for her. She thanked Penne for the 'ffaythfullnes and trewe saruys' that he had always shown to her.[134] Katherine assured Penne that she was 'yowr ready frend both now and allways'.[135]

Although the duchess of Somerset had denied knowledge of her son's marriage, following their imprisonment she attempted to intercede for her son and Katherine, writing to Cecil to seek mercy for 'thys yowng couple'. She visited court after the imprisonment of Hertford and his wife to plead their suit, with her son acknowledging 'her long and troublesome suit for us, to our most gracious queen' in a letter to Dudley, now ennobled as earl of Leicester, from whom Hertford had also sought assistance.[136] The duchess continued, even after the couple's release from the Tower and placement under house arrest, to petition the queen, Cecil and Leicester for her son's release, doing so in January 1566, for example.[137] That letter illustrates the duchess' efforts on the couple's behalf:

Good master Secretary after thys long sylens and for that as yet myne old occasyon lettes [hinders] myne attendans, I have presumed by leter to renew my sute for my sonne to the Quenes Majesty, and have

lykewyse wrytten to my lord of Leycester, prayng you to sett in your
helpyng hand to ende thys tedyous sute: wherin for me to reson how
moch her Hyghnes desplesure ys to long lastyng, or how unmeate
yt ys thys yowng couple should thus waxe olde in pryson, or how
farre beter yt were for them to be abrode and lerne to serve, I wyll
not; but leave those and such lyke speches to the frendly settyng forth
of my good Lord and you; only my sekyng ys, that as ther ys none
other cause syns her Majesties regne but hath had some favorable
order or ende, so by your ernest conferryng and joynyng with my
good Lord, thys yowng couple may fele some lyke of her Majesties
plentyfull mercy; to the procurement wherof, the more ernest my
Lord and yow shall shew your selfes, the more shall you sett forth the
Queenes Majesties honor; and as a mother I must nedes say, the beter
descharge your callynges and credyte. And so restyng in prayer, that
God wold blesse your travell [travail] to some comfortable ende I take
my leve.

    Your assured lovyng freynd,
    Anne Somerset[138]

In view of the queen's belief that Katherine and Hertford had committed treason by marrying without obtaining her permission, it was
essential for Anne to couch her suit on her son's behalf in suitably penitent terms, as Lord John had in his letters to Cecil. The penalty for those
found guilty of treason – of which both the Grey and Seymour families
were all too aware – explained the urgency of requesting mercy from
Elizabeth. The duchess wrote to Cecil again in April in a bid to obtain
that mercy:

Good Mr. Secretary, yf I have let you alone all thys whyle I pray you
thynke yt was to tary for my L. Leycesters assystans, to whom as I
have now wryten to take some occasyon to do good in my sonne's
cause, so are thyese to pray you to provoke hym, and joyne with hym
to further the same; trusting the occasyon of thyse Holy Weke and
charytable tyme of forgevenes ernestly sett forth by hys Lordship

and you, wyll bryng forth some comfortable frute of relyve to the long afflycted partyes: wherin my Lord and you cannot go so farre but God's cause and the Quene's honor bedd you go farther. Thus moch I thowght good to wret as gevyng occasyon for my Lord and you to move the Quenes Maty to mercy, and not styll to suffre this cause alone to rest withowt all favor and forgevenes. I can nomore but ons agayn pray yowre ernest dealyng herein; and lykwyse that myne humble duty of thanks for Mr. Mychells passport may be donne to her Hyghnes, and so do leave you to God.

Your asured lovyng frynd,
Anne Somerset[139]

Mercy was a virtue traditionally associated with queenship. A 'natural' woman and queen should be 'lyke a mother' in her acts of mercy.[140] In his *An Harborowe for Trewe and Faithfull Subjectes*, which was a defence of Elizabeth's queenship, John Aylmer characterised the queen as possessing 'mervelous mercy and no rigour' and 'using correction without severitie, by sekyng the loste with clemencie, by governing wisely without fury, with weying and judging withoute rashness'.[141] As noted earlier, Elizabeth's predecessor Mary had been praised for her acts of mercy following the coup of 1553. It was perceived by contemporaries to be an integral aspect of successful queenship, and that perception is confirmed by the letters of the duchess of Somerset.

This prevailing association of queenship with mercy may explain why public opinion on Elizabeth's actions was mixed. Sir John Mason, a member of Star Chamber, reported in January 1563 that:

There be abrode both in the Cite, and in sondry other Places of the Realme, very brode Speaches of the Case of Therl of Hertford: Summ following theyre lewde Affections, and summe others of Ignorance make such talks therof, as lyketh them; nott letting too say they be Man and Wief, and whye sholde Men and Wief be lett [prevented] from coming together? Theise Speaches and others, as I am informed be very common.[142]

Historians have offered alternative interpretations of Elizabeth's treatment of Hertford and Katherine following her discovery of their marriage. In the nineteenth century, A.F. Pollard opined that, in her determination to ensure that the marriage was pronounced invalid, Elizabeth 'pursued the unhappy countess with vindictive hostility'.[143] Similarly, writing in 1911, Richard Davey alleged that Katherine was 'tormented' by the 'feline cruelty' of Elizabeth, while even Cecil denounced the queen's harshness.[144] He concluded that 'Elizabeth's persecution of Lady Katherine and Hertford was very nearly, if not quite, as unrelenting as Mary's treatment of Jane Grey and Guildford Dudley; but far less justifiable. Her methods were those of Julian and not of Nero; but quite as efficacious!'[145] This condemnation of Elizabeth's actions is in a sense a reflection of the contemporary hostility that the queen faced from some quarters for her treatment of the couple.

In the seventeenth century, Fuller characterised Katherine as a 'Lady of Lamentation'.[146] By contrast, Elizabeth's biographers have usually adopted more nuanced perceptions of her actions. Carole Levin has suggested that the queen's treatment of Katherine indicates that she felt threatened by her, since Katherine's marriage to Hertford was 'a real risk to Elizabeth' in view of the perception at court that Katherine was an heir to the throne.[147] Susan Doran noted that the queen adopted a severe attitude towards Katherine and her sons because she wished to maintain cordial relations with Mary, Queen of Scots, both because she favoured Mary's claim to the English succession and in view of her awareness of the threat posed by Mary to her own security.[148] Other authors have indicated that Katherine was herself to blame for her predicament. Ives, for example, believed that she had a 'propensity to allow emotion to rule her head'.[149]

During the period of Katherine's disgrace, the succession remained unsettled and the question of which candidate enjoyed the strongest claim continued to be controversial. Katherine's exile from court meant that she personally played no part in the succession debates, although she surely would have learned of the efforts of Hales and others to promote her claim to succeed Elizabeth. The proliferation of tracts during the 1560s sought to resolve the succession question. They also aimed to influence public opinion in a culture characterised by 'the constant buzz of people talking to each other: asking for news, swapping stories, exchanging views'.[150] The market for print was increasingly commercialised and 'the proliferation of written media was conspiring in the creation of a new world of information'.[151] The tracts variously identified either Katherine or Mary, Queen of Scots as the candidate with the strongest claim to be Elizabeth's successor. The Scottish queen herself viewed Katherine as 'her competitor'.[152] The succession tracts usually warned of the dangers of failing to nominate a successor, for example by alluding to the civil wars of the fifteenth century, involving 'bloudie battells that were of longe tyme'.[153] The question of the queen's successor was of such import because it 'shall be for the benefitt of the whole comonwelthe'.[154]

The *Allegations against the Surmised Title of the Queen of Scots and the Favourers of the Same* (1565) rejected Mary's claim on the grounds that she was an alien, while warning of the dangers of subjecting England to foreign rule.[155] In addition, the Scots were 'a people by custom and almost nature our enemies, thirsty of our blood, poor and miserable by their country and envious of our welfare'.[156] The *Allegations* alluded to 'servitude and bondage' experienced under foreign rule, as well as 'subiection'.[157] Mary's claim would be strongest if Scotland could be considered as being subject to England, and if there were 'no other person that had better title by statute, or else by the will of Kinge Henrie the Eight, then by being next of blood', she would enjoy a superior claim.[158] The tract also refuted the suggestion that Mary's marriage to Lord Darnley strengthened her claim to be Elizabeth's successor: 'that by the mariage to the lord Darnley the Quene of Scotte title is no waye betterid.'[159]

In 1566, in response to Hales' tract favouring Katherine's claim, the lawyer Edmund Plowden published *A Treatise ... Proving the Queen of Scots by her Birth is Not Disabled by the Law of England to Receive the Crown of England*, in which Plowden denied that Edward III's 1351 statute prohibiting aliens from inheriting in England applied to the succession.

While the inheritance rule and the statute applied to bodies natural, it did not apply to the Crown, the body politic and the succession.[160] Similarly, Bishop John Leslie claimed that the crown was a corporation and therefore it 'doth not descend according to the common course of private inheritance but goeth by succession as other corporations do'.[161]

Mary's supporters also continued to question whether Henry VIII's will was valid; if it was not, then the Scottish queen arguably enjoyed a stronger claim than Katherine to succeed Elizabeth. An anonymous treatise of 1566, perhaps Plowden's, held that the king's will was invalid because it was signed by dry stamp and not 'with his most gracious hand' and thus, 'that if his will in writing be not signed with his hand, it is insufficient to make the crown pass', 'the authority of the act is not executed and so the limitation of the crown by that will is void'.[162] Yet none of the authors of the tracts had ever seen the original document, as it was kept concealed.[163]

While Katherine's supporters, including Hales, denied allegations of her illegitimacy, those who regarded Mary as Elizabeth's lawful successor argued that Katherine was illegitimate and, as such, was barred from the succession. The anonymous author of the *Allegations in behalf of the high and mighty Princes, the Lady Mary, now Queen of Scots ... touching the succession of the Crown* (1565) claimed that Charles Brandon 'had then an other Wyfe lyvinge' (Margaret Mortimer) when he married Mary Tudor and thus had lived with Mary 'in Adultery'; as a result, Katherine, 'beinge comme of one not legitimatly borne, cannot inherite, or be capable of the Crowne'.[164] Charles' marriage to Margaret meant that his union with Mary was 'voyde, and so all the Issues cleerly Bastardes', and as a result of her illegitimacy, Katherine could not succeed to the crown because 'for the Honor and Dignitie of the Realme, whosoever shuld be worthy or capable of the Crowne, it is meete, that not onely they shuld be free from eny Stayne or Spotte, but also from all suspicion of eny'.[165]

Katherine's supporters countered such claims by noting that, even if Charles' daughters by Mary were illegitimate, this would not overturn Katherine's title by Henry VIII's will, which assigned the succession not to Frances but to her heirs.[166] Perhaps aware of this counterargument, the *Allegations* also asserted that Katherine was disqualified from the succession as a result of her 'greate wickednes' and 'Whordome', for which 'she hath deservyd grevous Punishment', namely falling into 'carnall company' with Hertford despite already being lawfully married to Herbert: 'she the Wife of one Man, did gyve her Body to be used of an other Man unlawfully'.[167] Her unlawful marriage meant that she had 'cut off all hope of havinge lawfull Issue by her to succeede and possesse the Crowne heerafter'.[168] Finally, in Mary I's reign, it had been rumoured that both Katherine and Mary Grey were disqualified from the succession as a result of their sister Jane's conviction and execution for treason: 'her sisters likewise, being themselves reproached with the same crime, are consequently excluded from the succession'.[169]

Despite the proliferation of tracts, contemporaries failed to reach a consensus on the matter of the queen's successor. In October 1566, law students at Lincoln's Inn held a disputation on the succession, finding that Mary, as an alien, could not legally 'succeed to the crown, even if she were the nearest in birth and the ablest'. As Maitland noted, the disputation 'ruled against the Quene my sovereign'.[170] This event was intended to influence the proceedings of the upcoming parliament.[171] That month, a pamphlet claiming to be a 'Common Cry of Englishmen' addressed the queen, requesting her to settle the succession question in Parliament to prevent the 'certain ruin and destruction' of England. The 'Common Cry' reads as follows:

> We speak not ... of any private matter but of that which greatly toucheth us all, and you with us all, we say, high and low ...
>
> ... if you O Queen do die ... void of issue and wanting a known successor, as the case now standeth, what good can continue? what evil shall not come? ...
>
> ... it is not your marriage, most noble Queen, which can help this mischief, for a certain ruin cannot be stayed by an uncertain means. It is uncertain whether you shall marry; it is uncertain whether you shall have issue in your marriage; it is uncertain whether your issue shall

live to succeed you ... But this is most certain, that unless the succession after you be, and that in time, appointed and ordered, England runneth to certain ruin and destruction. And this is what we most humbly beg for England's sake, without verily it may be doubted whether England will long be England: that is, that you with your High Court of Parliament do both appoint your next successors and also set the succession and the inheritance in safe and sure order ...

And if the Queen, either of timorousness to attempt a matter of so great weight or of any other singular respect, should seem not willing to hear and help, as we desire presently; then we turn our cry to you our Lords and Commons assembled now in Parliament. Though the delay made upon your last most godly request in this behalf [in 1563] did daunt and grieve the hearts of you and of thousands which loved you for your good attempt, yet assay again. The matter is worth the labour, and it is meet, and only meet, for your travail ... You know whether your last answer received was a delay or a promise. If it was no refusal, was it a promise? It is time to claim the performance ... Was it a delay, peradventure but to try whether you did heartily affect the thing desired? Show forth again that affection which the cause requireth. But what if it was a refusal then? ... look not for it to happen again. If it should hap, yet considering the peril that hangeth thereon, as you do know what your authority is, so bestow your wisdom and power to put your country out of such peril. Princes ... sometimes let slip that which would be done. Sometimes they profit not. Sometimes they neglect it. Sometimes they go astray. Then do not only wise councillors stand instead, but chiefly such great assemblies of such persons so authorized and therewith privileged as Parliament men are. That is the place of free speaking. Speak there and let your action agree with your title. You be in place to consider as things arise and to provide remedy. Regard this matter duly. Deal for it with the Queen dutifully ... Good princes, because they have their authority not without their parliaments and states, are counted not to rule without them, but with them. Yea, ofttimes to be ruled by them ...[172]

Before the parliament of 1566 took place, Cecil wrote privately:

> To require both marriage and stablishing of succession is the utter-
> most that can be desired … To require marriage is most natural, most
> easy, most plausible to the Queen's Majesty. To require certainty of
> succession is most plausible to all the people [but] is hardest to be
> obtained both for the difficulty to discuss the right and for the loath-
> someness in the Queen's Majesty to consent thereto … Corollary: the
> mean betwixt these is to determine effectually to marry, and if it suc-
> ceed not, then proceed to discussion of the right of the successor.[173]

On 26 October, the imperial ambassador Diego Guzmán de Silva
reported that the succession was still being discussed in Parliament, and
that Elizabeth:

> is extremely annoyed as she fears that if the matter is carried fur-
> ther they will adopt Catharine, both she and her husband the earl
> of Hertford being strong Protestants, and most of the members of
> Parliament are heretics, and are going on that course to maintain
> their own party. I have always pointed out to the Queen the grave
> difficulties which might result from such a nomination, and the peril
> in which she and her affairs would be if Catharine were appointed
> her successor, contrasted with her security if she had direct heirs. She
> quite understands it, and three days ago told me that on no account
> would she allow this nomination to be discussed.[174]

The ambassador had previously asserted that the duke of Norfolk
intended to support Katherine's claim, believing that Cecil had
encouraged Norfolk to do so 'with the idea that the daughter of the
Duke may marry Catharine's son (although they are both children)'.[175]
For the supporters of Mary, Queen of Scots, however, her claim to
succeed Elizabeth had arguably been strengthened in 1566 as a result
of the disgrace of both Katherine and her sister Mary, alongside
the birth of a son, James, in June of that year to the Scottish queen.

Notwithstanding this, de Silva was to claim that 'it would be much better for the queen of Scotland that it [Parliament] should be dissolved, as the members of the Commons are, as I have said nearly all heretics and adherents of Catharine', and noted that there was an 'artful plot in favour of Catharine'.[176]

Parliament was determined that the queen name a successor and, for that reason, on 11 November the imperial ambassador reported that:

the members of Parliament who had met, as I wrote your Majesty on the 4th inst., resolved the same day to petition the Queen by common consent to deal with the matter of the succession. She summoned them the next day to give them her reply, and made them a long speech, pointing out the dangers that might result therefrom to the peace and order of the country. This she enforced by examples, and said she was not surprised at the members of the Lower Chamber treating this matter like inexperienced schoolboys instead of as a matter of so great importance, but she marvelled greatly that the lords had concurred and joined them in such action. There were some of these lords, that when her sister was Queen came to her and offered help, urging her to endeavour to obtain the crown during her sister's life, and it might well be understood that if her successor were nominated there would be no lack of people to go on a similar errand to her to disturb the common peace, and if it was necessary she would say who these men were. Then turning to the Bishops who were present, she said, "And you doctors," (she did not call them Bishops) "who are so fond of making speeches on this subject, whilst some of you dared to say in past times, that the Queen, my sister, and I were bastards it would be much better if you looked after your own reformation, and gave a good example in your own lives and families, instead of interfering in such matters as this. The lords in Parliament ought to have shown you this, but since they have not done so, I will do it myself. I might well excuse myself from marrying in the face of pressure from all of you, but having in view the good of the country, I am determined to marry. It will be, however, with someone who will not please you, which has been partly my reason for avoiding it hitherto, but I will refrain no longer. Those who have shown most anxiety that I should marry, have helped me but little to do so now, because the man who is to be my husband is a foreigner, and will not think himself very safe in your hands, if I, your lawful Queen, am to be so thwarted, and I will not put up with it."[177]

Elizabeth dissolved Parliament on 2 January 1567. Two days after its dissolution, Maitland wrote a letter to Cecil declaring that, 'by the civill and common lawes, and by the common lawes of Inglonde', Mary was 'undoubtedlie heire to the crowne next after the issue of Henrye theight lawfullie begotten'.[178] He challenged the claim of Katherine's supporters that Mary was barred from the succession on account of her 'forreyn birth', acknowledging that there was a question of 'whether the realme of Scotland be forth of the homage and legeaunce of Englonde'.[179] Maitland regretted that the 'bokes and writinges conteyning anye discussion of titles' had influenced public opinion to the extent that there was now 'a settled opinion against my soveriegn to the advauncement of the ladie Katherines title'.[180]

During the succession debates of the 1560s, Katherine was little more than a cipher in view of the circumstances of her existence. As the years passed, with no evidence that she would be forgiven by the queen, and separated from her husband and eldest son with no hope of seeing them again, Katherine gave way to despair. It remains uncertain – especially prior to her marriage to Hertford – whether she had ever harboured ambitions to be recognised as Elizabeth's successor. If she had once dreamed of becoming queen of England in the event of Elizabeth dying without an heir of her own, by the mid-1560s any such ambition was surely eclipsed by the desire to be reunited with her beloved husband and eldest son. That hope, however, was destined to remain unfulfilled.

9

'An Incomparable Pair'

In February 1567, Katherine would have learned at Gosfield of the murder of Scotland's king consort Henry, Lord Darnley, in Edinburgh. The scandal of Darnley's death was amplified by the suspicion that his wife was involved in his assassination. Robert Dudley, earl of Leicester, decided to offer his support for Katherine's claim to the succession as a result of the scandal surrounding Mary, Queen of Scots. De Silva related that:

> on the night that the king of Scotland's death was known here Lord Robert sent his brother the earl of Warwick to the earl of Hertford, Catharine's husband, to offer him his services in the matter of succession, and Lord Robert himself went to see the duchess of Somerset, the Earl's mother, with the same object, and had made friends with both of them, contrary to his former action as he has shown signs of a desire to help the queen of Scotland.[1]

Irrespective of Elizabeth's attitude to the subject, the events of 1567 were generally perceived to improve Katherine's succession prospects as a result of a decline in the Scottish queen's fortunes.[2] At court, 'the heretics' – including Katherine's supporters – openly voiced the opinion that Mary had been involved in her husband's death in 'revenge for her Italian Secretary',[3] although Elizabeth 'cannot believe the queen of Scotland can be to blame for so dreadful a thing notwithstanding the murmurs of the people'.[4] Allegations of Mary's complicity were rumoured to be 'set afloat by people who desire to injure her, and make her odious in this country in respect to the succession', and Elizabeth was advised 'to be on the alert to prevent undue elation of the opposite party who were strong and might cause trouble, meaning that of Catharine [Grey]'.[5] Elizabeth shrewdly took this advice and showed no sign of forgiving Katherine, let alone naming her as her heir presumptive in the wake of the Scottish queen's fall from grace. The conditions of Hertford's incarceration were made stricter in December since, according to de Silva, 'they are possibly afraid of some movement in his interest, as I am assured that certain negotiations are afoot respecting the succession to the crown'.[6]

By then, Katherine had moved for the final time. Wentworth had died in September 1567 and Elizabeth ordered the removal of the countess of Hertford from Gosfield to Cockfield Hall in Suffolk, where she was placed in the custody of Sir Owen Hopton. The queen instructed Hopton in October 'to keep her from the access of all strangers'.[7] To Elizabeth's relief, however, the problem of Katherine was soon to be resolved. On 27 January 1568, at the age of 27, Katherine died at Cockfield Hall.[8] Her illness had compelled Hopton to send to London for the queen's physician Dr Symonds.[9] Hopton had done so on 11 January because Katherine had kept to her bed for three days.[10] According to Camden, 'after certain years ... being taken with a grievous Sickness, [Katherine] craved Pardon of the Queen before Hopton Lieutenant of the Tower, that she had contracted Marriage without her Privity; and with Obtestations commending her Children and Hertford's Liberty to her Protection, slept piously and peaceably in Christ'.[11] This account of her demise is at odds with the suggestion of some modern historians that Katherine died of anorexia, apparently having starved herself to death in her despair. It is plausible that the 'grievous Sickness' that led to Katherine's death was consumption (nowadays known as tuberculosis). Nonetheless, the nature of the countess' demise that winter has strengthened the perception of her as an ultimately tragic figure who unjustly suffered for her decision to marry without seeking royal permission, with the attendant consequences. After her death, it was romantically believed by some authors that Katherine had died of a broken heart.[12]

Death was a constant presence in early modern England, operating 'at the center of life'.[13] Death was of profound importance to early modern individuals, as they organised their lives on the understanding that death was ever-present and could strike at any time. Dying what contemporaries viewed as a 'good' death offered early modern people spiritual and material benefits: they could look forward to eternal bliss while those of sufficient wealth participated in the glorification of their family as channelled through monuments, which honoured their personal virtues and family achievements. Preparation for death was regarded as 'the most important business of earthly existence'.[14] After the Reformation, the dying individual's faith 'assumed overriding importance' in the final hours.[15] The dying individual's comportment tended to be interpreted as an indicator of their elect status.[16] As argued by the theologian William Perkins, Protestants expected three things of the Christian nearing death. He should die in faith (expressing faith by the outward signs of prayer or thanksgiving), placing his reliance on God's special love and mercy; he should die readily and in submission to God's will; and, lastly, he should render up his soul into God's hands.[17] Outward comportment should reflect one's inward faith.[18]

On the eve of her execution in 1554, Jane Grey had written to Katherine advising her of the need to 'learn ... to die' so that she would enjoy 'an immortal and everlasting life'.[19] Likewise, John More would write in *A Lively Anatomie of Death* (1596):

Our very years are limited, God hath measured out our months, the days of our lives are dated, how long we have to live. So that our first lesson (even at the beginning) that we have to learn is this, to think of our ending ... As youth succeedeth childhood, and age youth, so childhood, youth and age all have their end.[20]

Early modern preachers reiterated that people should be ready for death at all times and should not resist it. Only the most dissolute who embraced 'the pleasures of this world … think no more of death than the brute beast that is without understanding', as would be argued by Robert Pricke in *A Verie Godlie and Learned Sermon, Treating of Mans Mortalitie* (1608).[21] As her final illness took its hold, Katherine began preparations for her death in line with this contemporary emphasis on fully preparing for the end of earthly life. It was essential that she be seen to die well, both to obtain eternal salvation and to uphold the honour of the Grey family. This latter point was especially important in view of Katherine's tainted reputation following her clandestine marriage and because the coup of 1553 had tarnished her family with the crime of treason, an offence that the queen seemingly never forgot nor forgave.

Chapman has reiterated the contemporary importance of enacting a respectable deathbed scene: 'it became Katherine Grey to show that she could die correctly and in the highest traditions of spiritual well-being.'[22] On her deathbed, Katherine was attended by Mrs Isham, Mrs Woodford, Mrs Page and Mrs Coffin. They were joined by her three menservants and a doctor.[23] A contemporary account recorded that:

> all the night she contynued in prayer, in sayenge of psalms & hering them red of others, and somtyme sayenge them after others; and as sone as one psalme was ended she wolde call for an other to be said. And dyvers tymes she her selfe wolde rehearse the prayers appoynted for the visitation of the syck. And five or sixe tymes in the same night she sayde the prayer appoynted to be sayde at the howre of deathe.[24]

The sixteenth-century author Thomas Churchyard obtained a manuscript copy of the eyewitness account of Katherine's death and retold it in verse. He described the deathbed scene thus:

> Her coulour changde her cheerefull lookes,
> and countenaunce wanted spreet;
> To sallow ashes turnde the hue

of beauties blossoms sweete.
And dreery dulnes had bespred,
the wearishe body throw;
Each vitall vaine did flat refuse
to do their dutie now.[25]

In her final hours Katherine was comforted by her attendants, who expressed the hope that she 'shall lyve and doe well many yeres', but the countess seemed resigned to her fate: 'No, no. No lyfe in this worlde; but in the worlde to come I hope to lyve ever. For here ys nothinge but care and myserye, and there ys lyfe everlastinge.'[26] Katherine began to feel faint and was comforted by Lady Hopton, reminding the countess that she had previously 'escaped many daungers when yow were as lykelye to dye as nowe yow bee'.[27] Katherine replied that 'my tyme is come, and yt ys not Gods will that I shall lyve any longer. And his will be donne and not myne.'[28] Thus, she vocally expressed acceptance of her fate as God's will. 'Then lokinge uppon those that were abowte her, she sayde, "I praye yow all praye for me that I maye dye in the faithe of Christe; for as I am, so shall you all be. Beholde the picture of your selves."'[29] At six or seven that morning, the countess asked Owen Hopton to come to her. She then beseeched him to:

beare witnes with me that I dye a true Christian and that I beleve to be saved by the deathe of Christe and that I truste I am one of those he shed his moste precyous blood for. And I aske God and the worlde forgivenes. And I forgeve all the worlde.[30]

As noted earlier, contemporaries believed that the dying individual's faith in their final hours demonstrated their elect status.[31] As Jane had done on the scaffold, Katherine's final speech proclaimed her Protestant faith and her belief in salvation through faith alone.

Katherine subsequently asked Hopton to forward her request to the queen that she forgive her, acknowledging that she had offended her. She also beseeched Elizabeth to be good to her children and not impute their mother's fault to them.[32] Following these requests, Katherine instructed her attendants to bring her 'the boxe wherin my weddinge ringe ys', and once it had been passed to her, she opened it and asked Hopton to deliver a ring with a pointed diamond to Hertford. It was not her wedding ring, but 'the ringe of my assurance unto my Lord'.[33] She then removed the wedding ring from the box and requested that Hopton also deliver it to the earl, while testifying that she had been 'a trewe and a faithfull wyfe' and beseeching Hertford to be 'a lovinge and a naturall father unto my children, unto whome I give the same blessinge that God gave un[to] Abraham, Isack, and Jacobe'.[34] Following this statement, Katherine removed a ring with a death's head from the box, professing that '"This shalbe the laste token unto my Lord that ever I shall sende him. Yt is the picture of myselfe." The wordes written abowte the deathes head were these: "While I lyved, yours."'[35]

Lucinda Becker has suggested that, for women facing death, there was a need to conform and present an acceptable image of oneself in death. 'Conformity and a level of self-effacement were necessary not simply in order to enact the longed for "good death", but also in order to ensure that one's last words and actions were heeded, respected, and acted upon.'[36] There was an onus on the dying woman to present a good example to others, especially to her offspring. The deathbed was a 'semi-public arena'.[37] In this context, it is significant that, as her death approached, Katherine reportedly welcomed her demise: 'And then, as yt were with a cherefull cowntenance, she sayd, "Welcome, Death."'[38] Like her sister, Katherine ensured that the manner of her death conformed to contemporary expectations of a 'good' death; this account of her demise indicates that, as Jane had hoped, Katherine had learned how to die. Indeed, the godly often played an active role in the drama of their own deathbeds by means of good advice and exhortations, declarations of faith, devout prayers and ready acceptance of death.[39] Katherine embraced 'her selfe with her armes' and lifted 'her eyes and hands towards heaven, knockinge often on her breste', and declared: '"O Lord, for thy many mercyes, blott owt of thy booke all my synnes."'[40] She began to pray: '"Lord, into thy handes I comytt my sowle. Lord Jesus receave my spyrite." So putting downe her owne eyes with her owne hands, she yelded up her meke sowle unto God at ix of the clock in the morning on twisdaye, the xxviith of January.'[41]

According to de Silva, when she learned of Katherine's passing, Elizabeth 'expressed sorrow to me at her death, but it is not believed that she feels it, as she was afraid of her'.[42] He also noted that:

> the heretics mourn her loss, as they had fixed their eyes on her for the succession in any eventuality. The Catholics are pleased, and are already beginning to say that the children are not legitimate owing to Catharine's having married against the law. I am told, however, that in her will she has again left the necessary declarations to prove her marriage.[43]

Elizabeth issued a warrant granting Hopton £76 towards the charges of Katherine's funeral.[44] He was paid an additional £140 the following month for household expenses and funeral charges.[45] By mid-February, news of the countess' demise had reached the Vatican: Katherine, 'the Queen's nearest kinswoman, is dead'.[46]

In a sense, Katherine's untimely death could have had the effect of clarifying, and indeed strengthening, the claim of Mary, Queen of Scots to succeed Elizabeth as queen. As this study has stressed, Katherine was the Scottish queen's greatest rival for the English succession and, at a stroke, her death removed her as a challenger to Mary's dynastic interests. However, Katherine's death occurred only months after Mary's abduction and rape by the earl of Bothwell and her enforced abdication and imprisonment at Loch Leven Castle. In May 1568, the deposed queen made the ultimately fatal decision to escape from the castle and seek assistance in England. As is well known, during her captivity, Mary's involvement in treasonous conspiracies that aimed to depose and replace Elizabeth led to her condemnation and execution in 1587, the fourth queen in the sixteenth century to suffer beheading for treason. With Katherine's sons having been declared illegitimate, her younger sister Mary was now Elizabeth's heir presumptive according to the last will and testament of Henry VIII, but there was never a concerted political effort to position her as a viable successor. Lord William Howard had reported of Mary's clandestine marriage that 'the offence to the queen's grace is very great, and her majesty taketh it much to heart'.[47] Mary died in 1578 and was buried in Westminster Abbey, having eventually been granted her freedom and even returning to court to serve the queen.[48]

After her death, Katherine's remains were interred at Yoxford church. Her burial took place on 21 February 1568. The antiquarian Robert Reyce (1555–1638) noted Katherine's resting place in his *The Breviary of Suffolk*:

> There lie buried in the Church and Chancel at Yoxford, the bowels of the Lady Katherine, wife of Edward Seimour Earl of Hartford. She was daughter of Henry Grey Duke of Suffolk, and of Mary the French Queen [her mother was Frances Brandon], the youngest of the two daughters of King Henry VII.: of the elder, K.James and K.Charles were descended.[49]

At Katherine's funeral, £4 17s 8d were given to the poor in alms, while the queen ordered 'the sum of threescore pounds and ten ... to be paid for the fees of officers of arms, banners, scutcheons, hearse, and other things about the said burial'.[50] This included 'the travelling expenses of the heralds, and the painter's work for a great banner of arms, for four banner rolls, six dozen scutcheons of paper in metal for garnishing the hearse, and six dozen of paper scutcheons in colours, six great scutcheons on buckram, &c. &c'. Thomas Spern was paid £6 'for the carrying and coffining of the Lady Katharine Gray', while 'singing men at the same funeral' were paid 20s.[51]

Some of Katherine's contemporaries represented hers as a tragic love story. The poet Churchyard retold Katherine's story in verse, in which the lady (Katherine) and her knight (Hertford) fall in love, 'ioynd, a hazard great', but they incur the 'prince displeasuer throw this prank'. Both are imprisoned after the knight initially goes abroad.[52] In the poem, the lady prepares for death by singing psalms and saying prayers, rejecting the encouragement of the bystanders and beseeching them to testify that she died as a good Christian. She requests 'a knight' in attendance to send a message to the prince acknowledging her fault and seeking forgiveness.[53]

About four years after Katherine's demise, John Philippe wrote a panegyric entitled 'The Honour of Fidelitie', in which he extolled Katherine's 'vertues', namely her patience, resignation and piety. The poet celebrated the love between Katherine and Hertford, for he was her 'trustie' and 'faithfull knight', while she was to him 'a loving spouse' and 'a constant wife'.[54] Hertford was described as experiencing 'sorow' and 'care and greif' following Katherine's death, but he could be comforted by the fact that Katherine would live 'in lasting Joy / and blys that shall endure'.[55] When the hour of death was upon her, Katherine's response to Lady Hopton's comforting message that 'yow shall not dye / but lyve and do full well' was that 'my tyme is come it is gods will / life shall not long indure', 'whose will must be obeyed yow knowe'.[56] Beseeching the queen to forgive her and not impute her fault to her sons, Katherine voiced her hope that she would one day see her husband and children 'in that blissfull place' (heaven).[57]

While contemporary and modern authors have depicted Katherine and Hertford as star-crossed lovers, it was her claim to the succession that most interested those writing at the time. For that reason, looking back over Katherine's life, her agency and political ambition with regard to the succession are issues that deserve consideration. As noted in the previous chapter, she was not personally involved in the succession debates of the 1560s, even if she may have been aware of the publication of various tracts supporting her claim to be recognised as heir presumptive. At the beginning of Elizabeth's reign, the imperial ambassador had described Katherine's dissatisfaction on two counts: first, the queen's refusal to recognise her as heir presumptive and, second, her dismissal from the Privy Chamber. Aside from the ambassador's report, the evidence is insufficient to conclude that Katherine was personally ambitious for her inheritance rights to be publicly recognised.

Her agency, moreover, was limited with regard to the succession question. The imperial envoys may have taken for granted her acquiescence in the conspiracy to marry her to Don Carlos that arose from Spanish hostility to the prospect of Mary, Queen of Scots – at that time married to the dauphin of France – being recognised as Elizabeth's successor. However, they were unaware of Katherine's relationship with Hertford and, once it became public, they no longer showed an interest in Katherine as a viable claimant. In contrast to the Scottish queen's actions during the 1570s and 1580s while imprisoned in England, in which she actively pressed for her right to succeed Elizabeth to be acknowledged by the queen and government (later turning her focus to replacing a deposed Elizabeth), Katherine never displayed any interest in being named heir presumptive following her loss of royal favour. Instead, the evidence reveals that she longed to be reunited with her husband and eldest son following their enforced separation. It is also true that the context of the 1570s and 1580s was very different from that of the 1560s, when Elizabeth's councillors continued to hope that the still-young queen would marry and produce an heir.

Katherine's claim to the throne continued to interest her contemporaries after her death. This was due to the queen's failure to resolve the succession question. Thus, on 5 December 1574, Antonio de Guaras reported that:

the Queen has been unwell last week, and the secret murmurs in Court, and amongst people all over the country as to what will become of the country in case of the Queen's death, were very remarkable. God grant her health, for upon the life of such depends the welfare of this realm. The Catholics wish in such case to proclaim the queen of Scots, and the heretics to take up arms against her and proclaim the son of the earl of Hertford. These tribulations are expected as a result of the refusal of the Queen and Parliament to allow a successor to be appointed. On the contrary, they have passed a law, making it treason to discuss the matter during the

Queen's life. The people threaten, in the event of the above happening, to kill all foreigners; but God preserve the life of the Queen for many happy years.[58]

In 1595, *A Conference about the next Succession to the Throne of England* was smuggled into England from Antwerp and was dedicated to the earl of Essex. It was written by the English Jesuit Robert Persons and discussed the claims of fourteen potential successors to the throne, concluding that the lawful successor was Infanta Isabella Clara Eugenia, daughter of Philip II of Spain.[59] The author noted that a marriage between the infanta and Thomas Seymour, younger son of Katherine, would be advantageous in 'making of compositions of peace and union with the opposite parties'.[60] Elizabeth's hostility to a Grey succession continued unabated. She ordered the book to be placed on record in the Tower and forbade it from being removed without her approval; a few months later, she sanctioned the imprisonment of Hertford for attempting to prove his son's legitimacy.[61] In 1589 and 1591, Katherine's younger son Thomas had appealed against the ruling that his parents' marriage was invalid and their children illegitimate.[62] It was only in the reign of Elizabeth's successor, however, that the official verdict on the Hertford–Grey marriage was overturned.

Meanwhile, the succession remained open to question. It is untrue that Puritans embraced James VI of Scotland following the execution of Mary, Queen of Scots as their preferred candidate to succeed Elizabeth; until the mid-1590s, Puritans differed in their favoured candidates, only one of whom was James, with both the earl of Huntingdon and Katherine's son Edward Seymour, Lord Beauchamp, considered as possible heirs.[63] Beauchamp's credentials were, however, weakened by his unsuitable marriage to Honora Rogers, a daughter of the Dorset knight Sir Richard Rogers, whom he had conceived 'a fond liking' for in 1581.[64] Hertford bitterly opposed his son's choice to the extent that Beauchamp threatened to kill himself rather than be parted from Honora.[65] The imperial ambassador Bernardino de Mendoza disclosed in June 1582 that 'the eldest son of the earl of Hertford, who is one of the pretenders to the crown, has made a love match with a lady of much lower quality than himself'.[66]

While Hertford was forced to come to terms with his eldest son's marriage, he instead turned his attention to Beauchamp's son Edward, for whom Hertford favoured a marriage with Arbella Stuart, great-granddaughter of Margaret Tudor, because a union between Edward Seymour and Arbella would unite the lines of Henry VIII's two sisters.[67] It may have been partly for that reason that the Venetian diplomat Giovanni Carlo Scaramelli reported in February 1603 that 'James and Arabella are the real claimants to the crown of England' and noted that 'the Queen has conceived some fear less Arabella should escape from the Castle where she is confined, as there are rumours that she is being sought in marriage'.[68] Scaramelli believed that Arbella 'has an inclination towards Thomas Seymour, the son, as I have already clearly set forth, of Catherine of Suffolk, and Edward Seymour, Earl of Hertford'.[69] The identification of Thomas Seymour was mistaken, given that he had died in 1600, and the following month the diplomat reported that:

> the business of Lady Arabella has reached such a pitch that the son of the Earl of Hertford, to whom they affirm she is betrothed, has suddenly disappeared and is nowhere to be found, and Arabella for this reason has been removed from the custody of the Countess of Shrewsbury, and taken to the same castle where Queen Mary of England kept her sister, the present Queen, a prisoner.[70]

Ultimately, Elizabeth ignored her father's last will and testament by refusing to recognise Katherine's eldest son Edward as her successor. Instead, on her death in 1603, the crown passed to James VI of Scotland, only son of the disgraced Mary, Queen of Scots. His accession to the English throne was not predestined. Even Elizabeth's supposed recognition of him on her deathbed as her heir is open to question. As Guy observed, the suggestion of the English queen's recognition of the Scottish king in her dying hours is not supported by solid evidence, and 'as she had by then lost the power of speech, the most she might have done was to signal her assent by a gesture. Even that is guesswork.'[71] The seeming inevitability of James' inheritance of the English throne has served to marginalise the arguable superiority of Katherine's claim to succeed Elizabeth.

Following James' accession, Arbella Stuart was invited to court but 'she remains without a mate and without estate'.[72] On 22 June 1610 at Greenwich Palace, she secretly married William Seymour, second son of Edward, Lord Beauchamp, and brother to the Edward linked with Arbella some years previously. Seymour was incarcerated in the Tower and Arbella placed under house arrest for marrying without royal permission: 'this law was passed to meet the case of the Earl of Hertford, grandfather of the youth, whose father was secretly born in the Tower.'[73] In June 1611, 'Seymour, who was chosen by the Lady Arabella as her husband against the King's wishes and who was therefore imprisoned in the Tower, made his escape; Lady Arabella also is fled.'[74] Unfortunately for Arbella, she was 'captured along with the ship she was in by a frigate of the guard a league away from Calais'[75] and imprisoned in the Tower. Arbella shared the same fate as her husband's grandmother, Katherine Grey – she never saw her husband again and may have starved herself to death, as Katherine was reputed to have done.

Katherine's husband, her 'good Ned', died in 1621 having remarried twice, to Frances Howard and Frances Pranell in 1582 and 1601, respectively. In the 1640s, Katherine's grandson William Seymour, now ennobled as earl of Hertford and duke of Somerset, established an elaborate monument to his father, uncle and paternal grandparents at Salisbury Cathedral and had the remains of his grandmother transferred from Yoxford. The monument at Salisbury Cathedral sought both to crown and to immortalise the Hertford–Grey marriage.[76] The monument 'bears witness to the legitimacy' of the blood line of Katherine and Hertford 'and thus of the Seymours' place in the succession', which was confirmed in 1606 when their marriage was declared valid.[77]

Nigel Llewellyn has suggested that early modern funeral monuments 'were intended to establish in the collective memory and set for ever the honourable reputation of the subjects they commemorated'.[78]

They preserved continuities between the present, future and past, while exhorting the living to follow the model set by the deceased.[79] The placing of Katherine's effigy above her husband's reflects her higher social status. The epitaph on the couple's monument describes Katherine's husband as 'most illustrious' and Katherine as 'his most dear and beloved Consort', 'A woman distinguished as an example of uprightness, piety, beauty, and faith, the best and most illustrious not only of her own but of every age'.[80] The couple were 'An Incomparable Pair' and the epitaph acknowledges that 'having experienced alternate changes of fortune here, at length they rest together in the same concord in which they lived'.[81] As has been noted, Hertford's love for Katherine is indicated in his request to be buried alongside her, rather than alongside either of his two other wives.[82] In death, having been cruelly separated in life, Katherine and Hertford were reunited for eternity.

Bibliography

Manuscripts

Bodleian Library
Ashmole 829

British Library
Add MS 26748
Add MS 33749
Add MS 35327
Cotton Faustina A XI
Cotton MS Titus C VII
Cotton MS Vitellius C XVI
Harley MS 249
Harley MS 6286
Lansdowne MS 6
Lansdowne MS 7
Lansdowne MS 819/13

Inner Temple Library
Petyt MS 538.47

Lambeth Palace Library
Lambeth MS 2872

National Archives
C 270/33
C 270/34
E 23/4
EXT 9/42/2
SP 46/10

Surrey History Centre
6729/3/4
6729/9/113

Printed Primary Sources

Anonymous. 'Allegations in behalf of the high and mighty Princes, the Lady Mary, now Queen of Scots, Against the Opinions and Books set forth in the Part and Favour of the Lady Katherine, And the rest of the Issues of the French Queen, Touching the Succession of the Crown. Written in the Time of Queen Elizabeth. London, Printed by J.D in the Year 1690' in William Atwood, *The Fundamental Constitution of the English Government* (Wilmington, DE: Scholarly Resources, Inc., 1973; first published in 1690).

Anonymous. *Aristotle's Master-Piece* (London, 1684).

Arber, Edward (ed.). *John Knox. The First Blast of the Trumpet Against the Monstrous Regiment of Women* (London: Southgate, 1878).

Ayre, John. *The Catechism of Thomas Becon* (Cambridge: Cambridge University Press,1844).

Bain, Joseph (ed.). *Calendar of the State Papers relating to Scotland and Mary, Queen of Scots 1547–1603* (Edinburgh: H.M. General Register House, 1898, 11 vols).

Blatcher, Marjorie (ed.). *Historical Manuscripts Commission. Report on the Manuscripts of the Most Honourable The Marquess of Bath, Preserved at Longleat, Wiltshire* (London: Her Majesty's Stationery Office, 1968, 5 vols).

Byrne, Muriel St. Clare (ed.), selected by Bridget Boland. *The Lisle Letters: An Abridgement* (Chicago, IL: University of Chicago Press, 1983).

Calendar of the Cecil Papers in Hatfield House (24 vols), accessed at www.british-history.ac.uk/search/series/cal-cecil-papers?page=2.

Calendar of the Patent Rolls Preserved in the Public Record Office: Philip and Mary (London: H.M. Stationery Office, 1936–39, 4 vols).

Calendar of State Papers Domestic: Elizabeth, Addenda 1580-1625, accessed at www.british-history.ac.uk/cal-state-papers/domestic/edw-eliz/addenda/1580-1625.

Calendar of State Papers, Foreign, accessed at www.british-history.ac.uk/search/series/cal-state-papers--foreign.

Calendar of State Papers, Simancas (4 vols), accessed at www.british-history.ac.uk/search/series/cal-state-papers--simancas.

Calendar of State Papers, Spain (13 vols), accessed at www.british-history.ac.uk/search/series/cal-state-papers--spain?page=1.

Calendar of State Papers, Vatican (2 vols), accessed at www.british-history.ac.uk/search/series/cal-state-papers--vatican.

Calendar of State Papers, Venice (38 vols), accessed at www.british-history.ac.uk/search/series/cal-state-papers--venice.

Camden, William. *The History of the Most Renowned and Victorious Princess Elizabeth, Late Queen of England; Containing All the most Important and Remarkable Passages of State, both at Home and Abroad (so far as they were linked with English Affairs) during her Long and Prosperous Reign* (London: Printed by M. Flesher, for R. Bentley at the Post-Office in Covent-Garden, 1688).

Clifford, Arthur (ed.). *The State Papers and Letters of Sir Ralph Sadler, Knight-Banneret* (Edinburgh: Constable and Co., 1809, 2 vols).

Cressy, David and Lori Anne Ferrell (eds). *Religion and Society in Early Modern England: A Sourcebook* (London and New York: Routledge, 1996).

Edwards, A.S.G. (ed.). *Metrical Visions by George Cavendish* (Columbia, SC: University of South Carolina Press, 1980).

Edwards, J. Stephan. *The Lady Jane Grey's Prayer Book: British Library Harley Manuscript 2342, Fully Illustrated and Transcribed* (Palm Springs, CA: Old John Publishing, 2016).

Ellis, Henry (ed.). *Holinshed's Chronicles of England, Scotland, and Ireland. In Six Volumes* (London: Printed for J. Johnson [etc.], 1808, 6 vols).

Ellis, Henry (ed.). *Grafton's Chronicle; or, History of England. To Which is Added His Table of the Bailiffs, Sheriffs, and Mayors, of the City of London. From the Year 1189, to 1558, Inclusive* (London: Printed for J. Johnson [etc.], 1809, 2 vols).

Ellis, Henry (ed.). *The New Chronicles of England and France, in Two Parts; By Robert Fabyan* (London: Printed for F.C. & J. Rivington [etc.], 1811).

Ellis, Henry (ed.). *Original Letters, Illustrative of English History; Including Numerous Royal Letters: From Autographs in the British Museum, and One or Two Other Collections* (London: Harding & Lepard, 1827, 4 vols).

d'Ewes, Sir Simond. *The Journals of All the Parliaments during the Reign of Queen Elizabeth, Both of the House of Lords and House of Commons.* (London: Printed for John Starkey at the Mitre in Fleetstreet near Temple-Bar, 1682).

Garnett, Richard (ed.). *The Accession of Queen Mary: Being the Contemporary Narrative of Antonio de Guaras, a Spanish Merchant Resident in London* (London: Lawrence & Bullen, 1892).

Giles, J.A. (ed.). *The Whole Works of Roger Ascham, Now First Collected and Revised, With a Life of the Author* (London: John Russell Smith, 1864, 4 vols).

Hamilton, William Douglas (ed.). *A Chronicle of England during the Reigns of the Tudors, from A.D. 1485 to 1559. By Charles Wriothesley, Windsor Herald.* (London: J.B. Nichols & Sons, 1875–77, 2 vols).

Harbin, George. *The Hereditary Right of the Crown of England Asserted The History of the Succession Since the Conquest Clear'd; and the True English Constitution Vindicated from the Misrepresentations of Dr. Higden's View and Defence. Wherein Some Mistakes Also of Our Common Historians are Rectify'd; and Several Particulars Relating to the Succession, and to the Title of the House of Suffolk, are Now First Publish'd from Ancient Records and Original Mss; Together with an Authentick Copy of King Henry VIII.'s Will* (London: Printed by G. James, for Richard Smith, at Bishop Beveridge's Head in Pater-Noster-Row, 1713).

Harris Nicolas, Nicholas. *The Literary Remains of Lady Jane Grey; with a Memoir of Her Life* (London: Harding, Triphook & Lepard, 1825).

Haynes, Samuel (ed.). *A Collection of State Papers, Relating to Affairs in the Reigns of King Henry VIII. King Edward VI. Queen Mary, and Queen Elizabeth, From the Year 1542 to 1570* (London: William Bowyer, 1740).

Hayward, Sir John. *The life, and raigne of King Edward the Sixt. Written by Sr. Iohn Hayward Kt. Dr. of Lawe* (London: Printed for Iohn Partridge ..., 1630).

Head, Richard. *The life and death of Mother Shipton being not only a true account of her strange birth and most important passages of her life, but also all her prophesies, now newly collected and historically experienced from the time of her birth, in the reign of King Henry the Seventh until this present year 1667, containing the most important passages of state during the reign of these kings and queens of England ... : strangely preserved amongst other writings belonging to an old monastary in York-shire, and now published for the information of posterity* (London: Printed for B. Harris ..., 1677).

HMC. *Report on the Manuscripts of Lord Middleton, Preserved at Wollaton Hall, Nottinghamshire* (London: Published by His Majesty's Stationery Office, 1911).

HMC. *Thirteenth Report, Appendix, Part IV. The Manuscripts of Rye and Hereford Corporations, Capt. Loder-Symonds, Mr. E. R. Wodehouse, M.P., and others.* (London: H.M. Stationery Office, 1892).

Iane, by the grace of God quene of England, Fraunce and Ireland, defendor of the faith, & of the Church of Englande, & also of Irelande under Christ in earth the supreme head to al our most louing, faithfull, and obedient subiects, and to euery of them greting (London: In ædibus Richardi Grafto[n], reg[inæa] typ[o]graphia [excu]sum, 1553) STC 7846.

Kervyn de Lettenhove, M. Le Baron (ed.). *Relations politiques des Pays-Bas et de l'Angleterre: Depuis l'abdication de Charles-Quint jusqu'au depart de Philippe II pour l'Espagne (25 Oct. 1555–24 Août 1559)* (Brussels: F. Hayez, 1882, 10 vols).

Lemon, Robert (ed.). *Calendar of State Papers, Domestic Series, of the Reigns of Edward VI., Mary, Elizabeth 1547–1580, Preserved in the State Paper Department of Her Majesty's Public Record Office* (London: Longman, Brown, Greene, Longmans & Roberts, 1856).

Lettere di Principi, le quali si scrivono o da principi, o ragionano di principi (Venice: Appresso Giordano Ziletti, 1569–77), translated by Dr J. Stephan Edwards and accessed at somegreymatter.com/lettereengl.htm.

Letters and Papers, Foreign and Domestic, Henry VIII (21 vols), accessed at www.british-history.ac.uk/search/series/letters-papers-hen8.

MacCulloch, Diarmaid (ed.). *The* Vita Mariae Angliae Reginae *of Robert Wingfield of Brantham* (London: Offices of the Royal Historical Society, University College London, 1984).

Marcus, Leah S., Janel Mueller and Mary Beth Rose (eds). *Elizabeth I: Collected Works* (Chicago, IL and London: University of Chicago Press, 2002).

Maxwell Lyte, H.C. (ed.). *The Manuscripts of His Grace the Duke of Rutland, G.C.B., Preserved at Belvoir Castle* (London: Printed for Her Majesty's Stationery Office, by Eyre & Spottiswoode, 1888, 4 vols).

Miola, Robert S. (ed.). *Early Modern Catholicism: An Anthology of Primary Sources* (New York: Oxford University Press, 2007).

Mulcaster, Richard. *THE PASSAGE of our most drad Soueraigne Lady Quene Elyzabeth through the citie of London to Westminster the daye before her coronacion* (London, 1559), accessed at mapoflondon.uvic.ca/QMPS1.htm.

Nichols, John (ed.). *The History of the Worthies of England: Endeavoured by Thomas Fuller, D.D. First Printed in 1662.* (London: F.C. & J. Rivington, 1811, 2 vols).

Nichols, John. *The Progresses and Public Processions of Queen Elizabeth* (London: John Nichols & Son, 1823, 3 vols).

Nichols, John Gough (ed.). *The Diary of Henry Machyn, Citizen and Merchant-Taylor of London, from A.D. 1550 to A.D. 1563* (London: Camden Society, 1848).

Nichols, John Gough (ed.). *The Chronicle of Queen Jane, and of Two Years of Queen Mary, and Especially of the Rebellion of Sir Thomas Wyat. Written by a Resident in the Tower of London* (London: Camden Society, 1850).

Nichols, John Gough (ed.). *Chronicle of the Grey Friars of London* (London: Camden Society, 1852).Nichols, John Gough (ed.). *Literary Remains of King Edward the Sixth* (London: J.B. Nichols & Sons, 1857, 2 vols).

Park, Thomas (ed.). *Nugae Antiquae: Being a Miscellaneous Collection of Original Papers, in Prose and Verse; Written during the Reigns of Henry VIII. Edward VI. Queen Mary, Elizabeth, and King James: By Sir John Harington, Knt. and by Others who Lived in Those Times* (London: Vernor and Hood, 1804, 2 vols).

Payne Collier, J. (ed.). *The Egerton Papers. A Collection of Public and Private Documents, Chiefly Illustrative of the Times of Elizabeth and James I* (London: Camden Society, 1840).

Pickering, Danby. *The Statutes at Large, from the First Year of K. Richard III. to the 31st Year of K. Henry VIII. inclusive.* (Cambridge: Printed by Joseph Bentham, 1763, 46 vols).

Reed Cattley, Stephen (ed.). *The Acts and Monuments of John Foxe: A New and Complete Edition* (London: R.B. Seeley & W. Burnside, 1838, 8 vols).

Robertson, James Craigie (ed.). *Ecclesia Restaurata; or, the History of the Reformation of the Church of England. By Peter Heylyn, D.D.* (Cambridge: Cambridge University Press, 1849, 2 vols).

Robinson, Hastings. *The Zurich Letters, Comprising the Correspondence of Several English Bishops and Others, with Some of the Helvetian Reformers, during the Early Part of the Reign of Queen Elizabeth* (Cambridge: Cambridge University Press, 1842).

Robinson, Hastings (ed.). *Original Letters Relative to the English Reformation, Written during the Reigns of King Henry VIII, King Edward VI, and Queen Mary: Chiefly from the Archives of Zurich* (Cambridge: Cambridge University Press, 1846, 2 vols).

Rollins, Hyder E. (ed.). *Old English Ballads 1553–1625 Chiefly from Manuscripts* (Cambridge: Cambridge University Press, 1920).

Rosso, Giulio Raviglio. *Historia delle cose occurse nel regno d'Inghilterra, in materia del Duca di Nortomberlan dopo la morte di Odoardo VI* (Venice: Academy of Venice, 1558; edited by Luca Contile), translated by Dr J. Stephan Edwards and accessed at somegreymatter.com/rossoengl.htm.

Rymer, Thomas. *Fœdera, conventiones, literæ, et cujuscunque generis acta publica, inter reges Angliæ et alios quosvis imperatores, reges, pontifices, principes, vel communitates, ab ineunte sæculo duodecimo, viz. ab anno 1101, ad nostra usque tempore habita aut tractata; ex autographis, infra secretiores Archivorum regiorum thesaurarias, per multa sæcula reconditis, fideliter exscripta... Accurante Thoma Rymer* (London: A. & J. Churchill, 1704–35).

Sharp Hume, Martin A. (ed.). *Chronicle of King Henry VIII. of England. Being a Contemporary Record of Some of the Principal Events of the Reigns of Henry VIII. and Edward VI.* (London: George Bell & Sons, 1889).

Stevenson, Joseph (ed.). *The Life of Jane Dormer Duchess of Feria by Henry Clifford* (London: Burns & Oates, 1887).

Strype, John. *Ecclesiastical Memorials, Relating Chiefly to Religion, and the Reformation of It, and the Emergencies of the Church of England, under King Henry VIII. King Edward VI. and Queen Mary I. With Large Appendixes, Containing Original Papers, Records, &c.* (Oxford: Clarendon Press, 1822, 7 vols).

Turnbull, William B. (ed.). *Calendar of State Papers, Foreign Series, of the Reign of Edward VI., 1547–1553, Preserved in the State Paper Department of Her Majesty's Public Record Office* (London: Longman, Green, Longman, & Roberts, 1861).

Tytler, Patrick Fraser. *England under the Reigns of Edward VI. and Mary, with the Contemporary History of Europe, Illustrated in Original Letters Never Before Printed* (London: Richard Bentley, 1839, 2 vols).

Von Klarwill, Victor (ed.). *Queen Elizabeth and Some Foreigners* (London: The Bodley Head, 1928).

Weller Singer, Samuel (ed.). *The Life of Cardinal Wolsey. By George Cavendish, His Gentleman Usher* (Chiswick: from the Press of C. Whittingham; for Harding, Triphook & Lepard, London, 1825, 2 vols).

Wright, Thomas (ed.). *Queen Elizabeth and Her Times, a Series of Original Letters* (London: Henry Colburn, 1838, 2 vols).

Yorke, Philip. *Miscellaneous State Papers. From 1501 to 1726. In Two Volumes* (London: W. Strahan & T. Cadell, 1778, 2 vols).

Secondary Sources

Adams, Simon. *Leicester and the Court: Essays on Elizabethan Politics* (Manchester: Manchester University Press, 2002).

Akkerman, Nadine and Birgit Houben. 'Introduction' in Nadine Akkerman and Birgit Houben (eds), *The Politics of Female Households: Ladies-in-Waiting across Early Modern Europe* (Leiden: Brill, 2014), pp. 1–31.

Alford, Stephen. *The Early Elizabethan Polity: William Cecil and the British Succession Crisis, 1558–1569* (Cambridge: Cambridge University Press, 1998).

Alford, Stephen. *Kingship and Politics in the Reign of Edward VI* (Cambridge: Cambridge University Press, 2002).

Archer, Ian W. (ed.), with Simon Adams, G.W. Bernard, Mark Greengrass, Paul E.J. Hammer and Fiona Kisby. *Religion, Politics, and Society in Sixteenth-Century England* (Cambridge: Cambridge University Press, 2003).

Attreed, Lorraine C. 'Preparation for Death in Sixteenth-Century Northern England', *The Sixteenth Century Journal* 13 (1982), 37–66.

Axton, Marie. *The Queen's Two Bodies: Drama and the Elizabethan Succession* (London: Royal Historical Society, 1977).

Baldwin, David. *Elizabeth Woodville: Mother of the Princes in the Tower* (Stroud: The History Press, 2010).

Becker, Lucinda M. *Death and the Early Modern Englishwoman* (Abingdon: Routledge, 2016).

Beem, Charles. 'The Tragic Queen: Dynastic Loyalty and the "Queenships" of Mary Queen of Scots' in Caroline Dunn and Elizabeth Carney (eds), *Royal Women and Dynastic Loyalty* (New York: Palgrave Macmillan, 2018), pp. 111–23.

Beer, Barrett L. *Rebellion and Riot: Popular Disorder in England during the Reign of Edward VI* (Kent, OH: Kent State University Press, 1982).

Bell, Ilona. *Elizabeth I: The Voice of a Monarch* (New York: Palgrave Macmillan, 2010).

Bernard, G.W. *The King's Reformation: Henry VIII and the Remaking of the English Church* (New Haven, CT and London: Yale University Press, 2005).

Betteridge, Tom. *Literature and Politics in the English Reformation* (Manchester: Manchester University Press, 2004).

Betteridge, Thomas. 'Maids and Wives: Representing Female Rule during the Reign of Mary Tudor' in Susan Doran and Thomas S. Freeman (eds), *Mary Tudor: Old and New Perspectives* (Basingstoke and New York: Palgrave Macmillan, 2011), pp. 138–53.

Bloxam, Andrew. *A Description of Bradgate Park, and the Adjacent Country; with Remarks on the Natural History of Charnwood Forest, and a Memoir of Lady Jane Grey* (Leicester: Thomas Combe & Son, 1829).

Braddock, Robert C. 'To Serve the Queen' in Alice Hunt and Anna Whitelock (eds), *Tudor Queenship: The Reigns of Mary and Elizabeth* (New York: Palgrave Macmillan, 2010), pp. 225–39.

Brigden, Susan. *New Worlds, Lost Worlds: The Rule of the Tudors 1485–1603* (London: Allen Lane, 2000).

Chapman, Hester W. *Two Tudor Portraits: Henry Howard, Earl of Surrey and Lady Katherine Grey* (London: Jonathan Cape, 1960).

Charlton, Kenneth. *Women, Religion and Education in Early Modern England* (Abingdon: Routledge, 1999).

Cleland, Katharine. *Irregular Unions: Clandestine Marriage in Early Modern English Literature* (Ithaca, NY and London: Cornell University Press, 2021).

Cooper, Elizabeth. *The Life and Letters of Lady Arabella Stuart, including Numerous Original and Unpublished Documents* (London: Hurst & Blackett, 1866, 2 vols).

Cornwall, Julian. *Revolt of the Peasantry 1549* (Abingdon and New York: Routledge, 2022).

Crawford, Patricia. *Women and Religion in England 1500–1720* (London and New York: Routledge, 1993).

Cressy, David. *Birth, Marriage, and Death: Ritual, Religion, and the Life-Cycle in Tudor and Stuart England* (New York: Oxford University Press, 1997).

Davey, Richard. *The Nine Days' Queen: Lady Jane Grey and Her Times* (London: Methuen & Co., 1909).

Davey, Richard. *The Sisters of Lady Jane Grey and their Wicked Grandfather* (London: Chapman & Hall, 1911).

De la Torre, Victoria. '"We Few of an Infinite Multitude": John Hales, Parliament, and the Gendered Politics of the Early Elizabethan Succession', *Albion: A Quarterly Journal Concerned with British Studies* 33 (2001), 557–82.

De Lisle, Leanda. *The Sisters Who Would Be Queen: The Tragedy of Mary, Katherine & Lady Jane Grey* (London: HarperPress, 2008).

De Lisle, Leanda. *Tudor: The Family Story* (London: Chatto & Windus, 2013).

Dolan, Frances E. '"Gentlemen, I Have One Thing More to Say": Women on Scaffolds in England, 1563–1680', *Modern Philology* 92 (1994), 157–78.

Doran, Susan. *Monarchy and Matrimony: The Courtships of Elizabeth I* (London: Routledge, 1996).

Doran, Susan and Paulina Kewes. 'Introduction: A Historiographical Perspective' in Susan Doran and Paulina Kewes (eds), *Doubtful and Dangerous: The Question of Succession in Late Elizabethan England* (Manchester: Manchester University Press, 2014), pp. 3–20.

Doran, Susan. *Elizabeth I and Her Circle* (Oxford: Oxford University Press, 2015).

Doran, Susan and Paulina Kewes. 'The Earlier Elizabethan Succession Question Revisited' in Susan Doran and Paulina Kewes (eds), *Doubtful and Dangerous: The Question of Succession in Late Elizabethan England* (Manchester: Manchester University Press, 2014), pp. 20–47.

Duffy, Eamon. *Fires of Faith: Catholic England under Mary Tudor* (New Haven, CT and London: Yale University Press, 2009).

Duncan, Sarah. '"Most godly heart fraight with al mercie": Queens' Mercy during the Reigns of Mary I and Elizabeth I' in Carole Levin and R.O. Bucholz (eds),

Queens and Power in Medieval and Early Modern England (Lincoln, NE and London: University of Nebraska Press, 2009), pp. 31–51.

Duncan, Sarah. *Mary I: Gender, Power, and Ceremony in the Reign of England's First Queen* (New York: Palgrave Macmillan, 2012).

Dunn, Jane. *Elizabeth and Mary: Cousins, Rivals, Queens* (London: HarperCollins, 2004).

Edwards, John. *Mary I: England's Catholic Queen* (New Haven, CT and London: Yale University Press, 2011).

Edwards, J. Stephan. '"Jane the Quene": A New Consideration of Lady Jane Grey, England's Nine-Days Queen', PhD thesis (University of Colorado, 2007).

Edwards, J. Stephan. 'On the Birthdate of Lady Jane Grey', *Notes and Queries* 54 (2007), 240–42.

Edwards, J. Stephan. 'A Further Note on the Date of Birth of Lady Jane Grey', *Notes and Queries* 55 (2008), 146–48.

Edwards, J. Stephan. *A Queen of a New Invention: Portraits of Lady Jane Grey Dudley, England's 'Nine Days Queen'* (Palm Springs, CA: Old John Publishing, 2015).

Edwards, J. Stephan. 'The Berry-Hill Portrait: An Update, November 2021' (2021), accessed at somegreymatter.com/berryhill.htm.

Fletcher, Anthony. 'The Protestant Idea of Marriage in Early Modern England' in Anthony Fletcher and Peter Roberts (eds), *Religion, Culture and Society in Early Modern Britain: Essays in Honour of Patrick Collinson* (Cambridge: Cambridge University Press, 1994), pp. 161–82.

Fox, Adam. *Oral and Literate Culture in England 1500–1700* (Oxford: Oxford University Press, 2000).

Fraser, Antonia. *Mary Queen of Scots* (London: Phoenix, 2009).

Gowing, Laura. 'Language, Power and the Law: Women's Slander Litigation in Early Modern London' in Jenny Kermode and Garthine Walker (eds), *Women, Crime and the Courts in Early Modern England* (London: UCL Press, 1994), pp. 26–48.

Gristwood, Sarah. *The Tudors in Love: The Courtly Code Behind the Last Medieval Dynasty* (London: Oneworld Publications, 2021).

Guy, John. *Tudor England* (Oxford: Oxford University Press, 1988).

Guy, John. *'My Heart is My Own': The Life of Mary Queen of Scots* (London: Fourth Estate, 2004).

Harkrider, Melissa Franklin. *Women, Reform and Community in Early Modern England: Katherine Willoughby, duchess of Suffolk, and Lincolnshire's Godly Aristocracy, 1519–1580* (Woodbridge: The Boydell Press, 2008).

Hayward, Maria. '"We Should Dress us Fairly for Our End": The Significance of the Clothing Worn at Elite Executions in England in the Long Sixteenth Century', *History* 101 (2016), pp. 222–45.

Hibbert, Christopher. *The Virgin Queen: A Personal History of Elizabeth I* (London: Tauris Parke Paperbacks, 2010).

Hickerson, Megan L. *Making Women Martyrs in Tudor England* (Houndmills: Palgrave Macmillan, 2005).

Hill Cole, Mary. 'Monarchy in Motion: An Overview of Elizabethan Progresses' in Jayne Elisabeth Archer, Elizabeth Goldring and Sarah Knight (eds), *The Progresses, Pageants, and Entertainments of Queen Elizabeth I* (New York: Oxford University Press, 2007), pp. 27–46.

Hoak, Dale. 'Rehabilitating the Duke of Northumberland: Politics and Political Control, 1549–53' in Jennifer Loach and Robert Tittler (eds), *The Mid-Tudor Polity c. 1540–1560* (London and Basingstoke: Macmillan, 1980), pp. 29–52.

Hoak, Dale. 'A Tudor Deborah? The Coronation of Elizabeth I, Parliament, and the Problem of Female Rule' in Christopher Highley and John N. King (eds), *John Foxe and His World* (Abingdon: Routledge, 2017), pp. 73–91.

Honig, Elizabeth. 'In Memory: Lady Dacre and Pairing by Hans Eworth' in Lucy Gent and Nigel Llewellyn (eds), *Renaissance Bodies: The Human Figure in English Culture c. 1540–1660* (London: Reaktion Books, 1990), pp. 60–86.

Horton, Louise. 'The Cleric and the Learned Lady: Intertextuality in the Religious Writings of Lady Jane Grey' in Patricia Pender (ed.), *Gender, Authorship, and Early Modern Women's Collaboration* (London: Palgrave Macmillan, 2017), pp. 149–75.

Houlbrooke, Ralph. *Death, Religion, and the Family in England, 1480–1750* (Oxford and New York: Oxford University Press, 1998).

Ingram, Martin. *Carnal Knowledge: Regulating Sex in England, 1470–1600* (Cambridge: Cambridge University Press, 2017).

Ives, Eric. *Lady Jane Grey: A Tudor Mystery* (Chichester: Wiley-Blackwell, 2011).

Jones, Nigel. *Tower: An Epic History of the Tower of London* (London: Hutchinson, 2011).

Jones, William. *Finger-ring Lore: Historical, Legendary, Anecdotal* (London: Chatto & Windus, 1877).

Kewes, Paulina. 'Two Queens, One Inventory: The Lives of Mary and Elizabeth Tudor' in Kevin Sharpe and Steven N. Zwicker (eds), *Writing Lives: Biography and Textuality, Identity and Representation in Early Modern England* (Oxford: Oxford University Press, 2008), pp. 187–207.

Kewes, Paulina. 'The Puritan, the Jesuit and the Jacobean Succession' in Susan Doran and Paulina Kewes (eds), *Doubtful and Dangerous: The Question of Succession in Late Elizabethan England* (Manchester: Manchester University Press, 2014), pp. 47–71.

Lee, Sidney (ed.). *Dictionary of National Biography* (New York: Macmillan and Co., 1896, 63 vols).

Levin, Carole. 'Elizabeth I as Sister and "Loving Kinswoman"' in Anne J. Cruz and Mihoko Suzuki (eds), *The Rule of Women in Early Modern Europe* (Urbana and Chicago, IL: University of Illinois Press, 2009), pp. 123–42.

Levine, Mortimer. 'A "Letter" on the Elizabethan Succession Question, 1566', *Huntington Library Quarterly* 19 (1955), pp. 13–38.

Levine, Mortimer. *The Early Elizabethan Succession Question 1558–1568* (Stanford, CA: Stanford University Press, 1966).

Levine, Mortimer. *Tudor Dynastic Problems 1460–1571* (London: George Allen & Unwin, 1973).

Licence, Amy. *Tudor Roses: From Margaret Beaufort to Elizabeth I* (Stroud: Amberley
   Publishing, 2022).
Lipscomb, Suzannah. *The King is Dead: The Last Will and Testament of Henry VIII*
   (London: Head of Zeus, 2015).
Llewellyn, Nigel. 'Honour in Life, Death and in the Memory: Funeral Monuments
   in Early Modern England', *Transactions of the Royal Historical Society* 6 (1996),
   pp. 179–200.
Loades, David. *Mary Tudor: A Life* (Oxford: Blackwell, 1992).
Loades, David. *John Dudley: Duke of Northumberland 1504–1553* (Oxford: Clarendon
   Press, 1996).
Loades, D.M. *Two Tudor Conspiracies* (Cambridge: Cambridge University Press, 1965).
Loades, D.M. *The Reign of Mary Tudor: Politics, Government, and Religion in England,
   1553–1558* (London: Ernest Benn, 1979).
MacCaffrey, Wallace. *Elizabeth I* (London: Arnold, 1993).
McClive, Cathy. 'The Hidden Truths of the Belly: The Uncertainties of Pregnancy
   in Early Modern Europe', *Social History of Medicine* 15 (2002), pp. 209–27.
MacCulloch, Diarmaid. *The Boy King: Edward VI and the Protestant Reformation*
   (Berkeley and Los Angeles, CA: University of California Press, 1999).
McLaren, Anne. 'The Quest for a King: Gender, Marriage, and Succession in
   Elizabethan England', *Journal of British Studies* 41 (2002), pp. 259–90.
Madden, Frederic, Bulkeley Bandinel and John Gough Nichols (eds). *Collectanea
   Topographica Et Genealogica* (London: John Bowyer Nichols & Son, 1838, 8 vols).
Mallick, Oliver. 'Clients and Friends: The Ladies-in-Waiting at the Court of Anne
   of Austria (1615–66)' in Nadine Akkerman and Birgit Houben (eds), *The Politics
   of Female Households: Ladies-in-Waiting across Early Modern Europe* (Leiden: Brill,
   2014), pp. 231–67.
Marshall, Peter. *Beliefs and the Dead in Reformation England* (Oxford: Oxford
   University Press, 2002).
Medvei, V.C. 'The Illness and Death of Mary Tudor', *Journal of the Royal Society of
   Medicine* 80 (1987), pp. 766–70.
Mendelson, Sara and Patricia Crawford. *Women in Early Modern England 1550–1720*
   (Oxford: Clarendon Press, 1998).
Neale, J.E. *Queen Elizabeth I* (Chicago, IL: Academy Chicago Publishers, 1992).
Norton, Elizabeth. *The Temptation of Elizabeth Tudor* (London: Head of Zeus, 2015).
O'Hara, Diana. *Courtship and Constraint: Rethinking the Making of Marriage in Tudor
   England* (Manchester: Manchester University Press, 2000).
Outhwaite, R.B. *Clandestine Marriage in England 1500–1850* (London and Rio
   Grande, OH: Hambledon Press, 1995).
Page, Augustine (ed.). *A Supplement to the Suffolk Traveller; or Topographical and
   Genealogical Collections, Concerning That County* (London: J.B. Nichols & Son, 1844).
Perry, Maria. *The Word of a Prince: A Life of Elizabeth I from Contemporary Documents*
   (Woodbridge: The Boydell Press, 1990).
Plowden, Alison. *Lady Jane Grey: Nine Days Queen* (Stroud: Sutton Publishing, 2003).

Pollard, A.F. 'Catherine Seymour', *Dictionary of National Biography, 1885–1900*, Volume 51, accessed at en.wikisource.org/wiki/Dictionary_of_National_Biography,_1885–1900/Seymour,_Catherine.

Pollock, Linda A. 'Embarking on a Rough Passage: The Experience of Pregnancy in Early-Modern Society' in Valerie Fildes (ed.), *Women as Mothers in Pre-industrial England* (Abingdon and New York: Routledge, 1990), pp. 39–67.

Post Walton, Kristen. *Catholic Queen, Protestant Patriarchy: Mary, Queen of Scots and the Politics of Gender and Religion* (Houndmills: Palgrave Macmillan, 2007).

Ravenscroft, Janet. 'Dwarfs – and a *Loca* – as Ladies' Maids at the Spanish Habsburg Courts' in Nadine Akkerman and Birgit Houben (eds), *The Politics of Female Households: Ladies-in-Waiting across Early Modern Europe* (Leiden: Brill, 2014), pp. 147–81.

Richards, Jennifer. 'How Lady Jane Grey May Have Used Her Education' in Elizabeth Scott-Baumann, Danielle Clarke and Sarah C.E. Ross (eds), *The Oxford Handbook of Early Modern Women's Writing in English, 1540–1700* (Oxford: Oxford University Press, 2022), pp. 39–53.

Richards, Judith M. *Mary Tudor* (Abingdon and New York: Routledge, 2008).

Rickman, Johanna. *Love, Lust, and License in Early Modern England: Illicit Sex and the Nobility* (Aldershot: Ashgate, 2008).

Ring, Morgan. *So High a Blood: The Life of Margaret, Countess of Lennox* (London: Bloomsbury, 2017).

St Maur, H. *Annals of the Seymours: Being a History of the Seymour Family, From Early Times to Within a Few Years of the Present* (London: Kegan Paul, 1902).

Samson, Alexander. 'Changing Places: The Marriage and Royal Entry of Philip, Prince of Austria, and Mary Tudor, July–August 1554', *The Sixteenth Century Journal* 36 (2005), pp. 761–84.

Schutte, William M. 'Thomas Churchyard's "Dollful Discourse" and the Death of Lady Katherine Grey', *The Sixteenth Century Journal* 15 (1984), pp. 471–87.

Seymour, William. *Ordeal by Ambition: An English Family in the Shadow of the Tudors* (London: Sidgwick & Jackson, 1972).

Sharpe, J.A. '"Last Dying Speeches": Religion, Ideology and Public Execution in Seventeenth-Century England', *Past & Present* 107 (1985), pp. 144–67.

Skidmore, Chris. *Edward VI: The Lost King of England* (London: Phoenix, 2008).

Somerset, Anne. *Elizabeth I* (London: Phoenix, 1997).

Spies, Martin. 'The Portrait of Lady Katherine Grey and Her Son: Iconographic Medievalism as a Legitimation Strategy' in Alicia C. Montoya, Sophie van Romburgh and Wim van Anrooij (eds), *Early Modern Medievalisms: The Interplay between Scholarly Reflection and Artistic Production* (Leiden: Brill, 2010), pp. 165–91.

Stone, Lawrence. *The Family, Sex and Marriage in England 1500–1800* (New York: Harper & Row, 1977).

Strickland, Agnes. *Lives of the Tudor Princesses including Lady Jane Gray and Her Sisters* (London: Longmans, Green & Co., 1868).

Tallis, Nicola. *Crown of Blood: The Deadly Inheritance of Lady Jane Grey* (London: Michael O'Mara, 2016).

Thomas, Melita. *The House of Grey: Friends & Foes of Kings* (Stroud: Amberley Publishing, 2019).

Villeponteaux, Mary. *The Queen's Mercy: Gender and Judgment in Representations of Elizabeth I* (New York: Palgrave Macmillan, 2014).

Walsham, Alexandra. *Providence in Early Modern England* (Oxford: Oxford University Press, 1999).

Warnicke, Retha M. *The Rise and Fall of Anne Boleyn: Family Politics at the Court of Henry VIII* (Cambridge: Cambridge University Press, 1989).

Warnicke, Retha M. *Mary Queen of Scots* (Abingdon and New York: Routledge, 2006).

Warnicke, Retha M. *Wicked Women of Tudor England: Queens, Aristocrats, Commoners* (New York: Palgrave Macmillan, 2012).

Weir, Alison. *The Six Wives of Henry VIII* (London: The Bodley Head, 1991).

Weir, Alison. *Children of England: The Heirs of King Henry VIII 1547–1558* (London: Jonathan Cape, 1996).

Weir, Alison. *The Lost Tudor Princess: A Life of Margaret Douglas, Countess of Lennox* (London: Jonathan Cape, 2015).

Whitelock, Anna. *Mary Tudor: England's First Queen* (London: Bloomsbury, 2009).

Whitelock, Anna. *Elizabeth's Bedfellows: An Intimate History of the Queen's Court* (London: Bloomsbury, 2013).

Whitelock, Anna. '"A Queen, and By the Same Title, a King Also": Mary I: Queen-in-Parliament' in Sarah Duncan and Valerie Schutte (eds), *The Birth of a Queen: Essays on the Quincentenary of Mary I* (New York: Palgrave Macmillan, 2016), pp. 89–113.

Whitelock, Anna. '"Woman, Warrior, Queen?"' Rethinking Mary and Elizabeth' in Alice Hunt and Anna Whitelock (eds), *Tudor Queenship: The Reigns of Mary and Elizabeth* (New York: Palgrave Macmillan, 2010), pp. 173–91.

Wiesner, Merry E. *Women and Gender in Early Modern Europe* (Cambridge: Cambridge University Press, 1993).

Williams, Kate. *Rival Queens: The Betrayal of Mary, Queen of Scots* (London: Hutchinson, 2018).

The Wiltshire Archaeological and Natural History Magazine, Published under the Direction of the Society Formed in that County A.D. 1853 (Devizes: H.F. & E. Bull, 1875), Vol. XV.

Wizeman, William, S.J. 'The Religious Policy of Mary I' in Susan Doran and Thomas S. Freeman (eds), *Mary Tudor: Old and New Perspectives* (Basingstoke and New York: Palgrave Macmillan, 2011), pp. 153–71.

Wood, Lynsey. '"The Very Next Blood of the King": The Rules Governing Female Succession to the Throne in English History' in Ana Maria S.A. Rodrigues, Manuela Santos Silva and Jonathan Spangler (eds), *Dynastic Change: Legitimacy and Gender in Medieval and Early Modern Monarchy* (Abingdon: Routledge, 2020), pp. 21–43.

Zahl, Paul F.M. *Five Women of the English Reformation* (Grand Rapids, MI: William B. Eerdmans, 2001).

Notes

Introduction

1. Katherine's life has also been explored in several group biographies, including Hester W. Chapman, *Two Tudor Portraits: Henry Howard, Earl of Surrey and Lady Katherine Grey* (London: Jonathan Cape, 1960) and Leanda de Lisle, *The Sisters Who Would Be Queen: The Tragedy of Mary, Katherine & Lady Jane Grey* (London: HarperPress, 2008).
2. For example, Alison Weir, *A Dangerous Inheritance* (London: Arrow, 2012), Elizabeth Fremantle, *Sisters of Treason* (London: Penguin, 2014) and Philippa Gregory, *The Last Tudor* (London: Simon & Schuster UK, 2017).
3. Hester W. Chapman, *Two Tudor Portraits: Henry Howard, Earl of Surrey and Lady Katherine Grey* (London: Jonathan Cape, 1960), p. 232.

Chapter 1: A Godly Family

1. Richard Davey, *The Sisters of Lady Jane Grey and their Wicked Grandfather* (London: Chapman & Hall, 1911), p. 83.
2. James Craigie Robertson (ed.), *Ecclesia Restaurata; or, the History of the Reformation of the Church of England. By Peter Heylyn, D.D.* (Cambridge: Cambridge University Press, 1849, 2 vols), Vol. II, p. 4. It is likely that Katherine's elder sister Jane was named for Queen Jane Seymour (who married Henry VIII in 1536) and her younger sister Mary named for Henry VIII's daughter (the future Queen Mary I).
3. Jane was traditionally believed to have been born in October 1537, but modern research has demonstrated that she was almost certainly born in the second half of 1536. See J. Stephan Edwards, 'On the Birthdate of Lady Jane Grey', *Notes*

and Queries 54 (2007), 240–42 and 'A Further Note on the Date of Birth of Lady Jane Grey', *Notes and Queries* 55 (2008), 146–48, and Nicola Tallis, *Crown of Blood: The Deadly Inheritance of Lady Jane Grey* (London: Michael O'Mara, 2016), pp. 2–3.

4. For the date of their marriage, see Leanda de Lisle, *The Sisters Who Would Be Queen*, p. 5.

5. William Douglas Hamilton (ed.), *A Chronicle of England during the Reigns of the Tudors, from A.D. 1485 to 1559. By Charles Wriothesley, Windsor Herald* (London: J.B. Nichols & Sons, 1875–77, 2 vols), Vol. I, p. 22.

6. John Nichols (ed.), *The History of the Worthies of England: Endeavoured by Thomas Fuller, D.D. First Printed in 1662* (London: F.C. & J. Rivington, 1811, 2 vols), Vol. I, p. 563.

7. Eric Ives, *Lady Jane Grey: A Tudor Mystery* (Chichester: Wiley-Blackwell, 2011), p. 35.

8. Melita Thomas, *The House of Grey: Friends & Foes of Kings* (Stroud: Amberley Publishing, 2019), p. 204.

9. Ibid., p. 229.

10. Ibid., p. 234.

11. Robertson, *Ecclesia Restaurata*, Vol. II, p. 3.

12. 'Henry VIII: October 1538 26–31', in *Letters and Papers, Foreign and Domestic, Henry VIII, Volume 13 Part 2, August–December 1538*, ed. James Gairdner (London, 1893), pp. 263–85. *British History Online*, www.british-history.ac.uk/letters-papers-hen8/vol13/no2/pp263-285.

13. Cited by Tallis, *Crown of Blood*, p. 5.

14. 'Henry VIII: Miscellaneous, 1538', in *Letters and Papers, Foreign and Domestic, Henry VIII, Volume 13 Part 2, August–December 1538*, ed. James Gairdner (London, 1893), pp. 496–539. *British History Online*, www.british-history. ac.uk/letters-papers-hen8/vol13/no2/pp496-539.

15. Alison Weir, *Children of England: The Heirs of King Henry VIII 1547–1558* (London: Jonathan Cape, 1996), p. 45.

16. Ibid.

17. Alison Plowden, *Lady Jane Grey: Nine Days Queen* (Stroud: Sutton Publishing, 2003), p. 39.

18. Ibid.

19. Elizabeth Honig, 'In Memory: Lady Dacre and Pairing by Hans Eworth' in Lucy Gent and Nigel Llewellyn (eds), *Renaissance Bodies: The Human Figures in English Culture c. 1540–1660* (London: Reaktion Books, 1990), p. 67.

20. Ibid., p. 68.

21. Leanda de Lisle, *Tudor: The Family Story* (London: Chatto & Windus, 2013), p. 417.

22. J.A. Giles (ed.), *The Whole Works of Roger Ascham, Now First Collected and Revised, With a Life of the Author* (London: John Russell Smith, 1864, 4 vols), Vol. III, p. 118.

23. Lawrence Stone, *The Family, Sex and Marriage in England 1500–1800* (New York: Harper & Row, 1977), pp. 7, 99.
24. Cited by Thomas, *The House of Grey*, pp. 303–4.
25. Ives, *Lady Jane Grey*, p. 53.
26. Hastings Robinson (ed.), *Original Letters Relative to the English Reformation, Written during the Reigns of King Henry VIII, King Edward VI, and Queen Mary: Chiefly from the Archives of Zurich* (Cambridge: Cambridge University Press, 1846, 2 vols), Vol. I, p. 276.
27. Tallis, *Crown of Blood*, p. 104; de Lisle, *Tudor*, p. 418.
28. Chapman, *Two Tudor Portraits*, p. 155.
29. Robertson, *Ecclesia Restaurata*, Vol. II, p. 4.
30. Thomas, *The House of Grey*, p. 259.
31. G.W. Bernard, *The King's Reformation: Henry VIII and the Remaking of the English Church* (New Haven, CT and London: Yale University Press, 2005).
32. 'Henry VIII: August 1540, 1–10', in *Letters and Papers, Foreign and Domestic, Henry VIII, Volume 15, 1540*, ed. James Gairdner and R.H. Brodie (London, 1896), pp. 481–88. *British History Online*, www.british-history.ac.uk/letters-papers-hen8/vol15/pp481-488.
33. Robinson, *Original Letters*, Vol. II, p. 406.
34. Thomas, *The House of Grey*, p. 266.
35. De Lisle, *Sisters Who Would Be Queen*, p. 16.
36. Chapman, *Two Tudor Portraits*, p. 154.
37. The perception of Katherine as the beauty of the family is repeated in numerous books about Lady Jane Grey and her family. For example: Weir, *Children of England*, p. 46; Plowden, *Lady Jane Grey*, p. 142; Tallis, *Crown of Blood*, p. 39.
38. Ives, *Lady Jane Grey*, p. 70.
39. Robinson, *Original Letters*, Vol. I, p. 277.
40. Thomas Park (ed.), *Nugae Antiquae: Being a Miscellaneous Collection of Original Papers, in Prose and Verse; Written during the Reigns of Henry VIII. Edward VI. Queen Mary, Elizabeth, and King James: By Sir John Harington, Knt. and by Others who Lived in Those Times* (London: Vernor & Hood, 1804, 2 vols), Vol. I, p. 28.
41. William B. Turnbull (ed.), *Calendar of State Papers, Foreign Series, of the Reign of Edward VI., 1547–1553, Preserved in the State Paper Department of Her Majesty's Public Record Office* (London: Longman, Green, Longman & Roberts, 1861), p. 101.
42. Robertson, *Ecclesia Restaurata*, Vol. II, p. 4.
43. De Lisle, *Sisters Who Would Be Queen*, p. 66.
44. Cited by de Lisle, *Sisters Who Would Be Queen*, p. 66.
45. Suzannah Lipscomb, *The King is Dead: The Last Will and Testament of Henry VIII* (London: Head of Zeus, 2015), p. 30.
46. John Edwards, *Mary I: England's Catholic Queen* (New Haven, CT and London: Yale University Press, 2011), p. 63.
47. Henry VIII's last will and testament optimistically nominated 'the Heires of our Body laufully begotten of the Body of our entierly beloved Wief

Quene Catheryn [Parr] that now is, or of any other our laufull Wief that We shall hereafter mary' to succeed Edward prior to the crown passing to Mary and Elizabeth. See NA E 23/4. The will is also reproduced in Thomas Rymer, *Fœdera, conventiones, literæ, et cujuscunque generis acta publica, inter reges Angliæ et alios quosvis imperatores, reges, pontifices, principes, vel communitates, ab ineunte sæculo duodecimo, viz. ab anno 1101, ad nostra usque tempore habita aut tractata; ex autographis, infra secretiores Archivorum regiorum thesaurarias, per multa sæcula reconditis, fideliter exscripta … Accurante Thoma Rymer* (London: A. & J. Churchill, 1704–35), p. 112.

48. Mortimer Levine, *Tudor Dynastic Problems 1460–1571* (London: George Allen & Unwin, 1973), p. 74.
49. NA E 23/4; Rymer, *Fœdera*, p. 113.
50. Tallis, *Crown of Blood*, p. 55.
51. Lipscomb, *The King is Dead*, p. 117.

Chapter 2: 'Tempests of Sedition'

1. David Loades, *Mary Tudor: A Life* (Oxford: Blackwell, 1992), p. 134.
2. John Strype, *Ecclesiastical Memorials, Relating Chiefly to Religion, and the Reformation of It, and the Emergencies of the Church of England, under King Henry VIII. King Edward VI. and Queen Mary I. With Large Appendixes, Containing Original Papers, Records, &c.* (Oxford: Clarendon Press, 1822, 7 vols), Vol. II(II), p. 291.
3. Ibid., pp. 292–93.
4. Ibid., p. 293.
5. Ibid., p. 297.
6. Ibid.
7. Ibid., p. 302.
8. Thomas, *The House of Grey*, p. 275.
9. Diarmaid MacCulloch, *The Boy King: Edward VI and the Protestant Reformation* (Berkeley and Los Angeles, CA: University of California Press, 1999), pp. 56 and 57 for the quotes.
10. Susan Brigden, *New Worlds, Lost Worlds: The Rule of the Tudors 1485–1603* (London: Allen Lane, 2000), p. 188.
11. Joseph Stevenson (ed.), *The Life of Jane Dormer Duchess of Feria by Henry Clifford* (London: Burns & Oates, 1887), p. 42.
12. Samuel Haynes (ed.), *A Collection of State Papers, Relating to Affairs in the Reigns of King Henry VIII. King Edward VI. Queen Mary, and Queen Elizabeth, From the Year 1542 to 1570* (London: William Bowyer, 1740), p. 83.
13. De Lisle, *Sisters Who Would Be Queen*, p. 29.
14. Haynes, *A Collection of State Papers*, p. 80.
15. Tallis, *Crown of Blood*, p. 61.
16. De Lisle, *Sisters Who Would Be Queen*, p. 29.

17. Patrick Fraser Tytler, *England under the Reigns of Edward VI. and Mary, with the Contemporary History of Europe, Illustrated in Original Letters Never Before Printed* (London: Richard Bentley, 1839, 2 vols), Vol. I, p. 138.
18. De Lisle, *Sisters Who Would Be Queen*, p. 31.
19. Chapman, *Two Tudor Portraits*, p. 167.
20. 'Spain: February 1547, 21–28', in *Calendar of State Papers, Spain, Volume 9, 1547–1549*, ed. Martin A.S. Hume and Royall Tyler (London, 1912), pp. 37–44. *British History Online*, www.british-history.ac.uk/cal-state-papers/spain/vol9/pp37-44.
21. 'Appendix: Miscellaneous 1547', in *Calendar of State Papers, Spain, Volume 9, 1547–1549*, ed. Martin A.S. Hume and Royall Tyler (London, 1912), pp. 491–530. *British History Online*, www.british-history.ac.uk/cal-state-papers/spain/vol9/pp491-530.
22. Ibid.
23. 'Spain: July 1547, 1–15', in *Calendar of State Papers, Spain, Volume 9, 1547–1549*, ed. Martin A.S. Hume and Royall Tyler (London, 1912), pp. 116–25. *British History Online*, www.british-history.ac.uk/cal-state-papers/spain/vol9/pp116-125.
24. 'Spain: June 1547, 16–30', in *Calendar of State Papers, Spain, Volume 9, 1547–1549*, ed. Martin A.S. Hume and Royall Tyler (London, 1912), pp. 100–16. *British History Online*, www.british-history.ac.uk/cal-state-papers/spain/vol9/pp100-116.
25. Martin A. Sharp Hume (ed.), *Chronicle of King Henry VIII. of England. Being a Contemporary Record of Some of the Principal Events of the Reigns of Henry VIII. and Edward VI.* (London: George Bell and Sons, 1889), pp. 157, 159.
26. Stephen Reed Cattley (ed.), *The Acts and Monuments of John Foxe: A New and Complete Edition* (London: R.B. Seeley & W. Burnside, 1838, 8 vols), Vol. V, p. 554.
27. Ibid., p. 553.
28. For this episode, see Elizabeth Norton, *The Temptation of Elizabeth Tudor* (London: Head of Zeus, 2015).
29. Haynes, *A Collection of State Papers*, p. 99.
30. Ibid.
31. Ibid.
32. Ibid., p. 96.
33. De Lisle, *Sisters Who Would Be Queen*, p. 41.
34. Chapman, *Two Tudor Portraits*, p. 158.
35. Haynes, *A Collection of State Papers*, p. 76.
36. Ibid.
37. Ibid.
38. Ibid., pp. 77–78.
39. NA EXT 9/42/2.
40. Haynes, *A Collection of State Papers*, p. 78.
41. Ibid.

42. Patricia Crawford, *Women and Religion in England 1500–1720* (London and New York: Routledge, 1993), p. 39.
43. Ibid.
44. Haynes, *A Collection of State Papers*, p. 78.
45. Chapman, *Two Tudor Portraits*, p. 158.
46. Haynes, *A Collection of State Papers*, p. 79.
47. Tytler, *England under the Reigns of Edward VI. and Mary*, p. 139.
48. Ibid.
49. Tallis, *Crown of Blood*, p. 83.
50. De Lisle, *Sisters Who Would Be Queen*, p. 50.
51. Haynes, *A Collection of State Papers*, pp. 95–99.
52. Cited by de Lisle, *Sisters Who Would Be Queen*, pp. 49–50.
53. 'Spain: January 1549', in *Calendar of State Papers, Spain, Volume 9, 1547–1549*, ed. Martin A.S. Hume and Royall Tyler (London, 1912), pp. 327–35. *British History Online*, www.british-history.ac.uk/cal-state-papers/spain/vol9/pp327-335.
54. Ibid.
55. Strype, *Ecclesiastical Memorials*, Vol. II(I), pp. 195–96.
56. Ibid., p. 197.
57. De Lisle, *Sisters Who Would Be Queen*, p. 52.
58. 'Spain: March 1549', in *Calendar of State Papers, Spain, Volume 9, 1547–1549*, ed. Martin A.S. Hume and Royall Tyler (London, 1912), pp. 347–60. *British History Online*, www.british-history.ac.uk/cal-state-papers/spain/vol9/pp347-360.
59. Hamilton, *A Chronicle of England*, Vol. II, p. 10.
60. Norton, *Elizabeth Tudor*, p. 281.
61. Sir John Hayward, *The life, and raigne of King Edward the Sixt. Written by Sr. Iohn Hayward Kt. Dr. of Lawe* (London: Printed for Iohn Partridge ..., 1630), p. 53.
62. Julian Cornwall, *Revolt of the Peasantry 1549* (Abingdon and New York: Routledge, 2022), p. 68.
63. Barrett L. Beer, *Rebellion and Riot: Popular Disorder in England during the Reign of Edward VI* (Kent, OH: Kent State University Press, 1982), p. 151.
64. De Lisle, *Sisters Who Would Be Queen*, p. 58.
65. Ives, *Lady Jane Grey*, pp. 36–37.
66. Tallis, *Crown of Blood*, p. 94.
67. *HMC Report on the Manuscripts of Lord Middleton, Preserved at Wollaton Hall, Nottinghamshire* (London: Published by His Majesty's Stationery Office, 1911), p. 521.
68. Ibid.
69. 'Spain: December 1549', in *Calendar of State Papers, Spain, Volume 9, 1547–1549*, ed. Martin A.S. Hume and Royall Tyler (London, 1912), pp. 481–90. *British History Online*, www.british-history.ac.uk/cal-state-papers/spain/vol9/pp481-490.
70. Ives, *Lady Jane Grey*, p. 57.

71. 'Venice: May 1557, 11–15', in *Calendar of State Papers Relating To English Affairs in the Archives of Venice, Volume 6, 1555–1558*, ed. Rawdon Brown (London, 1877), pp. 1041–95. *British History Online*, www.british-history.ac.uk/cal-state-papers/venice/vol6/pp1041-1095.

72. Thomas, *The House of Grey*, p. 294.

73. Ibid., p. 296. Ives, *Lady Jane Grey* (p. 58) suggested that Dorset was appointed warden in February 1551 and had resigned from that post by September.

74. 'Spain: April 1551, 6–10', in *Calendar of State Papers, Spain, Volume 10, 1550–1552*, ed. Royall Tyler (London, 1914), pp. 251–71. *British History Online*, www.british-history.ac.uk/cal-state-papers/spain/vol10/pp251-271.

75. De Lisle, *Sisters Who Would Be Queen*, p. 66.

76. Ibid.

77. Chapman, *Two Tudor Portraits*, p. 160.

78. Ives, *Lady Jane Grey*, p. 58.

79. Hamilton, *A Chronicle of England*, Vol. II, p. 50.

80. Ibid., p. 56.

81. Hayward, *The life, and raigne of King Edward the Sixt.*, p. 128.

82. See Chapter 3.

83. 'Spain: October 1551', in *Calendar of State Papers, Spain, Volume 10, 1550–1552*, ed. Royall Tyler (London, 1914), pp. 376–91. *British History Online*, www.british-history.ac.uk/cal-state-papers/spain/vol10/pp376-391.

84. Ibid.

85. 'Spain: December 1551, 1–15', in *Calendar of State Papers, Spain, Volume 10, 1550–1552*, ed. Royall Tyler (London, 1914), pp. 399–411. *British History Online*, www.british-history.ac.uk/cal-state-papers/spain/vol10/pp399-411.

86. 'Spain: December 1551, 16–31', in *Calendar of State Papers, Spain, Volume 10, 1550–1552*, ed. Royall Tyler (London, 1914), pp. 411–30. *British History Online*, www.british-history.ac.uk/cal-state-papers/spain/vol10/pp411-430.

87. Richard Garnett (ed.), *The Accession of Queen Mary: Being the Contemporary Narrative of Antonio de Guaras, a Spanish Merchant Resident in London* (London: Lawrence & Bullen, 1892), p. 83.

88. Hamilton, *A Chronicle of England*, Vol. II, p. 65.

89. 'Spain: February 1552', in *Calendar of State Papers, Spain, Volume 10, 1550–1552*, ed. Royall Tyler (London, 1914), pp. 450–64. *British History Online*, www.british-history.ac.uk/cal-state-papers/spain/vol10/pp450-464.

90. Tallis, *Crown of Blood*, p. 121.

91. 'Edward VI: May 1551', in *Calendar of State Papers Foreign: Edward VI 1547–1553*, ed. William B. Turnbull (London, 1861), pp. 98–115. *British History Online*, www.british-history.ac.uk/cal-state-papers/foreign/edw-vi/pp98-115.

92. John Gough Nichols (ed.), *Literary Remains of King Edward the Sixth* (London: J.B. Nichols & Sons, 1857, 2 vols), Vol. II, p. 319.

93. 'Edward VI: June 1551, 1–15', in *Calendar of State Papers Foreign: Edward VI 1547–1553*, ed. William B. Turnbull (London, 1861), pp. 115–29. *British History Online*, www.british-history.ac.uk/cal-state-papers/foreign/edw-vi/pp115-129.

94. 'Edward VI: August 1551', in *Calendar of State Papers Foreign: Edward VI 1547–1553*, ed. William B. Turnbull (London, 1861), pp. 158–64. *British History Online*, www.british-history.ac.uk/cal-state-papers/foreign/edw-vi/pp158-164.
95. Edwards, *Mary I*, pp. 68–69.
96. Ibid., p. 71.
97. 'Spain: January 1550, 1–15', in *Calendar of State Papers, Spain, Volume 10, 1550–1552*, ed. Royall Tyler (London, 1914), pp. 1–11. *British History Online*, www.british-history.ac.uk/cal-state-papers/spain/vol10/pp1-11.
98. Ibid.
99. 'Venice: May 1557, 11–15', in *Calendar of State Papers Relating To English Affairs in the Archives of Venice, Volume 6, 1555–1558*, ed. Rawdon Brown (London, 1877), pp. 1041–95. *British History Online*, www.british-history.ac.uk/cal-state-papers/venice/vol6/pp1041-1095.
100. Robinson, *Original Letters*, Vol. I, p. 304. For Jane's biographers, see for example Tallis, *Crown of Blood*, ch. 9, which provides details of Jane's correspondence with European reformers.
101. 'Venice: August 1554, 16–20', in *Calendar of State Papers Relating To English Affairs in the Archives of Venice, Volume 5, 1534–1554*, ed. Rawdon Brown (London, 1873), pp. 531–67. *British History Online*, www.british-history.ac.uk/cal-state-papers/venice/vol5/pp531-567.
102. 'Edward VI: November 1551', in *Calendar of State Papers Foreign: Edward VI 1547–1553*, ed. William B. Turnbull (London, 1861), pp. 188–200. *British History Online*, www.british-history.ac.uk/cal-state-papers/foreign/edw-vi/pp188-200.
103. Ibid.
104. John Gough Nichols (ed.), *Chronicle of the Grey Friars of London* (London: Camden Society, 1852), p. 72.
105. Strype, *Ecclesiastical Memorials*, Vol. II(I), p. 501.
106. Anna Whitelock, *Mary Tudor: England's First Queen* (London: Bloomsbury, 2009), p. 159.
107. Edwards, *Mary I*, p. 75.
108. Plowden, *Lady Jane Grey*, p. 80.
109. Ibid.
110. Robinson, *Original Letters*, Vol. I, p. 282.
111. De Lisle, *Sisters Who Would Be Queen*, p. 89.
112. Tallis, *Crown of Blood*, p. 125.
113. Strype, *Ecclesiastical Memorials*, Vol. II(II), p. 30.
114. Ibid.
115. Ibid., pp. 30–31.
116. Ibid., p. 30.

Chapter 3: Sister to the Queen

1. Edwards, *Mary I*, p. 80.
2. 'Spain: February 1553', in *Calendar of State Papers, Spain, Volume 11, 1553*, ed. Royall Tyler (London, 1916), pp. 6–14. *British History Online*, www.british-history.ac.uk/cal-state-papers/spain/vol11/pp6-14.
3. Ibid.
4. 'Spain: April 1553', in *Calendar of Papers, Spain, Volume 11, 1553*, ed. Royall Tyler (London, 1916), pp. 23–37. *British History Online*, www.british-history.ac.uk/cal-state-papers/spain/vol11/pp23-37.
5. Ibid.
6. Ibid.
7. Giulio Raviglio Rosso, *Historia delle cose occurse nel regno d'Inghilterra, in materia del Duca di Nortomberlan dopo la morte di Odoardo VI* (Venice: Academy of Venice, 1558; edited by Luca Contile), 10b, translated by Dr J. Stephan Edwards and accessed at somegreymatter.com/rossoengl.htm.
8. *Lettere di Principi, le quali si scrivono o da principi, o ragionano di principi* (Venice: Appresso Giordano Ziletti, 1569–77), fo. 222v, translated by Dr J. Stephan Edwards and accessed at somegreymatter.com/lettereengl.htm.
9. Thomas, *The House of Grey*, p. 303.
10. Cited by Thomas, *The House of Grey*, pp. 303–04.
11. Robinson, *Original Letters*, Vol. II, p. 432.
12. De Lisle, *Sisters Who Would Be Queen*, p. 101.
13. Surrey History Centre 6729/9/113.
14. Strype, *Ecclesiastical Memorials*, Vol. II(II), p. 112. See also Ives, *Lady Jane Grey*, p. 185.
15. Cited by Tallis, *Crown of Blood*, p. 140.
16. 'Spain: May 1553', in *Calendar of State Papers, Spain, Volume 11, 1553*, ed. Royall Tyler (London, 1916), pp. 37–48. *British History Online*, www.british-history.ac.uk/cal-state-papers/spain/vol11/pp37-48.
17. 'Spain: June 1553, 1–15', in *Calendar of State Papers, Spain, Volume 11, 1553*, ed. Royall Tyler (London, 1916), pp. 48–56. *British History Online*, www.british-history.ac.uk/cal-state-papers/spain/vol11/pp48-56.
18. Agnes Strickland, *Lives of the Tudor Princesses including Lady Jane Gray and Her Sisters* (London: Longmans, Green and Co., 1868), p. 186.
19. *Lettere di Principi*, fo. 222v, accessed at somegreymatter.com/lettereengl.htm.
20. Henry Ellis (ed.), *Grafton's Chronicle; or, History of England. To Which is Added His Table of the Bailiffs, Sheriffs, and Mayors, of the City of London. From the Year 1189, to 1558, Inclusive* (London: Printed for J. Johnson [etc.], 1809, 2 vols), Vol. II, p. 532.
21. Ibid.
22. Cited by Chris Skidmore, *Edward VI: The Lost King of England* (London: Phoenix, 2008), p. 249.
23. Robertson, *Ecclesia Restaurata*, Vol. I, p. 293.

24. David Loades, *John Dudley: Duke of Northumberland 1504–1553* (Oxford: Clarendon Press, 1996), p. 238.
25. Ives, *Lady Jane Grey*, p. 153.
26. Robertson, *Ecclesia Restaurata*, Vol. I, p. 294.
27. 'Spain: August 1553, 11–20', in *Calendar of State Papers, Spain, Volume 11, 1553*, ed. Royall Tyler (London, 1916), pp. 162–76. *British History Online*, www.british-history.ac.uk/cal-state-papers/spain/vol11/pp162-176.
28. Ibid.
29. Robertson, *Ecclesia Restaurata*, Vol. II, p. 383.
30. De Lisle, *Sisters Who Would Be Queen*, p. 128.
31. 'Spain: May 1553', in *Calendar of State Papers, Spain, Volume 11, 1553*, ed. Royall Tyler (London, 1916), pp. 37–48. *British History Online*, www.british-history.ac.uk/cal-state-papers/spain/vol11/pp37-48.
32. De Lisle, *Sisters Who Would Be Queen*, p. 103.
33. 'The thanksgiving of women after childbirth, commonly called the churching of women' in David Cressy and Lori Anne Ferrell (eds), *Religion and Society in Early Modern England: A Sourcebook* (London and New York: Routledge, 1996), p. 54.
34. Lipscomb, *The King is Dead*, p. 158.
35. Ellis, *Grafton's Chronicle*, Vol. II, p. 532.
36. Inner Temple Library Petyt MS 538.47, fo. 317.
37. Garnett, *The Accession of Queen Mary*, pp. 85, 86.
38. Ibid., p. 87.
39. Dale Hoak, 'Rehabilitating the Duke of Northumberland: Politics and Political Control, 1549–53' in Jennifer Loach and Robert Tittler (eds), *The Mid-Tudor Polity c. 1540–1560* (London and Basingstoke: Macmillan, 1980), p. 48.
40. Levine, *Tudor Dynastic Problems*, p. 81.
41. Ives, *Lady Jane Grey*, pp. 128, 136.
42. Skidmore, *Edward VI*, p. 249.
43. Stephen Alford, *Kingship and Politics in the Reign of Edward VI* (Cambridge: Cambridge University Press, 2002), p. 172.
44. Ibid.
45. John Guy, *Tudor England* (Oxford: Oxford University Press, 1988), p. 226.
46. 'Spain: July 1553, 1–10', in *Calendar of State Papers, Spain, Volume 11, 1553*, ed. Royall Tyler (London, 1916), pp. 69–80. *British History Online*, www.british-history.ac.uk/cal-state-papers/spain/vol11/pp69-80.
47. Skidmore, *Edward VI*, p. 251.
48. 'Spain: July 1553, 1–10', in *Calendar of State Papers, Spain, Volume 11, 1553*, ed. Royall Tyler (London, 1916), pp. 69–80. *British History Online*, www.british-history.ac.uk/cal-state-papers/spain/vol11/pp69-80.
49. Edwards, *Mary I*, p. 78.
50. 'Spain: July 1553, 1–10', in *Calendar of State Papers, Spain, Volume 11, 1553*, ed. Royall Tyler (London, 1916), pp. 69–80. *British History Online*, www.british-history.ac.uk/cal-state-papers/spain/vol11/pp69-80.

51. John Gough Nichols (ed.), *The Diary of Henry Machyn, Citizen and Merchant-Taylor of London, from A.D. 1550 to A.D. 1563* (London: Camden Society, 1848), p. 35.

52. 'Spain: July 1553, 16–20', in *Calendar of State Papers, Spain, Volume 11, 1553*, ed. Royall Tyler (London, 1916), pp. 90–109. *British History Online*, www.british-history.ac.uk/cal-state-papers/spain/vol11/pp90-109.

53. Garnett, *The Accession of Queen Mary*, p. 86.

54. Loades, *John Dudley*, p. 257.

55. Ellis, *Grafton's Chronicle*, Vol. II, p. 532.

56. 'Venice: August 1554, 16–20', in *Calendar of State Papers Relating To English Affairs in the Archives of Venice, Volume 5, 1534–1554*, ed. Rawdon Brown (London, 1873), pp. 531–67. *British History Online*, www.british-history.ac.uk/cal-state-papers/venice/vol5/pp531-567.

57. Edwards, *Mary I*, p. 81.

58. Ibid., p. 82.

59. Tallis, *Crown of Blood*, pp. 150, 152.

60. Rosso, *Historia delle cose occurse nel regno d'Inghilterra*, 13–13b, accessed at somegreymatter.com/rossoengl.htm.

61. Robertson, *Ecclesia Restaurata*, Vol. II, p. 23.

62. Nichols, *Diary of Henry Machyn*, p. 35.

63. Henry Ellis (ed.), *The New Chronicles of England and France, in Two Parts; By Robert Fabyan* (London: Printed for F.C. & J. Rivington [etc.], 1811), p. 712.

64. Nichols, *Diary of Henry Machyn*, p. 35.

65. John Gough Nichols (ed.), *The Chronicle of Queen Jane, and of Two Years of Queen Mary, and Especially of the Rebellion of Sir Thomas Wyat. Written by a Resident in the Tower of London* (London: Camden Society, 1850), p. 3.

66. 'Spain: July 1553, 1–10', in *Calendar of State Papers, Spain, Volume 11, 1553*, ed. Royall Tyler (London, 1916), pp. 69–80. *British History Online*, www.british-history.ac.uk/cal-state-papers/spain/vol11/pp69-80.

67. Richard Davey, *The Nine Days' Queen: Lady Jane Grey and Her Times* (London: Methuen & Co., 1909), p. 253.

68. De Lisle, *Sisters Who Would Be Queen*, p. 113.

69. Garnett, *The Accession of Queen Mary*, p. 88.

70. Chapman, *Two Tudor Portraits*, p. 166.

71. *Iane, by the grace of God quene of England, Fraunce and Ireland, defendor of the faith, & of the Church of Englande, & also of Irelande under Christ in earth the supreme head to al our most louing, faithfull, and obedient subiects, and to euery of them greting* (London: In ædibus Richardi Grafto[n], reg[inæa] typ[o]graphia [excu]sum, 1553) STC 7846. See also Nicholas Harris Nicolas, *The Literary Remains of Lady Jane Grey: With a Memoir of Her Life* (London: Harding, Triphook & Lepard, 1825), pp. xl–xlvi.

72. Surrey History Centre 6729/3/4.

73. Inner Temple Library Petyt MS 538.47, fo. 12.

74. Hamilton, *A Chronicle of England*, Vol. II, p. 88.
75. Ibid.
76. Inner Temple Library Petyt MS 538.47, fo. 13.
77. 'Spain: July 1553, 11–15', in *Calendar of State Papers, Spain, Volume 11, 1553*, ed. Royall Tyler (London, 1916), pp. 80–90. *British History Online*, www.british-history.ac.uk/cal-state-papers/spain/vol11/pp80-90.
78. Ibid.
79. Diarmaid MacCulloch (ed.), *The Vita Mariae Angliae Reginae of Robert Wingfield of Brantham* (London: Offices of the Royal Historical Society, University College London, 1984), pp. 182, 186.
80. Ibid., pp. 191, 244.
81. Sarah Duncan, *Mary I: Gender, Power, and Ceremony in the Reign of England's First Queen* (New York: Palgrave Macmillan, 2012), p. 12.
82. Ibid.
83. MacCulloch, *Vita Mariae*, p. 264.
84. Ibid., p. 265.
85. Ibid.
86. 'Venice: May 1557, 11–15', in *Calendar of State Papers Relating To English Affairs in the Archives of Venice, Volume 6, 1555–1558*, ed. Rawdon Brown (London, 1877), pp. 1041–95. *British History Online*, www.british-history.ac.uk/cal-state-papers/venice/vol6/pp1041-1095.
87. 'Spain: July 1553, 11–15', in *Calendar of State Papers, Spain, Volume 11, 1553*, ed. Royall Tyler (London, 1916), pp. 80–90. *British History Online*, www.british-history.ac.uk/cal-state-papers/spain/vol11/pp80-90.
88. 'Spain: July 1553, 16–20', in *Calendar of State Papers, Spain, Volume 11, 1553*, ed. Royall Tyler (London, 1916), pp. 90–109. *British History Online*, www.british-history.ac.uk/cal-state-papers/spain/vol11/pp90-109.
89. Ibid.
90. Rosso, *Historia delle cose occurse nel regno d'Inghilterra*, 19b, accessed at somegreymatter.com/rossoengl.htm.
91. 'Spain: July 1553, 16–20', in *Calendar of State Papers, Spain, Volume 11, 1553*, ed. Royall Tyler (London, 1916), pp. 90–109. *British History Online*, www.british-history.ac.uk/cal-state-papers/spain/vol11/pp90-109.
92. Garnett, *The Accession of Queen Mary*, p. 96.
93. *Lettere di Principi*, fo. 224v, accessed at somegreymatter.com/lettereengl.htm.
94. Nichols, *Chronicle of Queen Jane*, p. 12.
95. 'Spain: July 1553, 21–31', in *Calendar of State Papers, Spain, Volume 11, 1553*, ed. Royall Tyler (London, 1916), pp. 109–27. *British History Online*, www.british-history.ac.uk/cal-state-papers/spain/vol11/pp109-127.
96. Tallis, *Crown of Blood*, p. 187.
97. 'Spain: July 1553, 21–31', in *Calendar of State Papers, Spain, Volume 11, 1553*, ed. Royall Tyler (London, 1916), pp. 109–27. *British History Online*, www.british-history.ac.uk/cal-state-papers/spain/vol11/pp109-127.

98. De Lisle, *Sisters Who Would Be Queen*, p. 125.
99. 'Spain: July 1553, 16–20', in *Calendar of State Papers, Spain, Volume 11, 1553*, ed. Royall Tyler (London, 1916), pp. 90–109. *British History Online*, www.british-history.ac.uk/cal-state-papers/spain/vol11/pp90-109.
100. Chapman, *Two Tudor Portraits*, p. 167.
101. Robertson, *Ecclesia Restaurata*, Vol. II, pp. 382–83.
102. Nichols, *Worthies*, Vol. I, p. 563.
103. Ibid.
104. Strickland, *Tudor Princesses*, p. 190.
105. Thomas, *The House of Grey*, p. 310.
106. Anonymous, 'Allegations in behalf of the high and mighty Princes, the Lady Mary, now Queen of Scots, Against the Opinions and Books set forth in the Part and Favour of the Lady Katherine, And the rest of the Issues of the French Queen, Touching the Succession of the Crown. Written in the Time of Queen Elizabeth. London, Printed by J.D in the Year 1690' in William Atwood, *The Fundamental Constitution of the English Government* (Wilmington, DE: Scholarly Resources, Inc., 1973; first published in 1690), p. 12.
107. Hamilton, *A Chronicle of England*, Vol. II, p. 91.
108. De Lisle, *Sisters Who Would Be Queen*, p. 126.
109. 'Spain: August 1553, 11–20', in *Calendar of State Papers, Spain, Volume 11, 1553*, ed. Royall Tyler (London, 1916), pp. 162–76. *British History Online*, www.british-history.ac.uk/cal-state-papers/spain/vol11/pp162-176.
110. Ibid.
111. 'Spain: August 1553, 1–5', in *Calendar of State Papers, Spain, Volume 11, 1553*, ed. Royall Tyler (London, 1916), pp. 127–50. *British History Online*, www.british-history.ac.uk/cal-state-papers/spain/vol11/pp127-150.
112. Ellis, *Grafton's Chronicle*, Vol. II, p. 535.
113. Stevenson, *The Life of Jane Dormer*, p. 92.
114. Garnett, *The Accession of Queen Mary*, p. 109.
115. Ibid., p. 101.
116. Ibid., p. 102.
117. Hamilton, *A Chronicle of England*, Vol. II, p. 99.
118. Ellis, *Grafton's Chronicle*, Vol. II, p. 535.
119. Nichols, *Chronicle of Queen Jane*, p. 25.
120. Hyder E. Rollins (ed.), *Old English Ballads 1553–1625 Chiefly from Manuscripts* (Cambridge: Cambridge University Press, 1920), p. 14.
121. Nichols, *Chronicle of Queen Jane*, p. 28.
122. Ibid., p. 31.
123. Nichols, *Diary of Henry Machyn*, p. 45.

Chapter 4: 'The Ruin of a Family so Illustrious'

1. Plowden, *Lady Jane Grey*, p. 142.
2. 'Spain: November 1553, 1–5', in *Calendar of State Papers, Spain, Volume 11, 1553*, ed. Royall Tyler (London, 1916), pp. 331–37. *British History Online*, www.british-history.ac.uk/cal-state-papers/spain/vol11/pp331-337.
3. Tallis, *Crown of Blood*, p. 217.
4. 'Spain: November 1553, 11–15', in *Calendar of State Papers, Spain, Volume 11, 1553*, ed. Royall Tyler (London, 1916), pp. 352–63. *British History Online*, www.british-history.ac.uk/cal-state-papers/spain/vol11/pp352-363.
5. 'Spain: November 1553, 1–5', in *Calendar of State Papers, Spain, Volume 11, 1553*, ed. Royall Tyler (London, 1916), pp. 331–37. *British History Online*, www.british-history.ac.uk/cal-state-papers/spain/vol11/pp331-337.
6. Anne Boleyn in 1536. Her successor, Katherine Howard, was found guilty of treason by Act of Attainder in 1542.
7. Hamilton, *A Chronicle of England*, Vol. II, p. 104.
8. Nichols, *Chronicle of Queen Jane*, p. 32.
9. Nichols, *Diary of Henry Machyn*, p. 48.
10. 'Spain: November 1553, 11–15', in *Calendar of State Papers, Spain, Volume 11, 1553*, ed. Royall Tyler (London, 1916), pp. 352–63. *British History Online*, www.british-history.ac.uk/cal-state-papers/spain/vol11/pp352-363.
11. 'Spain: November 1553, 16–20', in *Calendar of State Papers, Spain, Volume 11, 1553*, ed. Royall Tyler (London, 1916), pp. 363–74. *British History Online*, www.british-history.ac.uk/cal-state-papers/spain/vol11/pp363-374.
12. BL Add MS 26748 fo. 15v.
13. 'Spain: July 1553, 21–31', in *Calendar of State Papers, Spain, Volume 11, 1553*, ed. Royall Tyler (London, 1916), pp. 109–27. *British History Online*, www.british-history.ac.uk/cal-state-papers/spain/vol11/pp109-127.
14. Anne McLaren, 'The Quest for a King: Gender, Marriage, and Succession in Elizabethan England', *Journal of British Studies* 41 (2002), 279.
15. Judith M. Richards, *Mary Tudor* (Abingdon and New York: Routledge, 2008), p. 145.
16. MacCulloch, *Vita Mariae*, p. 281.
17. 'Spain: February 1554, 1–5', in *Calendar of State Papers, Spain, Volume 12, 1554*, ed. Royall Tyler (London, 1949), pp. 66–82. *British History Online*, www.british-history.ac.uk/cal-state-papers/spain/vol12/pp66-82.
18. 'Spain: February 1554, 1–5', in *Calendar of State Papers, Spain, Volume 12, 1554*, ed. Royall Tyler (London, 1949), pp. 66–82. *British History Online*, www.british-history.ac.uk/cal-state-papers/spain/vol12/pp66-82.
19. Cited by Sarah Duncan, '"Most godly heart fraight with al mercie": Queens' Mercy during the Reigns of Mary I and Elizabeth I' in Carole Levin and R.O. Bucholz (eds), *Queens and Power in Medieval and Early Modern England* (Lincoln, NE and London: University of Nebraska Press, 2009), p. 34.

20. MacCulloch, *Vita Mariae*, p. 280.
21. Ibid., p. 281.
22. Ibid.
23. Paulina Kewes, 'Two Queens, One Inventory: The Lives of Mary and Elizabeth Tudor' in Kevin Sharpe and Steven N. Zwicker (eds), *Writing Lives: Biography and Textuality, Identity and Representation in Early Modern England* (Oxford: Oxford University Press, 2008), p. 203.
24. Ibid.
25. Edwards, *Mary I*, p. 172.
26. Nichols, *Chronicle of the Grey Friars*, p. 86.
27. Hamilton, *A Chronicle of England*, Vol. II, p. 109.
28. Cited by Whitelock, *Mary Tudor*, p. 215.
29. Ibid., pp. 215–16.
30. 'Spain: February 1554, 1–5', in *Calendar of State Papers, Spain, Volume 12, 1554*, ed. Royall Tyler (London, 1949), pp. 66–82. *British History Online*, www.british-history.ac.uk/cal-state-papers/spain/vol12/pp66-82.
31. Anna Whitelock, '"Woman, Warrior, Queen?" Rethinking Mary and Elizabeth' in Alice Hunt and Anna Whitelock (eds), *Tudor Queenship: The Reigns of Mary and Elizabeth* (New York: Palgrave Macmillan, 2010), p. 186.
32. 'Spain: February 1554, 1–5', in *Calendar of State Papers, Spain, Volume 12, 1554*, ed. Royall Tyler (London, 1949), pp. 66–82. *British History Online*, www.british-history.ac.uk/cal-state-papers/spain/vol12/pp66-82.
33. Ibid.
34. Thomas Betteridge, 'Maids and Wives: Representing Female Rule during the Reign of Mary Tudor' in Susan Doran and Thomas S. Freeman (eds), *Mary Tudor: Old and New Perspectives* (Basingstoke and New York: Palgrave Macmillan, 2011), p. 141.
35. Cited by D.M. Loades, *The Reign of Mary Tudor: Politics, Government, and Religion in England, 1553–1558* (London: Ernest Benn, 1979), p. 160.
36. Hamilton, *A Chronicle of England*, Vol. II, p. 111.
37. Tallis, *Crown of Blood*, p. 246.
38. Edwards, *Mary I*, p. 164.
39. Nichols, *Chronicle of Queen Jane*, p. 37.
40. Ibid.
41. Ibid.
42. Ibid.
43. 'Spain: January 1554, 26–31', in *Calendar of State Papers, Spain, Volume 12, 1554*, ed. Royall Tyler (London, 1949), pp. 50–66. *British History Online*, www.british-history.ac.uk/cal-state-papers/spain/vol12/pp50-66.
44. Ibid. For the acknowledgement in Jane's proclamation of this fear of foreign rule: 'that if the saied ladie Marie, or ladie Elizabeth should hereafter haue, & enioy the said Imperial croune of this realm and should then happen to marry with any Stranger borne out of this realme, that then the same Stranger hauing the gouernmente and the Imperiall croune in his handes, would adhere

and practise, not onely to bring this noble free realme, into the tirannie and seruitude of the Bishoppe of Rome, but also to haue the lawes and customes of his or their own natiue countrey or countreys to be practised, and put in vre within this realme, rather then the laws, statutes, and customes here of long time vsed, wherupon the title of inheritance of all and singular the subiects of this realme dooe depend, to the peril of conscience, and the vtter subuersion of the common weale of this realme' (*Iane, by the grace of God quene of England* ...; see also Nicolas, *Literary Remains of Lady Jane Grey*, pp. xl–xlvi).

45. De Lisle, *Sisters Who Would Be Queen*, pp. 141–42.
46. Ibid., p. 142.
47. 'Venice: February 1554', in *Calendar of State Papers Relating To English Affairs in the Archives of Venice, Volume 5, 1534–1554*, ed. Rawdon Brown (London, 1873), pp. 456–72. *British History Online*, www.british-history.ac.uk/cal-state-papers/venice/vol5/pp456-472.
48. 'Spain: February 1554, 1–5', in *Calendar of State Papers, Spain, Volume 12, 1554*, ed. Royall Tyler (London, 1949), pp. 66–82. *British History Online*, www.british-history.ac.uk/cal-state-papers/spain/vol12/pp66-82.
49. Ibid.
50. Hamilton, *A Chronicle of England*, Vol. II, p. 110.
51. 'Spain: February 1554, 6–10', in *Calendar of State Papers, Spain, Volume 12, 1554*, ed. Royall Tyler (London, 1949), pp. 82–93. *British History Online*, www.british-history.ac.uk/cal-state-papers/spain/vol12/pp82-93.
52. Rosso, *Historia delle cose occurse nel regno d'Inghilterra*, 48b, accessed at somegreymatter.com/rossoengl.htm.
53. Edward Warner (appointed Lieutenant of the Tower in 1552, removed from office the following year as a result of his rumoured support for Lady Jane Grey's claim and reinstalled in 1558) was arrested alongside the marquess of Northampton on suspicion of treason and the two were incarcerated on 26 January: Hamilton, *A Chronicle of England*, Vol. II, p. 107. Interestingly, Warner acted as Katherine Grey's custodian when she was imprisoned in the Tower in 1561 following the disclosure of her secret marriage.
54. D.M. Loades, *Two Tudor Conspiracies* (Cambridge: Cambridge University Press, 1965), p. 104.
55. Ibid., p. 103.
56. Ibid.
57. Cited by Tallis, *Crown of Blood*, p. 243.
58. 'Spain: February 1554, 11–15', in *Calendar of State Papers, Spain, Volume 12, 1554*, ed. Royall Tyler (London, 1949), pp. 93–100. *British History Online*, www.british-history.ac.uk/cal-state-papers/spain/vol12/pp93-100.
59. Ibid.
60. 'Spain: February 1554, 6–10', in *Calendar of State Papers, Spain, Volume 12, 1554*, ed. Royall Tyler (London, 1949), pp. 82–93. *British History Online*, www.british-history.ac.uk/cal-state-papers/spain/vol12/pp82-93.
61. Ives, *Lady Jane Grey*, p. 268.

62. Reed Cattley, *Acts and Monuments of John Foxe*, Vol. VI, pp. 417–18.
63. Ives, *Lady Jane Grey*, p. 20. See also de Lisle, *Tudor*, p. 497 n. 18.
64. J. Stephan Edwards, *The Lady Jane Grey's Prayer Book: British Library Harley Manuscript 2342, Fully Illustrated and Transcribed* (Palm Springs, CA: Old John Publishing, 2016), fos 78r–80r.
65. J. Stephan Edwards noted that both the original letter and the volume containing it are now lost, but it was transcribed in a number of texts during the sixteenth century: J. Stephan Edwards, '"Jane the Quene": A New Consideration of Lady Jane Grey, England's Nine-Days Queen', PhD thesis (University of Colorado, 2007), p. 79 n. 128.
66. Strickland, *Tudor Princesses*, p. 175.
67. Chapman, *Two Tudor Portraits*, p. 170.
68. Cited by David Cressy, *Birth, Marriage, and Death: Ritual, Religion, and the Life-Cycle in Tudor and Stuart England* (New York: Oxford University Press, 1997), p. 385.
69. Reed Cattley, *Acts and Monuments of John Foxe*, Vol. VI, p. 422.
70. Melissa Franklin Harkrider, *Women, Reform and Community in Early Modern England: Katherine Willoughby, Duchess of Suffolk, and Lincolnshire's Godly Aristocracy, 1519–1580* (Woodbridge: The Boydell Press, 2008), p. 63.
71. Louise Horton, 'The Cleric and the Learned Lady: Intertextuality in the Religious Writings of Lady Jane Grey' in Patricia Pender (ed.), *Gender, Authorship, and Early Modern Women's Collaboration* (London: Palgrave Macmillan, 2017), pp. 149, 156.
72. Ibid., p. 157.
73. Ibid.
74. Ibid., p. 158.
75. Jennifer Richards, 'How Lady Jane Grey May Have Used Her Education' in Elizabeth Scott-Baumann, Danielle Clarke and Sarah C.E. Ross (eds), *The Oxford Handbook of Early Modern Women's Writing in English, 1540–1700* (Oxford: Oxford University Press, 2022), p. 40.
76. Ibid., p. 41.
77. De Lisle, *Sisters Who Would Be Queen*, p. 159.
78. Horton, 'The Cleric and the Learned Lady', p. 153.
79. Ibid.
80. Cited by J.E. Neale, *Queen Elizabeth I* (Chicago, IL: Academy Chicago Publishers, 1992), p. 7.
81. Peter Marshall, *Beliefs and the Dead in Reformation England* (Oxford: Oxford University Press, 2002), p. 270.
82. Maria Hayward, '"We Should Dress us Fairly for Our End": The Significance of the Clothing Worn at Elite Executions in England in the Long Sixteenth Century', *History* 101 (2016), 223.
83. Ibid., 237.
84. Nichols, *Chronicle of Queen Jane*, p. 54.

85. 'Spain: February 1554, 11–15', in *Calendar of State Papers, Spain, Volume 12, 1554*, ed. Royall Tyler (London, 1949), pp. 93–100. *British History Online*, www.british-history.ac.uk/cal-state-papers/spain/vol12/pp93-100.

86. Nichols, *Chronicle of Queen Jane*, p. 55.

87. Henry Ellis (ed.), *Holinshed's Chronicles of England, Scotland, and Ireland. In Six Volumes* (London: Printed for J. Johnson [etc.], 1808, 6 vols), Vol. IV, p. 22.

88. Nichols, *Chronicle of Queen Jane*, p. 55.

89. Ibid., pp. 56–57.

90. Frances E. Dolan, '"Gentlemen, I Have One Thing More to Say": Women on Scaffolds in England, 1563–1680', *Modern Philology* 92 (1994), 175.

91. J.A. Sharpe, '"Last Dying Speeches": Religion, Ideology and Public Execution in Seventeenth-Century England', *Past & Present* 107 (1985), pp. 151, 155.

92. Nichols, *Chronicle of Queen Jane*, pp. 57–59.

93. Ellis, *Grafton's Chronicle*, Vol. II, pp. 543–44.

94. Ibid., p. 544.

95. Ellis, *Holinshed's Chronicles*, Vol. IV, p. 23.

96. Ibid.

97. Nichols, *Worthies*, Vol. I, p. 563.

98. Robertson, *Ecclesia Restaurata*, Vol. I, p. 295.

99. Richard Head, *The life and death of Mother Shipton being not only a true account of her strange birth and most important passages of her life, but also all her prophesies, now newly collected and historically experienced from the time of her birth, in the reign of King Henry the Seventh until this present year 1667, containing the most important passages of state during the reign of these kings and queens of England ... : strangely preserved amongst other writings belonging to an old monastary in York-shire, and now published for the information of posterity* (London: Printed for B. Harris ..., 1677), p. 28.

100. A.S.G. Edwards (ed.), *Metrical Visions by George Cavendish* (Columbia, SC: University of South Carolina Press, 1980), pp. 131–32.

101. 'Spain: February 1554, 11–15', in *Calendar of State Papers, Spain, Volume 12, 1554*, ed. Royall Tyler (London, 1949), pp. 93–100. *British History Online*, www.british-history.ac.uk/cal-state-papers/spain/vol12/pp93-100.

102. Loades, *Two Tudor Conspiracies*, p. 103.

103. Robinson, *Original Letters*, Vol. I, p. 305.

104. Ellis, *Holinshed's Chronicles*, Vol. IV, p. 24.

105. Nichols, *Chronicle of Queen Jane*, pp. 63–64.

106. 'Spain: February 1554, 21–28', in *Calendar of State Papers, Spain, Volume 12, 1554*, ed. Royall Tyler (London, 1949), pp. 123–29. *British History Online*, www.british-history.ac.uk/cal-state-papers/spain/vol12/pp123-129.

107. Robinson, *Original Letters*, Vol. I, p. 305.

108. Ellis, *Holinshed's Chronicles*, Vol. IV, p. 25.

109. Robinson, *Original Letters*, Vol. I, p. 303.

110. Ibid.

111. Ibid., p. 305.

112. Hamilton, *A Chronicle of England*, Vol. II, p. 115. John Grey was released in October 1554 and pardoned the following January: Loades, *Two Tudor Conspiracies*, p. 104.

Chapter 5: At the Court of Mary I

1. De Lisle, *Sisters Who Would Be Queen*, p. 161. De Lisle also noted (p. 168) that Mary Grey remained in the care of her mother following the duchess' retirement from court after her marriage. Indeed, at 10 years old, Mary was too young to attend on the queen.
2. Strickland, *Tudor Princesses*, p. 191.
3. Ibid., pp. 183–84.
4. William Camden, *The History of the Most Renowned and Victorious Princess Elizabeth, Late Queen of England; Containing All the most Important and Remarkable Passages of State, both at Home and Abroad (so far as they were linked with English Affairs) during her Long and Prosperous Reign* (London: Printed by M. Flesher, for R. Bentley at the Post-Office in Covent-Garden, 1688), p. 70.
5. 'Spain: April 1555', in *Calendar of State Papers, Spain, Volume 13, 1554–1558*, ed. Royall Tyler (London, 1954), pp. 153–68. *British History Online*, www.british-history.ac.uk/cal-state-papers/spain/vol13/pp153-168.
6. De Lisle, *Sisters Who Would Be Queen*, p. 168.
7. De Lisle, *Sisters Who Would Be Queen* (p. 168), suggested that Frances' marriage has been misdated to 1554 rather than 1555 in view of the dating of the year in sixteenth-century England (with New Year held to begin on 25 March rather than on 1 January), but ambassadors at court, including Renard, surely would have commented on Frances' pregnancy had she wed Stokes in March 1555, when her condition would have been apparent. Marrying while pregnant would surely have given rise to comment, but the ambassador's report of April 1555 proposing Courtenay as a husband for the duchess testifies to a degree of secrecy that was maintained about the circumstances of Frances' second marriage.
8. De Lisle, *Sisters Who Would Be Queen*, p. 168.
9. H. C. Maxwell Lyte (ed.), *The Manuscripts of His Grace the Duke of Rutland, G.C.B., Preserved at Belvoir Castle* (London: Printed for Her Majesty's Stationery Office, by Eyre and Spottiswoode, 1888, 4 vols), Vol. I, p. 67.
10. Kenneth Charlton, *Women, Religion and Education in Early Modern England* (Abingdon: Routledge, 1999), p. 66; Megan L. Hickerson, *Making Women Martyrs in Tudor England* (Houndmills: Palgrave Macmillan, 2005), p. 6. For Foxe, see Reed Cattley, *Acts and Monuments of John Foxe*, Vol. VI, p. 423.
11. Robinson, *Original Letters*, Vol. I, p. 304.
12. Ibid., p. 305.
13. 'Venice: May 1557, 11–15', in *Calendar of State Papers Relating To English Affairs in the Archives of Venice, Volume 6, 1555–1558*, ed. Rawdon Brown (London,

1877), pp. 1041–95. *British History Online*, www.british-history.ac.uk/cal-state-papers/venice/vol6/pp1041-1095.

14. Muriel St. Clare Byrne (ed.), selected by Bridget Boland, *The Lisle Letters: An Abridgement* (Chicago, IL: University of Chicago Press, 1983), p. 207.

15. Ibid., p. 208.

16. Oliver Mallick, 'Clients and Friends: The Ladies-in-Waiting at the Court of Anne of Austria (1615–66)' in Nadine Akkerman and Birgit Houben (eds), *The Politics of Female Households: Ladies-in-Waiting across Early Modern Europe* (Leiden: Brill, 2014), p. 256.

17. Janet Ravenscroft, 'Dwarfs – and a *Loca* – as Ladies' Maids at the Spanish Habsburg Courts' in Akkerman and Houben (eds), *Politics of Female Households*, p. 161. Elizabeth I's harsh response to the unwelcome news of Katherine's clandestine marriage with Hertford is explicable from this perspective.

18. Chapman, *Two Tudor Portraits*, p. 173.

19. 'Simancas: March 1559', in *Calendar of State Papers, Spain (Simancas), Volume 1, 1558–1567*, ed. Martin A.S. Hume (London, 1892), pp. 37–46. *British History Online*, www.british-history.ac.uk/cal-state-papers/simancas/vol1/pp37-46.

20. Alison Weir, *The Lost Tudor Princess: A Life of Margaret Douglas, Countess of Lennox* (London: Jonathan Cape, 2015), p. 151.

21. Nichols, *Chronicle of Queen Jane*, p. 24.

22. Robert S. Miola (ed.), *Early Modern Catholicism: An Anthology of Primary Sources* (New York: Oxford University Press, 2007), p. 404.

23. 'Venice: August 1554, 16–20', in *Calendar of State Papers Relating To English Affairs in the Archives of Venice, Volume 5, 1534–1554*, ed. Rawdon Brown (London, 1873), pp. 531–67. *British History Online*, www.british-history.ac.uk/cal-state-papers/venice/vol5/pp531-567.

24. 'Spain: July 1554, 26–31', in *Calendar of State Papers, Spain, Volume 13, 1554–1558*, ed. Royall Tyler (London, 1954), pp. 1–13. *British History Online*, www.british-history.ac.uk/cal-state-papers/spain/vol13/pp1-13.

25. Ibid.

26. Ibid.

27. Reed Cattley, *Acts and Monuments of John Foxe*, Vol. VI, p. 415.

28. 'Venice: February 1554', in *Calendar of State Papers Relating To English Affairs in the Archives of Venice, Volume 5, 1534–1554*, ed. Rawdon Brown (London, 1873), pp. 456–72. *British History Online*, www.british-history.ac.uk/cal-state-papers/venice/vol5/pp456-472.

29. Alexander Samson, 'Changing Places: The Marriage and Royal Entry of Philip, Prince of Austria, and Mary Tudor, July–August 1554', *The Sixteenth Century Journal* 36 (2005), 762.

30. Ibid.

31. Nichols, *Chronicle of Queen Jane*, p. 146.

32. MacCulloch, *Vita Mariae*, p. 281.

33. Ellis, *Holinshed's Chronicles*, Vol. IV, p. 76.
34. Ibid., p. 81.
35. William Wizeman, S.J., 'The Religious Policy of Mary I' in Doran and Freeman (eds), *Mary Tudor*, pp. 158–59.
36. Hamilton, *A Chronicle of England*, Vol. II, p. 136.
37. Cited by Eamon Duffy, *Fires of Faith: Catholic England under Mary Tudor* (New Haven, CT and London: Yale University Press, 2009), p. 120.
38. Reed Cattley, *Acts and Monuments of John Foxe*, Vol. VI, p. 422.
39. 'Venice: August 1554, 16–20', in *Calendar of State Papers Relating To English Affairs in the Archives of Venice, Volume 5, 1534–1554*, ed. Rawdon Brown (London, 1873), pp. 531–67. *British History Online*, www.british-history.ac.uk/cal-state-papers/venice/vol5/pp531-567.
40. De Lisle, *Sisters Who Would Be Queen*, p. 166.
41. Strickland suggested 31 March 1554, but Elizabeth was born the following year: Strickland, *Tudor Princesses*, p. 190.
42. De Lisle, *Sisters Who Would Be Queen*, p. 172.
43. 'Spain: September 1554', in *Calendar of State Papers, Spain, Volume 13, 1554–1558*, ed. Royall Tyler (London, 1954), pp. 39–55. *British History Online*, www.british-history.ac.uk/cal-state-papers/spain/vol13/pp39-55.
44. Ibid.
45. Rollins, *Old English Ballads*, p. 20.
46. Ibid.
47. Ibid., p. 21.
48. Tom Betteridge, *Literature and Politics in the English Reformation* (Manchester: Manchester University Press, 2004), p. 151.
49. Alexandra Walsham, *Providence in Early Modern England* (Oxford: Oxford University Press, 1999), p. 2.
50. De Lisle suggested that both Katherine and Mary Grey lived with their mother at Beaumanor in Leicestershire following the executions of Henry and Jane; de Lisle, *Sisters Who Would Be Queen*, p. 283.
51. 'Venice: August 1554, 16–20', in *Calendar of State Papers Relating To English Affairs in the Archives of Venice, Volume 5, 1534–1554*, ed. Rawdon Brown (London, 1873), pp. 531–67. *British History Online*, www.british-history.ac.uk/cal-state-papers/venice/vol5/pp531-567.
52. 'Spain: November 1554, 1–15', in *Calendar of State Papers, Spain, Volume 13, 1554–1558*, ed. Royall Tyler (London, 1954), pp. 76–95. *British History Online*, www.british-history.ac.uk/cal-state-papers/spain/vol13/pp76-95.
53. Ibid.
54. 'Spain: November 1554, 16–30', in *Calendar of State Papers, Spain, Volume 13, 1554–1558*, ed. Royall Tyler (London, 1954), pp. 96–112. *British History Online*, www.british-history.ac.uk/cal-state-papers/spain/vol13/pp96-112.
55. Ibid.

56. 'Spain: December 1554, 16–31', in *Calendar of State Papers, Spain, Volume 13, 1554–1558*, ed. Royall Tyler (London, 1954), pp. 123–31. *British History Online*, www.british-history.ac.uk/cal-state-papers/spain/vol13/pp123-131.

57. 'Spain: April 1555', in *Calendar of State Papers, Spain, Volume 13, 1554–1558*, ed. Royall Tyler (London, 1954), pp. 153–68. *British History Online*, www.british-history.ac.uk/cal-state-papers/spain/vol13/pp153-168.

58. Hamilton, *A Chronicle of England*, Vol. II, p. 128.

59. Linda A. Pollock, 'Embarking on a Rough Passage: The Experience of Pregnancy in Early-Modern Society' in Valerie Fildes (ed.), *Women as Mothers in Pre-industrial England* (Abingdon and New York: Routledge, 1990), p. 41.

60. Anonymous, *Aristotle's Master-Piece* (London, 1684), p. 150.

61. Cathy McClive, 'The Hidden Truths of the Belly: The Uncertainties of Pregnancy in Early Modern Europe', *Social History of Medicine* 15 (2002), pp. 211–12.

62. 'Venice: August 1554, 16–20', in *Calendar of State Papers Relating To English Affairs in the Archives of Venice, Volume 5, 1534–1554*, ed. Rawdon Brown (London, 1873), pp. 531–67. *British History Online*, www.british-history.ac.uk/cal-state-papers/venice/vol5/pp531-567.

63. *Calendar of the Patent Rolls Preserved in the Public Record Office: Philip and Mary* (London: H.M. Stationery Office, 1936–39, 4 vols), Vol. III, pp. 184–85; HMC Thirteenth Report, Appendix, Part IV. The Manuscripts of Rye and Hereford Corporations, Capt. Loder-Symonds, Mr. E.R. Wodehouse, M.P., and others (London: H.M. Stationery Office, 1892), p. 321.

64. 'Spain: March 1555', in *Calendar of State Papers, Spain, Volume 13, 1554–1558*, ed. Royall Tyler (London, 1954), pp. 143–53. *British History Online*, www.british-history.ac.uk/cal-state-papers/spain/vol13/pp143-153.

65. Nichols, Diary of Henry Machyn, p. 86.

66. 'Spain: May 1555, 11–20', in *Calendar of State Papers, Spain, Volume 13, 1554–1558*, ed. Royall Tyler (London, 1954), pp. 171–75. *British History Online*, www.british-history.ac.uk/cal-state-papers/spain/vol13/pp171-175.

67. 'Venice: May 1555, 16–25', in *Calendar of State Papers Relating To English Affairs in the Archives of Venice, Volume 6, 1555–1558*, ed. Rawdon Brown (London, 1877), pp. 72–82. *British History Online*, www.british-history.ac.uk/cal-state-papers/venice/vol6/pp72-82.

68. 'Spain: June 1555', in *Calendar of State Papers, Spain, Volume 13, 1554–1558*, ed. Royall Tyler (London, 1954), pp. 207–26. *British History Online*, www.british-history.ac.uk/cal-state-papers/spain/vol13/pp207-226.

69. Ibid.

70. Ibid.

71. 'Addenda, Queen Elizabeth - Volume 34: February 1600', in *Calendar of State Papers Domestic: Elizabeth, Addenda 1580-1625*, ed. Mary Anne Everett Green (London, 1872), pp. 404–405. *British History Online*, www.british-history.ac.uk/cal-state-papers/domestic/edw-eliz/addenda/1580-1625/pp404-405.

72. Ibid. There is no record of Katherine's relations with the baby Elizabeth, which would have been limited in view of the brevity of her half-sister's life.
73. 'Venice: August 1555, 1-15', in *Calendar of State Papers Relating To English Affairs in the Archives of Venice, Volume 6, 1555-1558*, ed. Rawdon Brown (London, 1877), pp. 145–163. *British History Online*, www.british-history.ac.uk/cal-state-papers/venice/vol6/pp145-163.
74. 'Spain: September 1555', in *Calendar of State Papers, Spain, Volume 13, 1554-1558*, ed. Royall Tyler (London, 1954), pp. 249–252. *British History Online*, www.british-history.ac.uk/cal-state-papers/spain/vol13/pp249-252.
75. 'Venice: May 1557, 11–15', in *Calendar of State Papers Relating To English Affairs in the Archives of Venice, Volume 6, 1555–1558*, ed. Rawdon Brown (London, 1877), pp. 1041–95. *British History Online*, www.british-history.ac.uk/cal-state-papers/venice/vol6/pp1041-1095.
76. Ibid.
77. Ibid.
78. www.tudorplace.com.ar/Documents/dudley_conspiracy.
79. Strype, *Ecclesiastical Memorials*, Vol. III(II), p. 67.
80. Stevenson, *Life of Jane Dormer*, p. 9.
81. Hamilton, *A Chronicle of England*, Vol. II, p. 138.
82. Ibid.
83. Nichols, *Diary of Henry Machyn*, p. 137.
84. Strype, *Ecclesiastical Memorials*, Vol. III(II), p. 69.
85. Ibid., p. 76.
86. 'Spain: June 1557', in *Calendar of State Papers, Spain, Volume 13, 1554–1558*, ed. Royall Tyler (London, 1954), pp. 293–300. *British History Online*, www.british-history.ac.uk/cal-state-papers/spain/vol13/pp293-300.
87. Loades, *Two Tudor Conspiracies*, p. 174.
88. Cited by Whitelock, 'Woman, Warrior, Queen?', p. 179.
89. Ellis, *The New Chronicles of England and France*, p. 718.
90. De Lisle, *Sisters Who Would Be Queen*, p. 173.
91. Strype, *Ecclesiastical Memorials*, Vol. III(II), p. 25.
92. Nichols, *Diary of Henry Machyn*, p. 163.
93. 'Spain: February 1558', in *Calendar of State Papers, Spain, Volume 13, 1554–1558*, ed. Royall Tyler (London, 1954), pp. 349–65. *British History Online*, www.british-history.ac.uk/cal-state-papers/spain/vol13/pp349-365.
94. 'Spain: March 1558', in *Calendar of State Papers, Spain, Volume 13, 1554–1558*, ed. Royall Tyler (London, 1954), pp. 365–74. *British History Online*, www.british-history.ac.uk/cal-state-papers/spain/vol13/pp365-374.
95. Ibid.
96. 'Spain: November 1553, 26–30', in *Calendar of State Papers, Spain, Volume 11, 1553*, ed. Royall Tyler (London, 1916), pp. 387–407. *British History Online*, www.british-history.ac.uk/cal-state-papers/spain/vol11/pp387-407.
97. Ibid.

98. Thomas, *The House of Grey*, p. 228.
99. Chapman, *Two Tudor Portraits*.
100. J. Stephan Edwards, 'The Berry-Hill Portrait: An Update, November 2021' (2021), accessed at somegreymatter.com/berryhill.htm.
101. J. Stephan Edwards, *A Queen of a New Invention: Portraits of Lady Jane Grey Dudley, England's 'Nine Days Queen'* (Palm Springs, CA: Old John Publishing, 2015), p. 147.
102. Ibid., p. 151.
103. bid.butterscotchauction.com/lots/view/1-56GPEA/english-school-16th-century.
104. 'Simancas: March 1559', in *Calendar of State Papers, Spain (Simancas), Volume 1, 1558–1567*, ed. Martin A.S. Hume (London, 1892), pp. 37–46. *British History Online*, www.british-history.ac.uk/cal-state-papers/simancas/vol1/pp37-46.
105. Robertson, *Ecclesia Restaurata*, Vol. II, p. 383.
106. Ellis, *Grafton's Chronicle*, Vol. II, p. 566.
107. BL Harley MS 249 fo. 57r; BL Harley MS 6286 p. 78.
108. BL Harley MS 6286 p. 45.
109. Ibid.
110. Ibid., p. 46.
111. Cited by Elizabeth Cooper, The Life and Letters of Lady Arabella Stuart, including Numerous Original and Unpublished Documents (London: Hurst & Blackett, 1866, 2 vols), Vol. I, p. 169.
112. 'Spain: October 1558, 21–31', in *Calendar of State Papers, Spain, Volume 13, 1554–1558*, ed. Royall Tyler (London, 1954), pp. 416–35. *British History Online*, www.british-history.ac.uk/cal-state-papers/spain/vol13/pp416-435.
113. 'Spain: November 1558', in *Calendar of State Papers, Spain, Volume 13, 1554–1558*, ed. Royall Tyler (London, 1954), pp. 435–42. *British History Online*, www.british-history.ac.uk/cal-state-papers/spain/vol13/pp435-442.
114. 'Venice: November 1558, 16–30', in *Calendar of State Papers Relating To English Affairs in the Archives of Venice, Volume 6, 1555–1558*, ed. Rawdon Brown (London, 1877), pp. 1547–62. *British History Online*, www.british-history. ac.uk/cal-state-papers/venice/vol6/pp1547-1562.
115. Ibid.
116. Nichols, *Diary of Henry Machyn*, p. 178.
117. V.C. Medvei, 'The Illness and Death of Mary Tudor', *Journal of the Royal Society of Medicine* 80 (1987), 770.
118. 'Venice: November 1558, 16–30', in *Calendar of State Papers Relating To English Affairs in the Archives of Venice, Volume 6, 1555–1558*, ed. Rawdon Brown (London, 1877), pp. 1547–62. *British History Online*, www.british-history. ac.uk/cal-state-papers/venice/vol6/pp1547-1562.
119. 'Simancas: November 1558', in *Calendar of State Papers, Spain (Simancas), Volume 1, 1558–1567*, ed. Martin A.S. Hume (London, 1892), pp. 1–6. *British History Online*, www.british-history.ac.uk/cal-state-papers/simancas/vol1/pp1-6.
120. Ibid.

121. Hamilton, *A Chronicle of England*, Vol. II, p. 142.
122. Nichols, *Diary of Henry Machyn*, pp. 182–83.
123. Ibid., p. 183.
124. Ibid.
125. Ibid.
126. Ibid., p. 184.
127. 'Simancas: November 1558', in *Calendar of State Papers, Spain (Simancas), Volume 1, 1558–1567*, ed. Martin A.S. Hume (London, 1892), pp. 1–6. *British History Online*, www.british-history.ac.uk/cal-state-papers/simancas/vol1/pp1-6.

Chapter 6: 'The Next Heir to the Throne'

1. 'Venice: January 1559, 16–31', in *Calendar of State Papers Relating To English Affairs in the Archives of Venice, Volume 7, 1558–1580*, ed. Rawdon Brown and G. Cavendish Bentinck (London, 1890), pp. 10–24. *British History Online*, www.british-history.ac.uk/cal-state-papers/venice/vol7/pp10-24.
2. Ibid.
3. Ibid.
4. Ibid.
5. Ibid.
6. Ibid.
7. Dale Hoak, 'A Tudor Deborah? The Coronation of Elizabeth I, Parliament, and the Problem of Female Rule' in Christopher Highley and John N. King (eds), *John Foxe and His World* (Abingdon: Routledge, 2017), pp. 78–79.
8. Ilona Bell, *Elizabeth I: The Voice of a Monarch* (New York: Palgrave Macmillan, 2010), p. 40.
9. Richard Mulcaster, THE PASSAGE of our most drad Soueraigne Lady Quene Elyzabeth through the citie of London to Westminster the daye before her coronacion (London, 1559), accessed online at mapoflondon.uvic.ca/QMPS1.htm.
10. Ibid.
11. 'Venice: January 1559, 16–31', in *Calendar of State Papers Relating To English Affairs in the Archives of Venice, Volume 7, 1558–1580*, ed. Rawdon Brown and G. Cavendish Bentinck (London, 1890), pp. 10–24. *British History Online*, www.british-history.ac.uk/cal-state-papers/venice/vol7/pp10-24.
12. Ibid.
13. Ibid.
14. De Lisle, *Sisters Who Would Be Queen* (p. 181) has suggested that Katherine did not attend the queen on the day before her state entry into London.
15. Susan Doran, *Monarchy and Matrimony: The Courtships of Elizabeth I* (London: Routledge, 1996), p. 3.
16. Retha M. Warnicke, *Mary Queen of Scots* (Abingdon and New York: Routledge, 2006), p. 3.

17. Susan Doran and Paulina Kewes, 'Introduction: A Historiographical Perspective' in Susan Doran and Paulina Kewes (eds), *Doubtful and Dangerous: The Question of Succession in Late Elizabethan England* (Manchester: Manchester University Press, 2014), p. 4.

18. Mortimer Levine, *The Early Elizabethan Succession Question 1558–1568* (Stanford: Stanford University Press, 1966), p. 1.

19. 'Simancas: March 1559', in *Calendar of State Papers, Spain (Simancas), Volume 1, 1558–1567*, ed. Martin A.S. Hume (London, 1892), pp. 37–46. *British History Online*, www.british-history.ac.uk/cal-state-papers/simancas/vol1/pp37-46.

20. Levine, *Early Elizabethan Succession Question*, p. 13. There is, of course, no evidence to suggest that Katherine was a Catholic and the ambassador may have believed that her outward conformity with the Marian religious settlement reflected her true beliefs.

21. 'Elizabeth: October 1559, 1–5', in *Calendar of State Papers Foreign: Elizabeth, Volume 2, 1559–1560*, ed. Joseph Stevenson (London, 1865), pp. 1–18. *British History Online*, www.british-history.ac.uk/cal-state-papers/foreign/vol2/pp1-18.

22. William M. Schutte, 'Thomas Churchyard's "Dollful Discourse" and the Death of Lady Katherine Grey', *The Sixteenth Century Journal* 15 (1984), p. 473.

23. Bell, *Elizabeth I*, p. 3.

24. Doran, *Monarchy and Matrimony*, p. 1. Bell, *Elizabeth I* (p. 62) likewise noted that the mistaken assumption that Elizabeth never considered marriage is derived from William Camden's posthumous history of the reign, in which he rewrote her first parliamentary speech to make it appear as if she was, from the outset, determined to live and die a virgin queen.

25. Edward Arber (ed.), John Knox. The First Blast of the Trumpet Against the Monstrous Regiment of Women (London: Southgate, 1878), p. 13.

26. Ibid.

27. Ibid.

28. Cited by Doran, *Monarchy and Matrimony*, p. 8.

29. Bell, *Elizabeth I*, p. 45.

30. Sir Simond d'Ewes, *The Journals of All the Parliaments during the Reign of Queen Elizabeth, Both of the House of Lords and House of Commons* (London: Printed for John Starkey at the Mitre in Fleetstreet near Temple-Bar, 1682), p. 46. See also Maria Perry, *The Word of a Prince: A Life of Elizabeth I from Contemporary Documents* (Woodbridge: The Boydell Press, 1990), p. 100.

31. MacCulloch, *Vita Mariae*, p. 278. Mary's belief that she should select her spouse as a 'kingly right', as her male predecessors had done, is noted by Anna Whitelock, '"A Queen, and By the Same Title, a King Also": Mary I: Queen-in-Parliament' in Sarah Duncan and Valerie Schutte (eds), *The Birth of a Queen: Essays on the Quincentenary of Mary I* (New York: Palgrave Macmillan, 2016), p. 94.

32. Victor van Klarwill (ed.), *Queen Elizabeth and Some Foreigners* (London: The Bodley Head, 1928), p. 41.

33. Bell, *Elizabeth I*, p. 4.

34. Klarwill, *Queen Elizabeth*, p. 29.
35. Ibid., p. 76.
36. Ibid., p. 78.
37. Ibid., p. 81.
38. 'Simancas: August 1559', in *Calendar of State Papers, Spain (Simancas), Volume 1, 1558–1567*, ed. Martin A.S. Hume (London, 1892), pp. 91–95. *British History Online*, www.british-history.ac.uk/cal-state-papers/simancas/vol1/pp91-95.
39. Ibid.
40. Simon Adams, *Leicester and the Court: Essays on Elizabethan Politics* (Manchester: Manchester University Press, 2002), p. 134.
41. 'Simancas: April 1559', in *Calendar of State Papers, Spain (Simancas), Volume 1, 1558–1567*, ed. Martin A.S. Hume (London, 1892), pp. 46–64. *British History Online*, www.british-history.ac.uk/cal-state-papers/simancas/vol1/pp46-64.
42. 'Venice: May 1559', in *Calendar of State Papers Relating To English Affairs in the Archives of Venice, Volume 7, 1558–1580*, ed. Rawdon Brown and G. Cavendish Bentinck (London, 1890), pp. 79–94. *British History Online*, www.british-history.ac.uk/cal-state-papers/venice/vol7/pp79-94.
43. Klarwill, *Queen Elizabeth*, p. 113.
44. Ibid.
45. Ibid., p. 114.
46. Ibid.
47. Ibid.
48. Ibid.
49. 'Simancas: September 1559', in *Calendar of State Papers, Spain (Simancas), Volume 1, 1558–1567*, ed. Martin A.S. Hume (London, 1892), pp. 95–97. *British History Online*, www.british-history.ac.uk/cal-state-papers/simancas/vol1/pp95-97.
50. Chapman, *Two Tudor Portraits*, p. 182.
51. 'Elizabeth: October 1559, 1–5', in *Calendar of State Papers Foreign: Elizabeth, Volume 2, 1559–1560*, ed. Joseph Stevenson (London, 1865), pp. 1–18. *British History Online*, www.british-history.ac.uk/cal-state-papers/foreign/vol2/pp1-18.
52. Ibid.
53. Klarwill, *Queen Elizabeth*, p. 154.
54. Ibid., p. 156.
55. De Lisle, *Sisters Who Would Be Queen*, pp. 199–200.
56. BL Add MS 33749 fo. 22v.
57. Ibid., fo. 24r.
58. BL Harley MS 249 fo. 57r.
59. Ibid.
60. NA SP 46/10.
61. Ibid.
62. BL Cotton MS Faustina A XI fo. 44r.
63. BL Harley MS 249 fo. 57r.

64. Ibid., fo. 57v. Stokes had drawn up a rough draft of a letter for his wife requesting the queen's permission for Hertford's marriage to Katherine, which 'was the only thing that she [Frances] desired before her death and should be an occasion to her to die the more quietly' (cited by de Lisle, *Sisters Who Would Be Queen*, pp. 194–95).
65. De Lisle, *Tudor*, p. 418.
66. John Nichols, *The Progresses and Public Processions of Queen Elizabeth* (London: John Nichols & Son, 1823, 3 vols), Vol. I, p. 80.
67. Ibid., p. 81.
68. Ibid.
69. Ibid.
70. Ibid.
71. 'Simancas: November 1559', in *Calendar of State Papers, Spain (Simancas), Volume 1, 1558–1567*, ed. Martin A.S. Hume (London, 1892), pp. 109–17. *British History Online*, www.british-history.ac.uk/cal-state-papers/simancas/vol1/pp109-117.
72. M. Le Baron Kervyn de Lettenhove (ed.), Relations politiques des Pays-Bas et de l'Angleterre: Depuis l'abdication de Charles-Quint jusqu'au depart de Philippe II pour l'Espagne (25 Oct. 1555–24 août 1559) (Brussels: F. Hayez, 1882, 10 vols), Vol. I, p. 612.
73. Ibid.
74. Ibid., p. 613.
75. 'Simancas: January 1560', in *Calendar of State Papers, Spain (Simancas), Volume 1, 1558–1567*, ed. Martin A.S. Hume (London, 1892), pp. 120–22. *British History Online*, www.british-history.ac.uk/cal-state-papers/simancas/vol1/pp120-122.
76. Anne Somerset, *Elizabeth I* (London: Phoenix, 1997), p. 178.
77. 'Simancas: January 1560', in *Calendar of State Papers, Spain (Simancas), Volume 1, 1558–1567*, ed. Martin A.S. Hume (London, 1892), pp. 120–22. *British History Online*, www.british-history.ac.uk/cal-state-papers/simancas/vol1/pp120-122.
78. Camden, History of the Most Renowned Princess Elizabeth, p. 67.
79. 'Simancas: September 1560', in *Calendar of State Papers, Spain (Simancas), Volume 1, 1558–1567*, ed. Martin A.S. Hume (London, 1892), pp. 174–76. *British History Online*, www.british-history.ac.uk/cal-state-papers/simancas/vol1/pp174-176.
80. 'Simancas: November 1559', in *Calendar of State Papers, Spain (Simancas), Volume 1, 1558–1567*, ed. Martin A.S. Hume (London, 1892), pp. 109–17. *British History Online*, www.british-history.ac.uk/cal-state-papers/simancas/vol1/pp109-117.
81. 'Simancas: March 1560', in *Calendar of State Papers, Spain (Simancas), Volume 1, 1558–1567*, ed. Martin A.S. Hume (London, 1892), pp. 132–42. *British History Online*, www.british-history.ac.uk/cal-state-papers/simancas/vol1/pp132-142.
82. See Chris Skidmore, *Death and the Virgin: Elizabeth, Dudley and the Mysterious Fate of Amy Robsart* (London: Weidenfeld & Nicolson, 2010) for Amy's death.

83. 'Simancas: February 1561', in *Calendar of State Papers, Spain (Simancas), Volume 1, 1558–1567*, ed. Martin A.S. Hume (London, 1892), pp. 180–84. *British History Online*, www.british-history.ac.uk/cal-state-papers/simancas/vol1/pp180-184.

84. 'Elizabeth: December 1560, 26–31', in *Calendar of State Papers Foreign: Elizabeth, Volume 3, 1560–1561*, ed. Joseph Stevenson (London, 1865), pp. 463–80. *British History Online*, www.british-history.ac.uk/cal-state-papers/foreign/vol3/pp463-480.

85. 'Venice: June 1566', in *Calendar of State Papers Relating To English Affairs in the Archives of Venice, Volume 7, 1558–1580*, ed. Rawdon Brown and G. Cavendish Bentinck (London, 1890), pp. 381–82. *British History Online*, www.british-history.ac.uk/cal-state-papers/venice/vol7/pp381-382.

86. 'Simancas: October 1560', in *Calendar of State Papers, Spain (Simancas), Volume 1, 1558–1567*, ed. Martin A.S. Hume (London, 1892), pp. 176–77. *British History Online*, www.british-history.ac.uk/cal-state-papers/simancas/vol1/pp176-177.

87. Ibid.

88. 'Cecil Papers: 1560', in *Calendar of the Cecil Papers in Hatfield House: Volume 1, 1306–1571* (London, 1883), pp. 190–200. *British History Online*, www.british-history.ac.uk/cal-cecil-papers/vol1/pp190-200.

89. 'Elizabeth: September 1560, 21–30', in *Calendar of State Papers Foreign: Elizabeth, Volume 3, 1560–1561*, ed. Joseph Stevenson (London, 1865), pp. 309–27. *British History Online*, www.british-history.ac.uk/cal-state-papers/foreign/vol3/pp309-327.

90. Nichols, *Worthies*, Vol. I, p. 563.

Chapter 7: A Second Marriage

1. In 1534, Mary Boleyn married for the second time, her first husband having died of the sweating sickness in 1528. When the king and queen learned of her clandestine marriage, they responded by dismissing her from court and she never regained royal favour. The phrase 'love overcame reason' comes from a letter sent by Mary to Thomas Cromwell seeking his intercession on her behalf.

2. BL Add MS 33749 fo. 83v; de Lisle, *Sisters Who Would Be Queen*, pp. 190–91.

3. H. St Maur, *Annals of the Seymours: Being a History of the Seymour Family, From Early Times to Within a Few Years of the Present* (London: Kegan Paul, 1902), p. 152.

4. BL Add MS 33749 fo. 22v.

5. Ibid., fo. 23r.

6. Ibid., fo. 83v.

7. Ibid.

8. Ibid., fo. 39v.

9. BL Harley MS 6286 p. 47.

10. BL Add MS 33749 fo. 39v.

11. Ibid.

12. Ibid., fo. 40r.

13. BL Harley MS 249 fo. 57v.
14. BL Add MS 33749 fos 40r–40v.
15. Retha M. Warnicke, *Wicked Women of Tudor England: Queens, Aristocrats, Commoners* (New York: Palgrave Macmillan, 2012), p. 35.
16. BL Add MS 33749 fo. 24r.
17. BL Harley MS 249 fo. 58r.
18. Chapman, *Two Tudor Portraits*, pp. 190–91.
19. BL Add MS 33749 fo. 81v.
20. Ibid., fo. 81r.
21. Ibid., fo. 24v.
22. Ibid.
23. BL Harley MS 6286 p. 88.
24. Ibid., p. 89.
25. BL Add MS 33749 fo. 24v.
26. BL Harley MS 6286 p. 85.
27. Ibid.
28. BL Add MS 33749 fo. 41r.
29. BL Harley MS 249 fo. 58v.
30. Her date of death is usually given as 19 March, but in his *Diary* Machyn reported that 'The xx day of Marche ded at the cowrt the yonge lade Jane Semer, the duke of Somerset('s) dowther, on of the quen('s) mayds.' Nichols, *Diary of Henry Machyn*, p. 253.
31. Almonry.
32. Other.
33. Nichols, *Diary of Henry Machyn*, p. 254.
34. BL Add MS 33749 fo. 40v.
35. Ibid., fo. 84r.
36. NA SP 46/10.
37. De Lisle, *Sisters Who Would Be Queen*, p. 208.
38. BL Add MS 33749 fo. 42r.
39. Ibid., fo. 42v.
40. BL Harley MS 6286 p. 91.
41. 'Elizabeth: May 1561, 11–20', in *Calendar of State Papers Foreign: Elizabeth, Volume 4, 1561–1562*, ed. Joseph Stevenson (London, 1866), pp. 109–17. *British History Online*, www.british-history.ac.uk/cal-state-papers/foreign/vol4/pp109-117.
42. Ibid.
43. Ibid.
44. BL Add MS 33749 fo. 41v.
45. Ibid.
46. John Guy, *'My Heart is My Own': The Life of Mary Queen of Scots* (London: Fourth Estate, 2004), p. 158.
47. BL Harley MS 6286 p. 92.

48. Ibid., p. 91.
49. 'Elizabeth: June 1561, 21–30', in *Calendar of State Papers Foreign: Elizabeth, Volume 4, 1561–1562*, ed. Joseph Stevenson (London, 1866), pp. 149–64. *British History Online*, www.british-history.ac.uk/cal-state-papers/foreign/vol4/pp149-164.
50. Ibid.
51. Levine, *Early Elizabethan Succession Question*, p. 144.
52. Anonymous, 'Allegations in behalf of the high and mighty Princes, the Lady Mary' in Atwood, *Fundamental Constitution*, p. 12.
53. 'Elizabeth: June 1561, 21–30', in *Calendar of State Papers Foreign: Elizabeth, Volume 4, 1561–1562*, ed. Joseph Stevenson (London, 1866), pp. 149–64. *British History Online*, www.british-history.ac.uk/cal-state-papers/foreign/vol4/pp149-164.
54. Nichols, *Progresses and Public Processions*, Vol. I, p. 91.
55. Ibid., pp. 91–92.
56. Bodleian Library Tanner MS 193 fo. 24, cited by de Lisle, *Sisters Who Would Be Queen*, pp. 212–13.
57. Mary Hill Cole, 'Monarchy in Motion: An Overview of Elizabethan Progresses' in Jayne Elisabeth Archer, Elizabeth Goldring and Sarah Knight (eds), *The Progresses, Pageants, and Entertainments of Queen Elizabeth I* (New York: Oxford University Press, 2007), p. 40.
58. Bodleian Library Tanner MS 193 fo. 227, cited by de Lisle, *Sisters Who Would Be Queen*, pp. 213–14.
59. Hill Cole, 'Monarchy in Motion', p. 40.
60. Warnicke, *Wicked Women*, p. 118.
61. De Lisle, *Sisters Who Would Be Queen*, p. 215.
62. BL Add MS 33749 fo. 42v.
63. Ibid.
64. Ibid., fo. 43v.
65. Several authors have suggested that she was imprisoned in the Bell Tower; for example, Davey, *Sisters of Lady Jane Grey*, p. 182 and Weir, *The Lost Tudor Princess*, p. 56.
66. Strickland, *Tudor Princesses*, pp. 225–27.
67. Haynes, *A Collection of State Papers*, p. 369.
68. Ibid.
69. Robert Lemon (ed.), *Calendar of State Papers, Domestic Series, of the Reigns of Edward VI., Mary, Elizabeth 1547–1580, Preserved in the State Paper Department of Her Majesty's Public Record Office* (London: Longman, Brown, Greene, Longmans & Roberts, 1856), p. 184.
70. Robert C. Braddock, 'To Serve the Queen' in Alice Hunt and Anna Whitelock (eds), *Tudor Queenship: The Reigns of Mary and Elizabeth* (New York: Palgrave Macmillan, 2010), p. 231.

71. 'Elizabeth: August 1561, 16–20', in *Calendar of State Papers Foreign: Elizabeth, Volume 4, 1561–1562*, ed. Joseph Stevenson (London, 1866), pp. 250–66. *British History Online*, www.british-history.ac.uk/cal-state-papers/foreign/vol4/pp250-266.

72. Ibid.

73. 'Elizabeth: September 1561, 21–25', in *Calendar of State Papers Foreign: Elizabeth, Volume 4, 1561–1562*, ed. Joseph Stevenson (London, 1866), pp. 318–28. *British History Online*, www.british-history.ac.uk/cal-state-papers/foreign/vol4/pp318-328.

74. 'Simancas: September 1561', in *Calendar of State Papers, Spain (Simancas), Volume 1, 1558–1567*, ed. Martin A.S. Hume (London, 1892), pp. 212–17. *British History Online*, www.british-history.ac.uk/cal-state-papers/simancas/vol1/pp212-217.

75. Nichols, *Diary of Henry Machyn*, p. 266.

76. 'Supplement: September 1561', in *Calendar of State Papers Foreign: Elizabeth, Volume 5, 1562*, ed. Joseph Stevenson (London, 1867), pp. 620–21. *British History Online*, www.british-history.ac.uk/cal-state-papers/foreign/vol5/pp620-621.

77. 'Rome: 1561, July–December', in *Calendar of State Papers Relating To English Affairs in the Vatican Archives, Volume 1, 1558–1571*, ed. J.M. Rigg (London, 1916), pp. 39–70. *British History Online*, www.british-history.ac.uk/cal-state-papers/vatican/vol1/pp39-70.

78. Ibid.

79. BL Add MS 33749 fo. 25r.

80. Diana O'Hara, *Courtship and Constraint: Rethinking the Making of Marriage in Tudor England* (Manchester: Manchester University Press, 2000), p. 38.

81. Katharine Cleland, *Irregular Unions: Clandestine Marriage in Early Modern English Literature* (Ithaca, NY and London: Cornell University Press, 2021), p. 3.

82. BL Add MS 33749 fo. 37r.

83. Cressy, *Birth, Marriage, and Death*, p. 308.

84. Cited by R.B. Outhwaite, *Clandestine Marriage in England 1500–1850* (London and Rio Grande, OH: Hambledon Press, 1995), p. 20.

85. 'Simancas: September 1561', in *Calendar of State Papers, Spain (Simancas), Volume 1, 1558–1567*, ed. Martin A.S. Hume (London, 1892), pp. 212–17. *British History Online*, www.british-history.ac.uk/cal-state-papers/simancas/vol1/pp212-217.

86. Laura Gowing, 'Language, Power and the Law: Women's Slander Litigation in Early Modern London' in Jenny Kermode and Garthine Walker (eds), *Women, Crime and the Courts in Early Modern England* (London: UCL Press, 1994), p. 32.

87. Ibid., p. 30.

88. Cited by Merry E. Wiesner, *Women and Gender in Early Modern Europe* (Cambridge: Cambridge University Press, 1993), p. 48.

89. Park, *Nugae Antiquae*, Vol. I, p. 28.

90. Sara Mendelson and Patricia Crawford, *Women in Early Modern England 1550–1720* (Oxford: Clarendon Press, 1998), pp. 66, 354–56.

91. John Ayre, *The Catechism of Thomas Becon* (Cambridge: Cambridge University Press, 1844), p. 361.
92. Ibid., p. 343.

Chapter 8: The Queen's Displeasure

1. Danby Pickering, *The Statutes at Large, from the First Year of K. Richard III. to the 31st Year of K. Henry VIII. inclusive* (Cambridge: Printed by Joseph Bentham, 1763, 46 vols), Vol. IV, p. 447.
2. Johanna Rickman, *Love, Lust, and License in Early Modern England: Illicit Sex and the Nobility* (Aldershot: Ashgate, 2008), p. 5.
3. Ibid., p. 28.
4. Samuel Weller Singer (ed.), *The Life of Cardinal Wolsey. By George Cavendish, His Gentleman Usher* (Chiswick: from the Press of C. Whittingham; for Harding, Triphook & Lepard, London, 1825, 2 vols), Vol. I, p. 59. There were even more pertinent precedents that Elizabeth could draw on in her treatment of Katherine and Hertford: when Henry VIII learned of his niece Lady Margaret Douglas' clandestine relationship with Lord Thomas Howard in the summer of 1536, he responded by ordering both parties to be incarcerated in the Tower.
5. Cited by Bell, *Elizabeth I*, p. 81.
6. Ibid., p. 88.
7. Martin Ingram, *Carnal Knowledge: Regulating Sex in England, 1470–1600* (Cambridge: Cambridge University Press, 2017), p. 311.
8. Arber, *John Knox*, p. 14.
9. Leah S. Marcus, Janel Mueller and Mary Beth Rose (eds), *Elizabeth I: Collected Works* (Chicago, IL and London: University of Chicago Press, 2002), p. 62.
10. Ibid., p. 63.
11. Ibid., p. 65.
12. Ibid.
13. Ibid., p. 66.
14. Ibid., p. 63.
15. Philip Yorke, *Miscellaneous State Papers. From 1501 to 1726. In Two Volumes* (London: W. Strahan and T. Cadell, 1778, 2 vols), Vol. I, p. 177.
16. Kervyn de Lettenhove, *Relations politiques*, Vol. II, p. 606.
17. 'Simancas: September 1561', in *Calendar of State Papers, Spain (Simancas), Volume 1, 1558–1567*, ed. Martin A.S. Hume (London, 1892), pp. 212–17. *British History Online*, www.british-history.ac.uk/cal-state-papers/simancas/vol1/pp212-217.
18. Ibid.
19. Ibid.
20. Warnicke, *Wicked Women*, p. 101.
21. Ibid.
22. Cited by Strickland, *Tudor Princesses*, p. 210.
23. Sharp Hume, *Chronicle of King Henry VIII*, p. 156.

24. As noted by Warnicke, *Wicked Women*, p. 82.

25. Strickland, *Tudor Princesses*, p. 242.

26. Alison Weir, *The Six Wives of Henry VIII* (London: The Bodley Head, 1991), p. 540.

27. William Seymour, *Ordeal by Ambition: An English Family in the Shadow of the Tudors* (London: Sidgwick & Jackson, 1972), p. 221.

28. Warnicke, *Wicked Women*, p. 104.

29. Sharp Hume, *Chronicle of King Henry VIII*, p. 164.

30. 'Simancas: September 1561', in *Calendar of State Papers, Spain (Simancas), Volume 1, 1558–1567*, ed. Martin A.S. Hume (London, 1892), pp. 212–17. *British History Online*, www.british-history.ac.uk/cal-state-papers/simancas/vol1/pp212-217.

31. 'Rome: 1561, July–December', in *Calendar of State Papers Relating To English Affairs in the Vatican Archives, Volume 1, 1558–1571*, ed. J.M. Rigg (London, 1916), pp. 39–70. *British History Online*, www.british-history.ac.uk/cal-state-papers/vatican/vol1/pp39-70.

32. The remains of the boy's aunt, Lady Jane Grey, were of course interred in the same chapel seven years previously.

33. 'Elizabeth: September 1561, 26–30', in *Calendar of State Papers Foreign: Elizabeth, Volume 4, 1561–1562*, ed. Joseph Stevenson (London, 1866), pp. 328–43. *British History Online*, www.british-history.ac.uk/cal-state-papers/foreign/vol4/pp328-343.

34. Hastings Robinson, *The Zurich Letters, Comprising the Correspondence of Several English Bishops and Others, with Some of the Helvetian Reformers, during the Early Part of the Reign of Queen Elizabeth* (Cambridge: Cambridge University Press, 1842), p. 103.

35. 'Rome: 1561, July–December', in *Calendar of State Papers Relating To English Affairs in the Vatican Archives, Volume 1, 1558–1571*, ed. J.M. Rigg (London, 1916), pp. 39–70. *British History Online*, www.british-history.ac.uk/cal-state-papers/vatican/vol1/pp39-70.

36. Victoria de la Torre, '"We Few of an Infinite Multitude": John Hales, Parliament, and the Gendered Politics of the Early Elizabethan Succession', *Albion: A Quarterly Journal Concerned with British Studies* 33 (2001), 572.

37. McLaren, 'The Quest for a King', 277.

38. Ibid.

39. Levine, *Tudor Dynastic Problems*, p. 105.

40. Ibid., p. 106.

41. Susan Doran, *Elizabeth I and Her Circle* (Oxford: Oxford University Press, 2015), p. 53.

42. Ibid.

43. Warnicke, *Mary Queen of Scots*, p. 98.

44. 'Simancas: January 1562', in *Calendar of State Papers, Spain (Simancas), Volume 1, 1558–1567*, ed. Martin A.S. Hume (London, 1892), pp. 222–28. *British History Online*, www.british-history.ac.uk/cal-state-papers/simancas/vol1/pp222-228.

45. Haynes, *A Collection of State Papers*, p. 378.
46. Ibid.
47. 'Elizabeth: June 1562, 6–10', in *Calendar of State Papers Foreign: Elizabeth, Volume 5, 1562*, ed. Joseph Stevenson (London, 1867), pp. 74–90. *British History Online*, www.british-history.ac.uk/cal-state-papers/foreign/vol5/pp74-90.
48. Ibid.
49. Camden, *History of the Most Renowned Princess Elizabeth*, p. 58.
50. Ibid., p. 59.
51. Somerset, *Elizabeth I*, p. 179.
52. Cited by Strickland, *Tudor Princesses*, p. 223.
53. De Lisle, *Sisters Who Would Be Queen*, p. 228.
54. Ibid.
55. Camden, *History of the Most Renowned Princess Elizabeth*, p. 59.
56. Ibid.
57. *The Wiltshire Archaeological and Natural History Magazine, Published under the Direction of the Society Formed in that County A.D. 1853* (Devizes: H.F. & E. Bull, 1875), Vol. XV, pp. 190–91.
58. De Lisle, *Tudor*, p. 331.
59. Martin Spies, 'The Portrait of Lady Katherine Grey and Her Son: Iconographic Medievalism as a Legitimation Strategy' in Alicia C. Montoya, Sophie van Romburgh and Wim van Anrooij (eds), *Early Modern Medievalisms: The Interplay between Scholarly Reflection and Artistic Production* (Leiden: Brill, 2010), p. 180.
60. Ibid., p. 187.
61. Ibid., p. 169.
62. 'Simancas: October 1562', in *Calendar of State Papers, Spain (Simancas), Volume 1, 1558–1567*, ed. Martin A.S. Hume (London, 1892), pp. 261–65. *British History Online*, www.british-history.ac.uk/cal-state-papers/simancas/vol1/pp261-265.
63. Ibid.
64. Ibid.
65. De Lisle, *Sisters Who Would Be Queen*, p. 230.
66. Levine, *Early Elizabethan Succession Question*, p. 146.
67. Ibid.
68. J. Payne Collier (ed.), *The Egerton Papers. A Collection of Public and Private Documents, Chiefly Illustrative of the Times of Elizabeth and James I* (London: Camden Society, 1840), pp. 47–48.
69. Levine, *Early Elizabethan Succession Question*, p. 162.
70. Mortimer Levine, 'A "Letter" on the Elizabethan Succession Question, 1566', *Huntington Library Quarterly* 19 (1955), 22.
71. Ibid., 23.
72. Levine, *Early Elizabethan Succession Question*, p. 46.
73. 'Simancas: October 1562', in *Calendar of State Papers, Spain (Simancas), Volume 1, 1558–1567*, ed. Martin A.S. Hume (London, 1892), pp. 261–65. *British History Online*, www.british-history.ac.uk/cal-state-papers/simancas/vol1/pp261-265.

74. 'Simancas: September 1562', in *Calendar of State Papers, Spain (Simancas), Volume 1, 1558–1567*, ed. Martin A.S. Hume (London, 1892), pp. 259–61. *British History Online*, www.british-history.ac.uk/cal-state-papers/simancas/vol1/pp259-261.
75. 'POLE, ARTHUR (1531–1570?)' in Sidney Lee (ed.), *Dictionary of National Biography* (New York: Macmillan & Co., 1896, 63 vols), Vol. 46, p. 19.
76. Anonymous, *A Brief account of the several plots, conspiracies, and hellish attempts of the bloody-minded papists against the princes and kingdoms of England, Scotland, and Ireland from the Reformation to this present year, 1678 as also their cruel practices in France against the Protestants in the massacre of Paris, &c., with a more particular account of their plots in relation to the late Civil War and their contrivances of the death of King Charles the First, of blessed memory* (London: Printed for J.R. & W.A., 1679), p. 4.
77. 'Simancas: November 1562', in *Calendar of State Papers, Spain (Simancas), Volume 1, 1558–1567*, ed. Martin A.S. Hume (London, 1892), pp. 265–73. *British History Online*, www.british-history.ac.uk/cal-state-papers/simancas/vol1/pp265-273.
78. Ibid.
79. Ibid.
80. Marcus, Mueller and Rose, *Elizabeth I*, pp. 73–74.
81. De Lisle, *Sisters Who Would Be Queen*, p. 233.
82. Arthur Clifford (ed.), *The State Papers and Letters of Sir Ralph Sadler, Knight-Banneret* (Edinburgh: Constable & Co., 1809, 2 vols), Vol. II, p. 557.
83. Ibid.
84. Kristen Post Walton, *Catholic Queen, Protestant Patriarchy: Mary, Queen of Scots and the Politics of Gender and Religion* (Basingstoke and New York: Palgrave Macmillan, 2007), p. 53.
85. Clifford, *State Papers*, Vol. II, p. 560.
86. Cited by Wallace MacCaffrey, *Elizabeth I* (London: Arnold, 1993), p. 91.
87. 'Simancas: February 1563', in *Calendar of State Papers, Spain (Simancas), Volume 1, 1558–1567*, ed. Martin A.S. Hume (London, 1892), pp. 295–305. *British History Online*, www.british-history.ac.uk/cal-state-papers/simancas/vol1/pp295-305.
88. Ibid.
89. Ibid.
90. 'Simancas: March 1563', in *Calendar of State Papers, Spain (Simancas), Volume 1, 1558–1567*, ed. Martin A.S. Hume (London, 1892), pp. 305–16. *British History Online*, www.british-history.ac.uk/cal-state-papers/simancas/vol1/pp305-316.
91. Ibid.
92. De la Torre, 'We Few of an Infinite Multitude', 557.
93. Doran, *Elizabeth I*, p. 54. Both Lord John and Francis Newdigate (second husband of Anne, duchess of Somerset and Hertford's stepfather) were interrogated in April 1564 for their actions in investigating the marriages of Charles Brandon and the legitimacy of Katherine's mother Frances (see Haynes, *A Collection of State Papers*, pp. 412–17). Both were shown Hales' tract

once it was written. Cecil reported in relation to the tract that 'My Lord John Gray is in trouble also for it'; Henry Ellis, *Original Letters, Illustrative of English History; Including Numerous Royal Letters: From Autographs in the British Museum, and One or Two Other Collections* (London: Harding and Lepard, 1827, 4 vols), Vol. II, p. 285. Nicholas Bacon, Elizabeth I's Lord Keeper, was also examined for his involvement in the scheme and was dismissed from court for a time.

94. Post Walton, *Catholic Queen, Protestant Patriarchy*, p. 58.
95. 'A Declaration of the Succession of the Crowne Imperiall of Ingland, made by J. Hales, 1563' in George Harbin, *The Hereditary Right of the Crown of England Asserted The History of the Succession Since the Conquest Clear'd; and the True English Constitution Vindicated from the Misrepresentations of Dr. Higden's View and Defence. Wherein Some Mistakes Also of Our Common Historians are Rectify'd; and Several Particulars Relating to the Succession, and to the Title of the House of Suffolk, are Now First Publish'd from Ancient Records and Original Mss; Together with an Authentick Copy of King Henry VIII.'s Will* (London: Printed by G. James, for Richard Smith, at Bishop Beveridge's Head in Pater-Noster-Row, 1713), p. xxxi. See also Lambeth MS 2872 fos 2–9v.
96. Ibid., p. xxxii.
97. Ibid., p. xxii.
98. Ibid., p. xxix.
99. Ibid., p. xxxvii.
100. Ibid., p. xxxix.
101. Ibid., p. xli.
102. Ellis, *Original Letters*, Vol. II, p. 285.
103. De Lisle, *Sisters Who Would Be Queen*, p. 245.
104. Spies, 'The Portrait of Lady Katherine Grey', p. 171.
105. Nichols, *Diary of Henry Machyn*, p. 300.
106. McLaren, 'The Quest for a King', 263.
107. BL Add MSS 35830, fo. 159v, cited by McLaren, 'The Quest for a King', 261.
108. Ibid., 289.
109. Strickland, *Tudor Princesses*, pp. 225–26.
110. Chapman, *Two Tudor Portraits*, p. 218.
111. 'Cecil Papers: 1563', in *Calendar of the Cecil Papers in Hatfield House: Volume 1, 1306–1571* (London, 1883), pp. 272–88. *British History Online*, www.british-history.ac.uk/cal-cecil-papers/vol1/pp272-288.
112. Ibid.
113. De Lisle, *Tudor*, p. 331.
114. *Wiltshire Archaeological and Natural History Magazine*, Vol. XV, p. 192.
115. Ibid.
116. De Lisle, *Sisters Who Would Be Queen*, p. 240.
117. BL Lansdowne MS 6/27. See also Ellis, *Original Letters*, Vol. II, pp. 275–76.
118. BL Lansdowne MS 6/32.
119. Ellis, *Original Letters*, Vol. II, pp. 279–80. See also BL Lansdowne MS 6/33.

120. BL Lansdowne MS 6/36.
121. BL Lansdowne MS 6/37.
122. BL Lansdowne MS 6/44.
123. Cited by Strickland, *Tudor Princesses*, p. 238.
124. BL Lansdowne MS 7/52; Strickland, *Tudor Princesses*, p. 239.
125. Lemon, *Calendar of State Papers, Domestic*, p. 240.
126. Strickland, *Tudor Princesses*, p. 240.
127. Ibid., p. 241.
128. Ellis, *Original Letters*, Vol. II, pp. 273–74. The letter actually dates to March 1564 in view of the fact that, in the sixteenth century, the New Year was held to begin on Lady Day (25 March).
129. De Lisle, *Sisters Who Would Be Queen*, p. 246.
130. Joseph Bain (ed.), *Calendar of the State Papers relating to Scotland and Mary, Queen of Scots 1547–1603* (Edinburgh: H.M. General Register House, 1900, 11 vols), Vol. II, p. 175. The wedding took place at Holyrood Palace on 29 July 1565.
131. De Lisle, *Sisters Who Would Be Queen*, pp. 251–52.
132. Ellis, *Original Letters*, Vol. II, p. 299.
133. Lemon, *Calendar of State Papers, Domestic*, p. 272.
134. BL Lansdowne MS 819/13 fo. 108.
135. Ibid., fo. 109.
136. Cited by Strickland, *Tudor Princesses*, p. 240.
137. Warnicke, *Wicked Women*, p. 101.
138. Ellis, *Original Letters*, Vol. II, pp. 286–87.
139. Ibid., pp. 287–88.
140. Mary Villeponteaux, *The Queen's Mercy: Gender and Judgment in Representations of Elizabeth I* (New York: Palgrave Macmillan, 2014), p. 2.
141. Ibid.
142. Haynes, *A Collection of State Papers*, p. 396.
143. A.F. Pollard, 'Catherine Seymour', *Dictionary of National Biography, 1885–1900, Volume 51*, accessed at en.wikisource.org/wiki/Dictionary_of_National_Biography,_1885-1900/Seymour,_Catherine.
144. Davey, *Sisters of Lady Jane Grey*, p. vii.
145. Ibid., p. 235.
146. Nichols, *Worthies*, Vol. I, p. 563.
147. Carole Levin, 'Elizabeth I as Sister and "Loving Kinswoman"' in Anne J. Cruz and Mihoko Suzuki (eds), *The Rule of Women in Early Modern Europe* (Urbana and Chicago, IL: University of Illinois Press, 2009), p. 134.
148. Doran, *Elizabeth I*, p. 53.
149. Ives, *Lady Jane Grey*, p. 271.
150. Adam Fox, *Oral and Literate Culture in England 1500–1700* (Oxford: Oxford University Press, 2000), p. 336.
151. Ibid.
152. Bain, *Calendar of State Papers*, Vol. II, p. 175.

153. Bodleian Library Ashmole 829 'A Discourse about the Succession to the Crowne, from Hen. 7 & c', fo. 32r.
154. Ibid.
155. Levine, *Early Elizabethan Succession Question*, p. 90.
156. Ibid.
157. Bodleian Library Ashmole 829 'Allegations against the Surmised Title of the Queen of Scots and the Favourers of the Same', fo. 55r.
158. Ibid., fo. 55v.
159. Ibid., fo. 60r.
160. Warnicke, *Mary Queen of Scots*, p. 98.
161. Cited by Levine, *Early Elizabethan Succession Question*, p. 110.
162. Lipscomb, *The King is Dead*, p. 161.
163. Levine, *Tudor Dynastic Problems*, p. 112.
164. Anonymous, 'Allegations in behalf of the high and mighty Princes, the Lady Mary' in Atwood, *Fundamental Constitution*, p. 5.
165. Ibid., pp. 7, 10.
166. Levine, *Tudor Dynastic Problems*, p. 111.
167. Anonymous, 'Allegations in behalf of the high and mighty Princes, the Lady Mary' in Atwood, *Fundamental Constitution*, p. 12.
168. Ibid., p. 13.
169. 'Venice: May 1557, 11–15', in *Calendar of State Papers Relating To English Affairs in the Archives of Venice, Volume 6, 1555–1558*, ed. Rawdon Brown (London, 1877), pp. 1041–95. *British History Online*, www.british-history.ac.uk/cal-state-papers/venice/vol6/pp1041-1095.
170. Collier, *Egerton Papers*, p. 48.
171. Levine, *Tudor Dynastic Problems*, p. 115.
172. Cited by Levine, *Tudor Dynastic Problems*, pp. 181–82.
173. Cited by Guy, *Tudor England*, p. 270.
174. 'Simancas: October 1566', in *Calendar of State Papers, Spain (Simancas), Volume 1, 1558–1567*, ed. Martin A.S. Hume (London, 1892), pp. 582–91. *British History Online*, www.british-history.ac.uk/cal-state-papers/simancas/vol1/pp582-591.
175. Ibid.
176. 'Simancas: December 1566', in *Calendar of State Papers, Spain (Simancas), Volume 1, 1558–1567*, ed. Martin A.S. Hume (London, 1892), pp. 598–606. *British History Online*, www.british-history.ac.uk/cal-state-papers/simancas/vol1/pp598-606.
177. 'Simancas: November 1566', in *Calendar of State Papers, Spain (Simancas), Volume 1, 1558–1567*, ed. Martin A.S. Hume (London, 1892), pp. 591–98. *British History Online*, www.british-history.ac.uk/cal-state-papers/simancas/vol1/pp591-598.
178. Collier, *Egerton Papers*, p. 43.
179. Ibid.
180. Ibid., pp. 48–49.

Chapter 9: 'An Incomparable Pair'

1. 'Simancas: February 1567', in *Calendar of State Papers, Spain (Simancas), Volume 1, 1558–1567*, ed. Martin A.S. Hume (London, 1892), pp. 615–21. *British History Online*, www.british-history.ac.uk/cal-state-papers/simancas/vol1/pp615-621.
2. Levine, *Early Elizabethan Succession Question*, p. 201.
3. David Rizzio, secretary to Mary, Queen of Scots, was murdered on 9 March 1566 at Holyrood Palace in the presence of the queen, in the culmination of a conspiracy in which Darnley was involved.
4. 'Simancas: February 1567', in *Calendar of State Papers, Spain (Simancas), Volume 1, 1558–1567*, ed. Martin A.S. Hume (London, 1892), pp. 615–21. *British History Online*, www.british-history.ac.uk/cal-state-papers/simancas/vol1/pp615-621.
5. Ibid.
6. 'Simancas: December 1567', in *Calendar of State Papers, Spain (Simancas), Volume 1, 1558–1567*, ed. Martin A.S. Hume (London, 1892), pp. 685–90. *British History Online*, www.british-history.ac.uk/cal-state-papers/simancas/vol1/pp685-690.
7. Lemon, *Calendar of State Papers, Domestic*, p. 300.
8. Katherine's death is often given as 26 January, but the contemporary account referred to in this chapter clearly states that she died on the morning of 27 January.
9. Strickland, *Tudor Princesses*, p. 248.
10. Lemon, *Calendar of State Papers, Domestic*, p. 304.
11. Camden, *History of the Most Renowned Princess Elizabeth*, p. 59.
12. Levin, 'Elizabeth I as Sister', p. 134.
13. Lorraine C. Attreed, 'Preparation for Death in Sixteenth-Century Northern England', *The Sixteenth Century Journal* 13 (1982), 37.
14. Ralph Houlbrooke, *Death, Religion, and the Family in England, 1480–1750* (Oxford and New York: Oxford University Press, 1998), p. 57.
15. Ibid., p. 154.
16. Ibid.
17. Ibid., p. 160.
18. Ibid., p. 198.
19. Reed Cattley, *Acts and Monuments of John Foxe*, Vol. VI, p. 422.
20. Cited by Cressy, *Birth, Marriage, and Death*, p. viii.
21. Ibid., p. 381.
22. Chapman, *Two Tudor Portraits*, p. 233.
23. Ibid.
24. BL Cotton MS Titus C VII fo. 124r.
25. Schutte, 'Thomas Churchyard's "Dollful Discourse"', 482.
26. BL Cotton MS Titus C VII fo. 124r.
27. Ibid.
28. Ibid.
29. Ibid.

30. Ibid.
31. Houlbrooke, *Death, Religion, and the Family*, p. 154.
32. BL Cotton MS Titus C VII fo. 124v.
33. Ibid.
34. Ibid.
35. Ibid.
36. Lucinda M. Becker, *Death and the Early Modern Englishwoman* (Abingdon: Routledge, 2016), p. 2.
37. Ibid., p. 6.
38. BL Cotton MS Titus C VII fo. 131.
39. Houlbrooke, *Death, Religion, and the Family*, p. 161.
40. BL Cotton MS Titus C VII fo. 131.
41. Ibid.
42. 'Simancas: February 1568', in *Calendar of State Papers, Spain (Simancas), Volume 2, 1568–1579*, ed. Martin A.S. Hume (London, 1894), pp. 3–12. *British History Online*, www.british-history.ac.uk/cal-state-papers/simancas/vol2/pp3-12.
43. Ibid.
44. Lemon, *Calendar of State Papers, Domestic*, p. 306.
45. Ibid., p. 308.
46. 'Rome: 1568, January–June', in *Calendar of State Papers Relating To English Affairs in the Vatican Archives, Volume 1, 1558–1571*, ed. J.M. Rigg (London, 1916), pp. 268–81. *British History Online*, www.british-history.ac.uk/cal-state-papers/vatican/vol1/pp268-281.
47. Strickland, *Tudor Princesses*, p. 265.
48. De Lisle, *Sisters Who Would Be Queen*, pp. 281–90.
49. Augustine Page (ed.), A Supplement to the Suffolk Traveller; or Topographical and Genealogical Collections, Concerning That County (London: J.B. Nichols & Son, 1844), p. 287.
50. Strickland, *Tudor Princesses*, pp. 253–54.
51. Ibid., p. 254.
52. Schutte, 'Thomas Churchyard's "Dollful Discourse"', 481.
53. Ibid., 483.
54. BL Add MS 35327 fos. 5r, 12r, 12v.
55. Ibid., fos. 6r–6v.
56. Ibid., fo. 9r.
57. Ibid., fo. 12r.
58. 'Simancas: December 1574', in *Calendar of State Papers, Spain (Simancas), Volume 2, 1568–1579*, ed. Martin A.S. Hume (London, 1894), pp. 490–91. *British History Online*, www.british-history.ac.uk/cal-state-papers/simancas/vol2/pp490-491.
59. Anna Whitelock, *Elizabeth's Bedfellows: An Intimate History of the Queen's Court* (London: Bloomsbury, 2013), p. 283.
60. Ibid.
61. Ibid., p. 284.

62. De Lisle, *Sisters Who Would Be Queen*, pp. 294–95.
63. Paulina Kewes, 'The Puritan, the Jesuit and the Jacobean Succession' in Doran and Kewes (eds), *Doubtful and Dangerous*, pp. 47–48.
64. Marjorie Blatcher (ed.), *Historical Manuscripts Commission. Report on the Manuscripts of the Most Honourable The Marquess of Bath, Preserved at Longleat, Wiltshire* (London: Her Majesty's Stationery Office, 1968, 5 vols), Vol. IV, p. 191.
65. Ibid., p. 192.
66. 'Simancas: June 1582', in *Calendar of State Papers, Spain (Simancas), Volume 3, 1580–1586*, ed. Martin A.S. Hume (London, 1896), pp. 379–82. *British History Online*, www.british-history.ac.uk/cal-state-papers/simancas/vol3/pp379-382.
67. De Lisle, *Sisters Who Would Be Queen*, pp. 296–97.
68. 'Venice: February 1603, 16–28', in *Calendar of State Papers Relating To English Affairs in the Archives of Venice, Volume 9, 1592–1603*, ed. Horatio F. Brown (London, 1897), pp. 531–48. *British History Online*, www.british-history.ac.uk/cal-state-papers/venice/vol9/pp531-548.
69. Ibid.
70. 'Venice: March 1603', in *Calendar of State Papers Relating To English Affairs in the Archives of Venice, Volume 9, 1592–1603*, ed. Horatio F. Brown (London, 1897), pp. 548–62. *British History Online*, www.british-history.ac.uk/cal-state-papers/venice/vol9/pp548-562. The castle in question was probably Woodstock.
71. Guy, 'My Heart is My Own', p. 503.
72. 'Venice: May 1607, 26–31', in *Calendar of State Papers Relating To English Affairs in the Archives of Venice, Volume 10, 1603–1607*, ed. Horatio F. Brown (London, 1900), pp. 501–24. *British History Online*, www.british-history.ac.uk/cal-state-papers/venice/vol10/pp501-524.
73. 'Venice: July 1610, 16–31', in *Calendar of State Papers Relating To English Affairs in the Archives of Venice, Volume 12, 1610–1613*, ed. Horatio F. Brown (London, 1905), pp. 16–21. *British History Online*, www.british-history.ac.uk/cal-state-papers/venice/vol12/pp16-21.
74. 'Venice: June 1611', in *Calendar of State Papers Relating To English Affairs in the Archives of Venice, Volume 12, 1610–1613*, ed. Horatio F. Brown (London, 1905), pp. 160–71. *British History Online*, www.british-history.ac.uk/cal-state-papers/venice/vol12/pp160-171.
75. Ibid.
76. Chapman, *Two Tudor Portraits*, p. 151.
77. Spies, 'The Portrait of Lady Katherine Grey', p. 171.
78. Nigel Llewellyn, 'Honour in Life, Death and in the Memory: Funeral Monuments in Early Modern England', *Transactions of the Royal Historical Society* 6 (1996), 179.
79. Ibid., 200.
80. Strickland, *Tudor Princesses*, p. 259.
81. Ibid.
82. St Maur, *Annals of the Seymours*, p. 152.

Index

By the same author

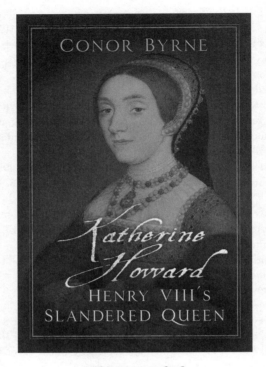

978 0 7509 9060 8

Over the years, Henry VIII's fifth wife has been slandered as a 'juvenile delinquent', 'empty-headed wanton' and 'natural born tart', who engaged in promiscuous liaisons prior to her marriage and committed adultery after. This in-depth biography poses the questions: who was the real Katherine Howard and has society been wrong to judge her so harshly for the past 500 years?